The Crusades

Other Books in the Turning Points Series:

The American Revolution
The Black Death
The Civil Rights Movement
The Collapse of the Soviet Union
The French Revolution
The Great Depression
North American Indian Wars
The Reformation
The Renaissance
The Rise of Christianity
The Rise of Nazi Germany
The Spread of Islam
Victorian England

Turning | Points
IN WORLD HISTORY

The Crusades

Brenda Stalcup, *Book Editor*

David L. Bender, *Publisher*
Bruno Leone, *Executive Editor*
Bonnie Szumski, *Editorial Director*
David M. Haugen, *Managing Editor*

Greenhaven Press, Inc., San Diego, California

Every effort has been made to trace the owners of copyrighted material. The articles in this volume may have been edited for content, length, and/or reading level. The titles have been changed to enhance the editorial purpose.

Library of Congress Cataloging-in-Publication Data

The Crusades / Brenda Stalcup, book editor.
    p.   cm. — (Turning points in world history)
    Includes bibliographical references and index.
    ISBN 1-56510-993-7 (lib. bdg. : alk. paper). —
ISBN 1-56510-992-9 (pbk. : alk. paper)
    1. Crusades. I. Stalcup, Brenda. II. Series: Turning points in world history (Greenhaven Press)
D159.C77 2000
909.07—dc21

99-29283
CIP

Cover photo: Superstock

©2000 by Greenhaven Press, Inc.
P.O. Box 289009, San Diego, CA 92198-9009

Printed in the U.S.A.

Contents

Foreword   9

Introduction   11

A Brief History of the Crusades   14

Chapter 1: The Origins of the Holy Wars

1. An Upheaval of Empires *by Alfred Duggan*   40
The unique circumstances that made the Crusades possible were hundreds of years in the making, the direct result of political turmoil and empire-building in Europe
and the Middle East.

2. The Feudal System and Church Reform
by Sidney Painter   50
In the eleventh century, European society experienced
some important changes that would allow the Crusades
to take place. Two of the most significant changes were
the expansion of the feudal system and the strengthening
of papal authority.

3. The Importance of Pope Urban II *by Robert Payne*   58
Pope Urban II played a crucial role in launching the
First Crusade and thereby beginning the crusading
movement. His personal blend of spirituality, charisma,
and practicality helped him to build enormous enthusiasm for the First Crusade throughout Europe.

4. The Pilgrimage Origins of the Crusades
by Marcus Bull   63
In many respects, the Crusades were similar to the pilgrimages that Western Europeans made to the Holy
Land. Also, one of the crusaders' primary goals was to
keep Jerusalem and other sacred sites available to Christian pilgrims.

5. Economic Factors *by Hans Eberhard Mayer*   73
The medieval practice of strictly limiting the number of
heirs to a family's land helped to avert agricultural disaster, but it also left many young men with few options
except to seek their fortune in military campaigns such
as the Crusades.

Chapter 2: Why Participants Went on the Crusades

1. A Variety of Reasons for Crusading
by Ronald C. Finucane   79
Crusaders were motivated by a number of factors, both
religious and practical. Many people were sincerely inspired by the call to save the Holy Land, but others went
for less honorable reasons.

2. Taking the Cross: Responsibilities and Rewards
by Jonathan Riley-Smith   85
The ceremonies surrounding a crusader's vow to fight in
the Middle East were fraught with religious symbolism.
Crusaders were promised many spiritual rewards in return for their military service.

3. The Military Orders *by Henry Treece*   93
The Christian military orders of the Middle East that
arose during the Crusades combined religious fervor
with military prowess. The Knights Hospitallers and the
Knights Templar were powerful forces that commanded
respect from both the Muslims and the European kings
of Jerusalem.

4. Religious Hysteria Led to Participation
by Norman P. Zacour   99
The Children's Crusade was closely related to other
mass movements of religious hysteria during the Middle
Ages. Its combination of religious enthusiasm and mob
psychology led to a disastrous outcome for many of the
participants.

Chapter 3: Social Changes and Cultural Influences of the Crusades

1. Life in the Crusader Kingdoms *by Antony Bridge*   109
The crusaders who remained in the Middle East established kingdoms based on those in Europe, but gradually
they adopted much of the Eastern way of life.

2. Relations Between Eastern and Western Christians
by R.C. Smail   119
Many Eastern Christians lived in the crusader kingdoms.
Relations between the Western and the Eastern Christians were usually good, but their cultural and religious
differences sometimes created problems.

3. **The Crusades' Impact on Women and Jews**
   by Ronald C. Finucane   125
   The ruthless military mindset and unyielding Christian
   fervor of the crusaders often created dangerous situations for European women and Jews.
4. **Expansion of Trade** *by Hilmar C. Krueger*   135
   The Crusades enabled Italian merchants to greatly expand their trading practices. The Italians established
   outposts in the crusader kingdoms in order to meet the
   demand for Middle Eastern goods in Western Europe.
5. **An Influx of Knowledge from the East**
   by Martin Erbstösser   143
   Western Europeans benefitted from agricultural, techni-
   cal, and scientific knowledge that they obtained from the
   Arabs during the time of the Crusades.

Chapter 4: Were the Crusades a Success?

1. **The Crusades Were Successful**
   by T.A. Archer and Charles Lethbridge Kingsford   153
   Taken as a whole, the Crusades were a success. If the
   crusading movement had not taken place, Western Europe would have been invaded and possibly conquered
   by the Muslims.

2. **The Crusades Were a Partial Success**
   by James A. Brundage   157
   The Crusades failed in their immediate goals; however,
   in their long-range impact on Europe, they succeeded in
   ways that the original crusaders would never have imagined.

3. **The Crusades Were a Failure** *by Steven Runciman*   161
   Destructive and barbaric, the Crusades represent a tragic
   episode in history. Not only did the crusaders fail to
   achieve their goals, but they caused irrevocable damage
   to the Byzantines and the Muslims.

Chapter 5: The Legacy of the Crusades

1. **The Crusades Led to the Decay of Near Eastern
   Civilization** *by J.J. Saunders*   175
   Primarily because they were weakened during the Crusades, the Byzantine Empire and the Islamic world lost
   their position of cultural dominance to Western European civilization.

2. **The Crusades Precipitated the Discovery of the New World** *by Joshua Prawer*   183

Christopher Columbus and other explorers were motivated by the idea of renewing the Crusades. Some hoped to find a western route to the Islamic countries, while others were inspired by a missionary movement that traced its origins to the crusading ideology.

3. **The Crusades Gave Rise to the Modern Conflict in the Middle East** *by Karen Armstrong*   188

The legacy of the Crusades is reflected in the twentieth-century conflict between the Israelis and the Palestinians in the Middle East. European and American reactions to this conflict stem directly from attitudes that formulated during the Crusades.

Map: Europe at the Time of the Crusades   203

Appendix: Excerpts from Original Documents
    Pertaining to the Crusades   204

Discussion Questions   235

Chronology   239

For Further Research   249

Index   252

Foreword

Certain past events stand out as pivotal, as having effects and outcomes that change the course of history. These events are often referred to as turning points. Historian Louis L. Snyder provides this useful definition:

> A turning point in history is an event, happening, or stage which thrusts the course of historical development into a different direction. By definition a turning point is a great event, but it is even more—a great event with the explosive impact of altering the trend of man's life on the planet.

History's turning points have taken many forms. Some were single, brief, and shattering events with immediate and obvious impact. The invasion of Britain by William the Conqueror in 1066, for example, swiftly transformed that land's political and social institutions and paved the way for the rise of the modern English nation. By contrast, other single events were deemed of minor significance when they occurred, only later recognized as turning points. The assassination of a little-known European nobleman, Archduke Franz Ferdinand, on June 28, 1914, in the Bosnian town of Sarajevo was such an event; only after it touched off a chain reaction of political-military crises that escalated into the global conflict known as World War I did the murder's true significance become evident.

Other crucial turning points occurred not in terms of a few hours, days, months, or even years, but instead as evolutionary developments spanning decades or even centuries. One of the most pivotal turning points in human history, for instance—the development of agriculture, which replaced nomadic hunter-gatherer societies with more permanent settlements—occurred over the course of many generations. Still other great turning points were neither events nor developments, but rather revolutionary new inventions and innovations that significantly altered social customs and ideas, military tactics, home life, the spread of knowledge, and the human condition in general. The developments of writing, gunpowder, the printing press, antibiotics, the electric light, atomic energy, television, and the computer, the last two of which have recently ushered in the world-altering information age, represent only some of these innovative turning points.

Each anthology in the Greenhaven Turning Points in World History series presents a group of essays chosen for their accessibility. The anthology's structure also enhances this accessibility. First, an introductory essay provides a general overview of the principal events and figures involved, placing the topic in its historical context. The essays that follow explore various aspects in more detail, some targeting political trends and consequences, others social, literary, cultural, and/or technological ramifications, and still others pivotal leaders and other influential figures. To aid the reader in choosing the material of immediate interest or need, each essay is introduced by a concise summary of the contributing writer's main themes and insights.

In addition, each volume contains extensive research tools, including a collection of excerpts from primary source documents pertaining to the historical events and figures under discussion. In the anthology on the French Revolution, for example, readers can examine the works of Rousseau, Voltaire, and other writers and thinkers whose championing of human rights helped fuel the French people's growing desire for liberty; the French *Declaration of the Rights of Man and Citizen*, presented to King Louis XVI by the French National Assembly on October 2, 1789; and eyewitness accounts of the attack on the royal palace and the horrors of the Reign of Terror. To guide students interested in pursuing further research on the subject, each volume features an extensive bibliography, which for easy access has been divided into separate sections by topic. Finally, a comprehensive index allows readers to scan and locate content efficiently. Each of the anthologies in the Greenhaven Turning Points in World History series provides students with a complete, detailed, and enlightening examination of a crucial historical watershed.

Introduction

After the fall of the Roman Empire in the fifth century, Western Europe sank into the Dark Ages. Governments disintegrated; economic structures fell apart; education and the arts declined. The majority of the population lived in ignorance and poverty. They feared the violence that accompanied the frequent political battles among the nobles, as well as the periodic raids and invasions by the Vikings, the Arabs, and the Turks. Life was difficult, uncertain, and often very short.

But although Western Europe was repeatedly attacked and its cities plundered, it was never completely conquered. Gradually, both the invasions from external enemies and the internal hostilities began to taper off, giving the continent some breathing room and the ability to concentrate on more than sheer survival. By the eleventh century, the Dark Ages were coming to a close as Western Europe entered a period of intellectual, cultural, political, and economic revival.

The Crusades were part and parcel of this European renaissance. They could not have taken place during the Dark Ages, when resources and manpower were scarce, when the European countries were overwhelmed with protecting their own borders against aggressive invaders. As historians Joseph R. Strayer and Dana C. Munro write, the Crusades demonstrate "the terrific energy and unbounded optimism" that Europe experienced during its recovery from the Dark Ages. Strayer and Munro assert, "It took supreme confidence . . . to dream of establishing a Christian outpost in the heart of the Moslem world, at a time when Europe had barely recovered from the last invasions." Not only did the European resurgence lead men to dream of such victories, but it also enabled the crusaders to make those dreams a reality. The revitalized strength of the Catholic Church gave impetus to the idea of fighting a holy war, the relative peace and cooperation between the rulers of Europe allowed the Crusades to be organized, and the lack of external threats made it safe for massive armies to leave Europe for the Holy Land.

In many ways, however, the Crusades also contributed to the revitalization of Western European society. For instance, the Byzantine Greeks and the Middle Eastern Muslims had retained much of the scientific and cultural knowledge of the ancient Greeks and Romans that had been lost to Western Europe during the Dark Ages. During the crusading period, many crusaders and European settlers in the Holy Land were exposed to these ideas and transmitted the knowledge back to Europe, where it added to the resurgence of education taking place. The Crusades also enabled the establishment of new trade routes between Western Europe and the Middle East, which strengthened and expanded the economic revival in Europe. If not for the Crusades, many historians believe, Western Europe would never have been able to establish itself as a major world power in later centuries.

The Crusades also had a significant impact on the other societies involved: the Muslims, the Byzantine Greeks, and the European Jews. Each of these peoples was diminished in strength, territory, or numbers by the Crusades. Indeed, some historians argue that the Crusades—and the consequent settlement of Western Europeans in the Middle East—represent the first harbinger of the European impulse toward colonialism and imperialism that in subsequent centuries would reshape the world. Furthermore, as many historians and social commentators have pointed out, attitudes and prejudices formulated during the period of the Crusades still affect modern perceptions, and even political policy. According to these experts, to thoroughly understand such modern-day problems as the conflict in the Middle East, the tensions between the Roman Catholic and Greek Orthodox churches, and the widespread persecution of European Jews during World War II, one must examine the crusading movement and its legacy.

Turning Points in World History: The Crusades provides a thorough overview of the varied aspects of the Crusades. The essays included in this volume explore the historical events that led to the Crusades, the impact of the crusading movement and of the settlement of the crusader kingdoms in the Middle East, and the Crusades' long-lasting influence on western society. These readings are supplemented by an appendix of primary source documents that present the Crusades in the words of those who actually experienced them. The documents include voices from all sides involved in the Holy Wars: the crusaders and their descendants who settled in the Middle East, the Muslims whose homelands were invaded by the crusaders, the Byzantine Greeks who instigated the Crusades by asking Western Europe for aid and later suffered themselves from the crusaders' rapacity, and the European Jews whose communities were destroyed by armies on their way to fight in the Crusades. In addition, both the historical essay that begins this volume and the detailed chronology place in context the events discussed in the articles and documents.

The Crusades are complex in their historical significance, encompassing religious, cultural, economic, political, and societal changes that affected several different regions and ethnicities. The selections featured in this volume are intended to introduce readers to the multifaceted impact that the Crusades made on the world of the Middle Ages, as well as the aftershocks of that impact that still remain today.

A Brief History of the Crusades

In the chill of a late autumn day, a crowd gathered in a field outside the city of Clermont in the province of Auvergne, in south-central France. More than two hundred bishops, knights, and barons were present, as well as many curious villagers and peasants who had heard rumors that Pope Urban II was to make an important announcement.

The pope ascended an elevated platform and began to address the assembly, describing in bloody detail Muslim atrocities against the Orthodox Christians of the East. Not only were these Christians suffering, Urban declared, but Western Europeans on pilgrimages to the Holy Land were also encountering hostility from the Muslims who controlled the region. Worst of all, the sacred city of Jerusalem itself was under Muslim rule, its holy places desecrated. The pope called on his listeners to embark on a holy war to assist their beleaguered Christian brethren and to free Jerusalem. The crowd responded immediately and enthusiastically, shouting "God wills it!" as nobles fell to their knees to vow allegiance to the pope and his great cause.

It was November 27, 1095, and the First Crusade had just begun.

Religious Conflicts

To fully grasp the motivation behind the military expeditions known as the Crusades, it is helpful to understand the religious and territorial conflicts that preceded them. The practitioners of three major world religions—Christianity, Islam, and Judaism—were significantly affected by the Crusades, yet in many respects the Crusades were simply a continuation of historical conflict among these three beliefs.

Judaism is the oldest of the three religions, with origins traced to approximately 1850 B.C. Jerusalem, the site of the Temple of Solomon, was originally the holy city of the Jewish people alone. However, Jerusalem and the rest of what is now Israel fell under the control of the Roman Empire during the first century A.D., the period in which Christianity arose. The Christian religion began as a sect of Judaism, but soon attracted many non-Jewish converts and diverged further and further from Jewish practices and beliefs. Christians also considered Jerusalem to be their most sacred city because it was the site of many important events in the life of Christ.

For centuries, adherents of Christianity were persecuted by the Roman Empire. In 313, however, Emperor Constantine converted to Christianity and declared it the official religion of the Empire, enabling Christianity to spread throughout the vast territory under Roman domination. The official validation of their religion also allowed Christians to exercise more control over the holy places in Jerusalem, which was still part of the Empire.

By the beginning of the fifth century, the Roman Empire had grown so large and unwieldy that it was divided into western and eastern sections, to be ruled by two emperors. Rome remained the capital of the western region, while the ancient city of Byzantium—renamed Constantinople in honor of Constantine—served as the capital of the eastern section. Almost immediately after the division, the western section of the empire was wracked by the first of many invasions by the Visigoths and other warlike barbarian tribes. These invasions eventually resulted in the fall of the western empire in 476. On the other hand, the eastern section, called the Byzantine Empire, remained strong and even expanded its boundaries through conquest.

This division of the Roman Empire, as well as the different fates of the two areas, contributed to a growing disparity between the eastern and western branches of Christianity. The Western Church was governed by the pope in Rome, whereas the Byzantine emperor was the head of the Eastern Church. Over time, the Byzantine emperors and the Roman popes began to challenge each other for ultimate control of the church. Basic cultural differences also deepened: For example, the liturgy of the Western Church was in Latin, while the language of the Eastern Church was Greek. Gradually, the two branches of Christianity developed irreconcilable theological differences as well. Tensions boiled over in 1054, when the pope excommunicated the patriarch of Constantinople, one of the highest-ranking clergy of the Eastern Church. At this point, known as the Great Schism, the Christian Church split into two separate entities: the Roman Catholic (or Latin) Church in Western Europe and the Eastern (or Greek) Orthodox Church in the Byzantine Empire.

Meanwhile, a new religion had risen in the Middle East. During the 610s, an Arab named Muhammad began preaching the doctrine that became the religion Islam, whose believers are Muslims. Like Christianity, Islam had deep roots in Judaism. Muhammad also taught that Jesus was an important prophet, although not God incarnate as Christians believed. He considered Islam to be a continuation of these two religions, the final revelation of the Judeo-Christian faith. Islam's most sacred sites were the Arabic cities of Mecca and Medina, but Jerusalem held an important place as the third holiest city.

Islam spread rapidly throughout the Arab world, and believers were enjoined to propagate the new religion through political conquest. The Muslims obeyed this injunction with stunning speed. During the mid-600s, they conquered Syria, Egypt, and Persia and wrested control of Jerusalem from the Eastern Christians. By the early 700s, the Muslims ruled over an empire that included central India and the northern coastline of Africa. Encroaching on Byzantine lands, they threatened Constantinople numerous times but were repeatedly turned back.

The Muslims also posed a threat to the Western Christians. The southern regions of Spain fell to Muslim invaders in the early 700s, Sardinia and Corsica were toppled a century later, and Sicily came under Muslim domination in 902. Throughout the eighth century, the Muslims made unsuccessful advances on France; during the ninth century they raided several cities in southern Italy and terrorized the outskirts of Rome. During the tenth and eleventh centuries, popes led armies in repulsing the Muslims from Italy, and Spanish Christians began the long reconquest of their lands. Thus, by the time of the First Crusade, Western Europeans were long accustomed to fighting Muslims. Indeed, many considered the Crusades as simply an extension of their struggle to drive the Muslims out of Europe.

Jerusalem Under Muslim Rule

In 638 the city of Jerusalem surrendered to the Muslim army after a year-long siege. The majority of the city's inhabitants were either Christian or Jewish, but though they must have been concerned about their fate, they soon discovered that life under Muslim rule was fairly benign. According to Muhammad's teachings, Jews and Christians were People of the Book (that is, their religions are based on biblical scripture, as is Islam) and were therefore entitled to practice their religions freely and peaceably. They were allowed to retain their synagogues and churches and were also granted a measure of political autonomy within their religious communities. The Muslim rulers did subject Jews and Christians to some restrictive regulations: For example, they were required to wear distinctive clothing, were forbidden to bear arms or ride on horseback, and had to pay special taxes. But these restrictions were mild in comparison with the type of persecution Christians and Jews feared, and they found that the taxes imposed by the Muslims were much lower than those levied by the Byzantine emperor. The inhabitants of Jerusalem, as well as those Christians and Jews in other sections of the Middle East that had been conquered by the Muslims, "had never enjoyed such freedom," writes historical author Henry Treece. "[T]axes were low, business was good, administration was efficient. . . . Moslem rule, social and political, was the best the Mediterranean world had known since the finest days of the Roman empire."

The Jews in particular fared better under Muslim rule than they had under Byzantine authority. Although the Christians acknowledged that their own religion was indebted to the earlier religion of Judaism, in general they were less tolerant toward other faiths than the Muslims were. The Byzantine rulers had placed the Jews under strict civil disabilities and had actively sought to convert them. Many Christians also distrusted or even hated Jews, holding them responsible for Christ's death on the cross. On the other hand, many Jews resented the fact that Christians controlled traditionally Jewish territory, especially their holy city of Jerusalem. During the Byzantine reign of Jerusalem, Christians and Jews had lived together uneasily, with periodic outbreaks of Christian oppression or violence against the Jewish population. "In return," notes historian Steven Runciman, the Jews "seized every opportunity for doing harm to the Christians." In fact, the Jews so disliked the rule of the Byzantine Empire that many provided aid and information to the invading Muslim forces.

By and large, the Muslim rulers, or caliphs, were able to keep peace in Jerusalem. Under their reign, both Christians and Jews had unimpeded access to their holy shrines. The caliphs allowed the Christian churches in Jerusalem to maintain religious ties with the emperor in Constantinople and other important leaders of the Orthodox Church. The only notable exception occurred during the regime of the insane caliph, Hakim, who persecuted both Christians and Jews from 1004 until he was deposed in 1021, after which the policy of religious tolerance was restored. Furthermore, the Muslims welcomed Christian pilgrims who made the long journey from the Byzantine Empire or Western Europe to visit the sacred sites in Jerusalem. Even during Hakim's oppressive rule, a steady stream of pilgrimages to the Holy Land continued with few interruptions.

However, this state of affairs would soon change with the arrival of new players on the scene: the Seljuk Turks.

The Turks and the Battle of Manzikert

The Turkish peoples of Central Asia lived primarily in nomadic tribes and clans. In the tenth century, they came under the rule of the Muslims and converted to Islam. During the eleventh century, one of these Turkish clans, called the Seljuks, began to make inroads into the Muslim world. The Seljuks started by taking control of Baghdad in 1055, then conquering Persia and Syria. During the late 1050s, they also began to invade Armenia, which was part of the Byzantine Empire.

In 1071, the Seljuks achieved two military victories that

would set the stage for the Crusades. First, the Seljuks over-threw the Egyptian Muslims who ruled Jerusalem, gaining control of the city as well as much of the Holy Land. Tired of the Seljuk incursions into Byzantine territory, Emperor Romanus IV Diogenes decided to crush the Turkish threat once and for all. The Seljuk forces came face to face with the Byzantine army at Manzikert in Armenia. Though far out-numbered, the Seljuks destroyed the Byzantine army and captured the emperor. After this devastating defeat, the Byzantines were unable to stop the Seljuks from overrun-ning most of Asia Minor and reducing the Byzantine Empire to a small strip of land surrounding Constantinople.

Before the Seljuk victories of 1071, pilgrims from West-ern Europe crossed through the Byzantine Empire and then bought safe passage into Jerusalem from the Egyptian Mus-lims who governed the Holy Land. After 1071, the Seljuk Turks controlled almost all of the pilgrimage route, and they were not inclined to be as helpful to European pilgrims. As Runciman explains:

> Anatolia could now be traversed only if the voyager took an armed escort; and even so the way was full of danger, and wars or hostile authorities often held him up. Syria was little better. Everywhere there were brigands on the roads; and at each small town the local lord tried to levy a tax on passers-by. The pilgrims that succeeded in overcoming all the diffi-culties returned to the West weary and impoverished, with a dreadful tale to tell.

When, in his speech at Clermont, Pope Urban II com-plained of Muslim harassment of Christian pilgrims, it was the Seljuk Turks to whom he referred.

An Appeal for Help

While the new dangers encountered by pilgrims from the West were a matter of concern, the Turks' decisive victory at the Battle of Manzikert and subsequent conquest of much of the Christian East were even more worrisome to the reli-gious and secular leaders of Western Europe. The French and the Italians had battled Muslim invaders on their own soil within recent memory, and the Spanish Christians were still fighting the Muslims for control of their territory. They were naturally alarmed by their common enemy's rampage through Eastern Christendom. And despite the Great Schism, the Latin Church had no desire to see the Greek Church fall to the Muslims. As early as 1074, Pope Gregory VII, the predecessor of Urban II, made plans to lead an army to drive the Seljuks out of the Byzantine Empire, but for a variety of reasons he was unable to put these plans into effect.

In 1081, Alexius I Comnenus became the emperor of Byzantium. Alexius, a skilled military leader, immediately began to stem the tide of the Seljuk invasion. But although he was able to stop the Turks from further encroaching on his land, Alexius realized that he could not regain the territory that the Byzantines had already lost to the Turks without aid. So in the early 1090s, he turned to the West for help. He wrote letters to lords and nobles, describing Muslim atrocities against the Byzantine Christians and asking for military assistance; at least one of these letters came to the attention of Pope Urban II. In February 1095, Alexius made a direct appeal to Urban, sending diplomatic envoys to a church council that was being held in Piacenza, Italy. According to writer Antony Bridge:

> [Alexius] did not appeal to the Christians of the West to help him restore the fortunes of his own Empire, nor did he ask them directly to help him turn the Turks out of Asia Minor, which was almost certainly his true concern; instead he appealed to the Pope in Rome to help him rescue the Christians of the East and their churches from the tyranny of their Moslem conquerors. It was intolerable that they and the holy places of their faith, to which so many pilgrims had travelled in the past, should now be crushed under the oppressive heel of infidel Turks, he said.

Alexius's plea to his fellow Christians deeply touched the pope and the other listeners at the council. It is highly likely that Urban had already given serious consideration to aiding the Byzantines, but after the Council of Piacenza he began to make concrete plans. Urban laid the groundwork for a council to be held in November at Clermont, where he would announce the First Crusade.

The overwhelming response Urban received from the crowd at Clermont in November 1095 far exceeded his expectations. Almost certainly Urban only intended to enlist nobles, knights, and other trained military men in his holy war against the Muslims. But from the first, his message had tremendous appeal to the common people and the poor, the villagers and the peasants. For nine months after the Council of Clermont, Urban journeyed across France to preach the Crusade. Throughout Europe, Catholic bishops, priests, and monks spread the word and gathered recruits, especially in France, Italy, and Germany. As men and women of the lower classes flocked to take the cross, it became increasingly clear that, in historian Simon Lloyd's words, "Urban had lost control in the matter of personnel." In particular, a monk known as Peter the Hermit attracted thousands of commoners to the cause.

Another unexpected response to the call for a holy war was the outbreak of persecution against European Jews. As historian Robert Chazan explains, "Certain crusading bands interpreted the papal initiative as a call to overcome *all* infidelity and chose to begin their mission with an assault on the infidels immediately at hand, the Jews." Although both unruly peasant mobs and noble armies attacked European Jews, the knights were far more brutal and efficient than the peasants, ruthlessly massacring entire Jewish communities. The bloodshed was greatest during the period preceding the First Crusade, but it became something of a tradition throughout the crusading period for armies to terrorize Jewish communities on their way to the Holy Land. The Jewish settlements in the Rhineland of Germany were especially vulnerable, as crusaders typically passed through this route. According to author Malcolm Billings, "The road to the Holy Land ran through what Jews later came to describe as the first Holocaust."

Crusaders on the March

Urban had fixed the Crusade's departure date for August 15, 1096, but the commoners who flocked to Peter the Hermit's side were impatient and began to leave in April. They traveled in several contingents, which historians refer to collectively as the People's Crusade, the Peasants' Crusade, or the Paupers' Crusade. Their total number is uncertain; various estimates range from twenty thousand to three hundred thousand people. Only eight of these were knights; the rest were foot soldiers, peasants, women, and children. Peter was unable to control this horde, which caused trouble as it went, scouring the countryside for food and other supplies. The crusaders started a riot in Hungary and then sacked Belgrade.

The different bands of the People's Crusade arrived in Constantinople from mid-July to early August. News of their exploits had preceded them, but Emperor Alexius was undoubtedly surprised by the nature of the "army" that had arrived to help him. Nevertheless, he treated the crusaders respectfully and helped settle them in a large military camp in Asia Minor. Correctly assessing their military skill, Alexius advised them to wait there for the arrival of reinforcements from Western Europe rather than set out to fight the Seljuks. However, they began to provoke the Turks, raiding and pillaging nearby villages. On October 21, they decided to engage the Turks in battle, and were predictably massacred by the vastly superior Seljuk army. Only three thousand survivors managed to return to Constantinople.

The first contingent of the army of the nobles entered Constantinople shortly after the crushing defeat of the People's Crusade. Unlike the peasants who had arrived before them, the nobles had taken the time to recruit and equip competent troops and to raise money for the journey. Between August and October, the troops had set off in separate groups, each led by a powerful prince or lord. The majority of the forces were French, although the Germans and Italians were also well represented. The various military companies continued to arrive in Constantinople throughout the winter and into the spring of 1097. Although these were obviously elite troops rather than ragtag hordes of peasants, Emperor Alexius must have again been dismayed, for he had expected that the pope would send a much smaller number of mercenaries who would place themselves under his command. Instead, he found entire armies on his doorstep, with their own lords in charge.

Onward to Jerusalem

At first, the crusaders and the Byzantines worked together. Once the last troops had arrived from Western Europe, the combined armies made their first move against the Seljuk Turks. Their objective was the strategic city of Nicaea, which lay directly across the Bosporus Strait from Constantinople. They lay siege to the city in May, and on June 19, Nicaea surrendered to Alexius. The crusader army and a number of Greek troops then continued onward to Dorylaeum, where they were taken by surprise by the Seljuk sultan Qilij Arslan and his army. The ensuing battle was bloody, hard-fought, and lasted for hours, but the crusaders eventually turned the tide to their favor and routed the Seljuk forces.

In the wake of their stunning victory at Dorylaeum, the cooperation between the different contingents of crusaders began to fall apart. Two of the lesser nobles, Baldwin of Boulogne and Tancred, decided they were tired of fighting for Alexius's cause. Each split his troops off from the main army and headed into Cilicia to gain cities for himself. Meanwhile, the main army continued on to the heavily fortified city of Antioch and lay siege to it in October. In contrast to their previous victories, the siege of Antioch was long and hard. The crusaders remained camped outside the city through the winter, many of their number dying of starvation or illness. The last of the Greek contingent gave up and left for Constantinople, further reducing morale. Not until June 3, 1098, after a siege of more than seven months, did Antioch fall to the crusaders. Rather than restoring the city to Byzantine rule, one of the nobles, Bohemond of Taranto, claimed it for himself.

Almost immediately after the crusaders occupied Antioch, they were themselves besieged by a large Turkish army that had come to the defense of the city. The crusaders were already seriously weakened from the privations they had endured over the winter; now they found themselves in a besieged city, completely cut off from their food supplies. As author Robert Payne notes, their "joy over the conquest of the city was exchanged for a melancholy knowledge that they could hold out only for a few weeks and would be forced to surrender." Some discouraged and frightened crusaders deserted and headed back to Constantinople. These deserters included Count Stephen of Blois, one of the high-ranking leaders of the crusading forces, who took a number of his soldiers and knights with him when he fled. As he retreated, Stephen joined Alexius, who was leading a massive army toward Antioch. Stephen convinced the Byzantine emperor that the crusaders' situation was hopeless and that it would be suicidal to attempt to come to their aid. Alexius turned his army back. News of Alexius's fateful decision eventually reached the crusaders at Antioch. In the words of historians Joseph R. Strayer and Dana C. Munro, "To the crusaders this was the final proof of his treachery, and their natural indignation led to a series of incidents which made further coöperation with the Eastern Empire almost impossible."

With no hope of rescue, the remaining crusaders at Antioch sank into despair until a strange event occurred. One of the common soldiers, a peasant by the name of Peter Bartholomew, announced that he had had a vision in which St. Andrew had revealed to him the hiding place of the lance used to pierce Christ's side on the cross. This hiding place, Peter swore, was under the floor of St. Peter's Cathedral in Antioch itself. On June 15 a group of crusaders dug into the cathedral floor and did indeed uncover an iron lance head, which they proclaimed to be the sacred relic. As news of the miracle spread throughout the city, morale improved dramatically. On June 28, bearing the holy lance at its head, the crusader army marched outside the city gates and engaged the Muslim forces. In the ensuing battle, the ragged and gaunt crusaders fought with unusual—almost supernatural—determination and strength, until the Turkish army disintegrated into a panicked retreat.

The Battle for the Holy City

Against all odds, the crusaders had triumphed in Antioch. Now, hungry and exhausted, they decided to rest in Antioch until November, and the end of the horrendous summer heat. They also bickered among themselves, especially concerning the fate of the city. Bohemond of Taranto continued to assert his claim to the city, designating himself the prince of Antioch. Most of the crusaders no longer felt any allegiance to Emperor Alexius and therefore did not object to Bohemond's decision to keep the city. However, Count Raymond of Toulouse challenged this decision, not so much because he truly believed Antioch should be returned to Alexius as to spite Bohemond, who was his fierce rival. Bohemond also announced that rather than advancing on Jerusalem, he intended to stay in Antioch and build a kingdom in Syria. Meanwhile, a deadly epidemic swept through Antioch, killing a number of the Europeans. Not until January 1099 did the crusader army leave for Jerusalem.

While the crusaders dawdled in Antioch, the Egyptian Muslims were busy in Palestine. The crusaders' victory at Antioch alerted the Egyptian Muslims to the weakened state of the Turkish military. They seized this opportunity to invade Palestine and recover much of the land they had previously lost to the Seljuk Turks, including the city of Jerusalem. By this point, however, it mattered little to the crusaders that Jerusalem had been restored to rulers who had typically accommodated Christian pilgrims. They had come to the Middle East to free their holy city from Muslim infidels, and it made no difference to them which particular Muslims they had to fight to do so.

The crusaders' journey from Antioch to Jerusalem was slow but easy; the Muslim rulers of the towns and cities along the way surrendered quickly, often without a fight. The situation in Jerusalem itself was entirely different. The Muslim governor of the city had realized long before that the crusaders intended to conquer Jerusalem, and he had had plenty of time to prepare. When the crusading army arrived at the gates of Jerusalem on June 7, 1099, they found that the wells outside the city had been poisoned and all the livestock from the surrounding countryside had been herded behind the city walls. Inside the city, the governor had stored vast quantities of food, water, and weapons in anticipation of a long siege.

He had also expelled all the local Christians from Jerusalem, lest they prove traitorous. Perhaps most importantly, he had dispatched messengers to Egypt to ask the caliph to send an army to defend the city against the crusaders.

Realizing that Jerusalem was well protected against a siege, the crusaders decided to attack immediately, but their assault on the city walls failed. A siege seemed to be the only option left, but the crusaders lacked sufficient water, food, and supplies to carry out a prolonged siege. Matters improved somewhat on June 17, when a small fleet of ships arrived from England and Genoa, bearing food and supplies that could be used to build siege machinery. Still, it was difficult work in the searing heat of summer, with water and food extremely scarce. Again army morale began to suffer; the leaders fought among themselves while discouraged soldiers snuck out of camp and headed home under cover of night. On July 8, in an attempt to revitalize morale, the priests led a barefoot procession of soldiers and lords around the walls of the city, singing hymns and blowing trumpets. The Muslims crowded onto the city walls to mock the procession below, which only bolstered the Christians' resolve to fight.

By July 13, the crusaders had constructed two tall wooden siege towers. That night, they launched their assault against the city. For two days the crusaders worked to maneuver the siege towers against the city wall as the Muslims poured down a steady bombardment of stones, flaming arrows, and Greek fire (an incendiary substance that ignited when exposed to water). On July 15, a group of crusaders managed to cross from one of the siege towers to the top of the city wall; they then fought their way to the gates of the city and forced them open. The main body of the crusading army rushed inside. The massacre that followed was one of the bloodiest in history. After three years of hunger, thirst, sickness, and warfare in the desert, the crusaders abandoned all restraint, killing everything that moved. But they also were spurred on by prejudice and religious fervor, as Bridge relates:

> [The crusaders] did not doubt for a moment that the
> Moslem defenders of Jerusalem were hateful to God, pro-

faners of holy places, servants of anti-Christ . . . ; so they killed every man, woman and child whom they could find in the city with enjoyment and a complete assurance that they were doing the will of God.

The Jews of Jerusalem were not put to the sword, but neither were they spared. They had sought sanctuary in their chief synagogue; when the crusaders discovered them, they set the building on fire, burning the Jews alive.

When there was no one left to kill, the crusaders gathered at the Church of the Holy Sepulchre to give thanks for their victory and the deliverance of Jerusalem, folding their bloodstained hands in prayer.

The Kingdom of Jerusalem

Now the crusaders set about establishing a government for the conquered city. One of the primary leaders of the army, Godfrey of Bouillon, was elected as Jerusalem's ruler, but he refused the title of king, saying he could not wear a crown of gold in the city where Christ had worn a crown of thorns. Instead, he took the title of advocate (or defender) of the Holy Sepulchre. Godfrey did accept all the military and administrative powers of a king. He was to be the primary ruler of Outremer, a French word meaning "the land overseas," which the crusaders used to refer to the small string of towns and cities they had conquered on their journey to Jerusalem.

However, the crusaders had one last battle to fight to consolidate their claim to the Holy Land. The messengers whom the Muslim governor of Jerusalem had dispatched to Egypt had succeeded in convincing the Egyptian caliph to send a sizable army against the crusaders. The Egyptian army had not arrived soon enough to save the Muslims of Jerusalem, but posed a serious threat nevertheless: They greatly outnumbered the crusaders and were eager to avenge the Jerusalem massacre. In early August the Egyptians camped at the town of Ascalon and readied themselves to march against the crusaders. They never expected that the much smaller crusader army would attack *them* first, but on August 12, at dawn, the crusaders launched a surprise attack, riding right through the middle of the Muslims' camp and cutting down soldiers who had just been startled awake. The Egyptians panicked and fled; most were slaughtered as they ran.

After the resounding defeat of the Egyptian army, the Muslims in the area offered very little further resistance. With Jerusalem safe in Christian hands, the crusading army began to disperse. Some of the crusaders headed home to Europe, but others decided to settle in Jerusalem or the other cities they had conquered. Several high-ranking lords hoped to carve out their own kingdoms and set off with their small armies to attack other Muslim cities. In July 1100, Godfrey died, and his brother Baldwin succeeded him as ruler of Jerusalem. Unlike Godfrey, Baldwin had no qualms about accepting the title of king of Jerusalem and eventually established a hereditary monarchy. The rulers of the other crusader kingdoms—the principality of Antioch, the county of Edessa, and the county of Tripoli—were considered subject to the ultimate authority of the king of Jerusalem. Naturally, Emperor Alexius was not pleased that the Western European knights had taken over land that had been his, but his protests went unheeded.

Those crusaders who chose to remain in Outremer gradually adopted some native customs and habits. They traded their heavy woolen and fur clothing for comfortable silk robes better suited for the desert. They learned at least a smattering of Arabic, necessary for communication. Their children and grandchildren who were born and reared in the Middle East adopted an even more pronounced Eastern lifestyle. Although the crusaders and their descendants would continue to fight both the Muslims and the Byzantine Greeks, there were also periods when they would live together in peace. Despite the wholesale massacre at Jerusalem, the city soon regained its cosmopolitan nature, with Muslims, Jews, Greek Christians, and Latin Christians living side by side. Business relationships and even close friendships developed among the disparate inhabitants of the region.

The crusaders tended to refer to all Muslims as Saracens, a word they adopted from the Byzantines. The exact origin of the word is unclear, but it seems to have been derived from the Arabic word *Sharkeyn*, which simply meant "eastern peoples." On the other hand, the majority of the participants in the First Crusade had been French—or Franks, as they were then called—so the Muslims began to refer to all Latin Christians indiscriminately as "the Franj." Despite this tendency to lump disparate groups together under one name, the Franks were sufficiently astute to exploit conflicts that arose between different factions of the Saracens, and vice versa. During the existence of the crusader kingdoms, it was not uncommon for the Franks to quarrel among themselves and therefore to seek alliances with the Saracens. Likewise, rival Saracen rulers might ally themselves with different crusader kingdoms. Such behavior never ceased to amaze new arrivals from Europe, who were shocked that good Christians would make treaties with the dreaded Muslim infidels.

The Second Crusade

This is not to say, however, that relations between the crusader kingdoms and the Muslims remained peaceful. In fact, most of the subsequent Crusades began when the Franks of the Middle East appealed to the pope and the European kings for help in battling their Saracen foes. The Second Crusade is a good example. For several decades, the Franks had taken advantage of divisions between various Muslim factions to gain even more territory for themselves. But beginning in 1128, a Turkish ruler named 'Imad ad-Din Zangi began to make incursions into the crusader kingdoms. Slowly but surely, Zangi captured several strategic Christian fortresses and towns. Then in 1144, he struck a powerful blow by capturing the city of Edessa, the capital of one of the four main crusader kingdoms. Just as the Christians had decimated Jerusalem, so Zangi and his forces slaughtered the Franks to the last man and sold the surviving women and children into slavery.

The king of Jerusalem appealed to the Western Europeans for help, and—appalled by the details of the massacre at Edessa—the pope declared a new Crusade. This time the crusading armies were led by Louis VII, the king of France, and Conrad III, the emperor of Germany. The two armies took different routes to Outremer; along the way, both armies encountered Muslim forces and sustained heavy losses in battle or raids. When the crusader armies regrouped in Jerusalem, they decided to march against the city of Damascus. This turned out to be a terrible mistake: Although Damascus was ruled by Muslims, it had also been threatened by Zangi's forces, and its leader had formed an alliance with the Christians in Jerusalem against their mutual enemy. As soon as the crusader army besieged Damascus, the governor of Damascus appealed to Zangi's son Nur ed-Din to send his forces to defend the city. Thus the crusaders made an enemy of Damascus, the one city willing to remain allied with them. In less than a week of fighting, Louis and Conrad simply gave up and retreated to Jerusalem. Whereas the soldiers of the First Crusade had won an almost miraculous victory, the Second Crusade ended in a humiliating fiasco and achieved nothing.

During the next few years, Nur ed-Din benefited from the crusading armies' foolishness, taking control of Damascus and making more inroads into the Franks' territory. However, he spent most of his time and energy fighting the Egyptian Muslims, as did his successor Saladin. By 1175, Saladin had consolidated his control over the Muslim world, establishing himself as the ruler of both Egypt and Syria. At this point, he turned his sights to the crusader kingdoms. There followed several years in which Saladin conquered parts of the Franks' territory but did not unleash the full power of his army against the Christians. On two occasions, he agreed to a truce with the king of Jerusalem. Both of these truces were broken by the same man, Reynald of Châtillon, the Christian ruler of Antioch. When Reynald broke the truce for the second time by attacking a Muslim caravan, Saladin mobilized his troops and declared outright war on the Franks.

On July 1, 1187, Saladin's army stormed the Christian town of Tiberias, near the Sea of Galilee. They captured the city easily but were unable to take the citadel, where a small contingent of Frankish knights protected the Christians who had sought refuge there. Saladin lay siege to the citadel, and the Franks assembled an army and marched toward Tiberias. On July 3, the Frankish army camped in the desert near two hills known as the Horns of Hattin. The next morning, they awoke to find themselves surrounded by Saladin's army. The Muslims had set fire to the brush surrounding the Franks' camp so that smoke blew into the Christians' eyes as they struggled to defend themselves against the Saracen archers and swordsmen. Only a few managed to escape; most were cut down or captured by Saladin's troops. King Guy of Jerusalem was among those captured and held prisoner.

The Battle of Hattin was a decisive moment in the history of the Crusades. Having annihilated the Christian army, the Muslims swept down onto the crusader kingdoms and easily conquered every Frankish city except Tyre, Antioch, and Tripoli. Jerusalem fell on October 2, 1187. Showing more mercy than the First Crusaders had shown, Saladin gave strict orders that the Christians of Jerusalem were not to be massacred. He did, however, sell thousands of Latin Christians into slavery.

The Third Crusade

News of the loss of Jerusalem and the devastation of the crusader kingdoms shocked Western Europe, and the pope immediately declared a new Crusade. Frederick Barbarossa, the emperor of Germany, set out first but drowned while trying to cross a river in Cilicia, and his army fell apart after his death. The kings of France and England, Phillip II and Richard I, respectively, also vowed to join the Crusade, but they did not arrive in the Holy Land until 1191. By that time, King Guy had gained his freedom from Saladin and had pulled together an army capable of laying siege to the town of Acre. Phillip and Richard added their troops to the siege, and Acre fell to the crusaders on July 12. Shortly after the victory at Acre, Phillip departed for Europe, having had enough of crusading. But King Richard—known as Richard the Lionheart—remained and took command of the crusaders.

The Third Crusade is probably best known for the year of fighting that followed, especially the relationship that developed between the two enemy leaders. Richard the Lionheart and Saladin were both bloodthirsty and vengeful, but both displayed courage and compassion as well. Both embodied the code of chivalry that characterized the Middle Ages, and many stories describe their exploits and the respect each felt for the other. During one battle, for instance, Richard was fighting furiously when his horse was killed from under him; seeing this, Saladin ordered a pair of horses to be sent to Richard under a flag of truce so that the king would not have to fight on foot.

Richard was able to reclaim several towns for the Franks, but he never reached Jerusalem. In September 1192, he and Saladin agreed to a treaty by which the Franks would keep a strip of land along the coast from Tyre to Jaffa. The Muslims would continue to control the rest of the territory, including Jerusalem, but they guaranteed the right of Christian pilgrims to visit Jerusalem unmolested. After concluding the treaty, Richard returned to England.

Although Richard had failed to recover Jerusalem, he had ensured the safety of Christian pilgrimages to the Holy City, restored strategic territory to the Franks, and strengthened their military position in Outremer. These achievements did not satisfy Pope Innocent III, however, who considered the Third Crusade a dismal failure. In 1198 he proclaimed the Fourth Crusade, with the goal of liberating Jerusalem. Ironically, the Fourth Crusade would go down in history as the most corrupt and immoral Crusade of all.

The Fourth Crusade

The French lords who volunteered for the Fourth Crusade needed passage by ship to the Holy Land. In 1201 some wealthy merchants from the Italian city of Venice agreed to provide transport, but when the nobles arrived in Venice, they discovered that they could not raise enough money to cover the cost. The merchants persuaded the crusaders to help them capture the Hungarian city of Zara, a rival seaport. Zara's treasury, the merchants said, contained enough money to meet their price and still leave plenty of booty for the crusaders. Some of the crusaders were hesitant because

Zara was a Christian city, but eventually—without informing the pope—they agreed to the Venetians' terms. In 1202 they sailed to the coast of Dalmatia and attacked Zara, which fell on November 15.

The crusaders decided to winter in Zara and head for the Holy Land in the spring. However, over the winter they became involved in the intrigues of the Byzantine court. Emperor Isaac II had recently been overthrown by his brother, who then had himself crowned as Emperor Alexius III. Isaac's son, Alexius Angelus, escaped to the west and approached the crusaders, begging their assistance in ousting his uncle and regaining his rightful throne. In return, Alexius Angelus promised to cover the cost of the Crusade and provide the crusaders with an army of ten thousand Greek soldiers. The crusaders found it difficult to resist such a lucrative offer, and in June 1203 they arrived at the gates of Constantinople.

At first, everything seemed to go smoothly. After a brief period of skirmishes, Alexius III and his followers fled the city, and the people of Constantinople gladly welcomed Alexius Angelus as their new emperor. Soon, though, the situation soured. The crusaders realized that Alexius Angelus had promised them much more than he could deliver, and the people of Constantinople discovered that he was an incompetent ruler as well. In 1204 the Greeks rose up against Alexius and then expelled the crusaders from the city. Frustrated and angry, the crusaders decided to retaliate by attacking Constantinople. On April 12 they breached the city walls and set out on a rampage fueled by insatiable greed and rage. In Bridge's words,

> [The] massacre . . . beggars description. For three days twenty thousand armed men roved the city in bands, often drunk and always totally out of control, raping, murdering, robbing and looting as they went. The destruction was immense. . . . Priests robbed the churches. . . . In the streets no one was spared; nuns were stripped and violated, . . . children had their heads cracked like egg-shells against the walls as soldiers swung them by the heels.

After the crusaders had thoroughly sacked Constantinople, they forgot their promise to free Jerusalem. Instead, they elected one of their own as emperor of Constantinople and established Latin rule over most of the territory that had been the Byzantine Empire. Their reign lasted less than sixty years; in 1261 a descendant of the royal house of the Byzantines took Constantinople by force. The only true lasting effect of the Fourth Crusade was the solidification of the mistrust and hatred between the Eastern Orthodox and Roman Catholic Churches.

The Later Crusades

Pope Innocent III was understandably upset by the outcome of the Fourth Crusade, but this failure did not prevent him from trying a second time. During the 1210s, he once again encouraged the nobles of Europe to rescue Jerusalem from the Saracens. The nobles and their armies arrived in the Holy Land in 1218 and decided to attack Egypt first. They began by laying siege to the city of Damietta in the Nile Delta. The siege dragged on for over a year before Damietta finally fell in November 1219. Many historians believe that the Fifth Crusaders could have repeated the amazing successes of the First Crusade if they had taken immediate advantage of their victory and advanced farther into Egypt. Instead, the crusaders began to argue among themselves and did not budge from Damietta for another eighteen months, allowing the Egyptian Muslims sufficient time to regroup. In the summer of 1221 the crusader army finally engaged the Egyptians at Mansourah, but then sued for peace when they found themselves hopelessly trapped by the floodwaters of the Nile. The Egyptian sultan agreed on the condition that the crusaders surrender Damietta and sign an eight-year truce. The weary crusaders acquiesced, and thus the Fifth Crusade ended without effecting any permanent changes.

The Sixth Crusade was basically the undertaking of one man, Frederick II, the emperor of Germany. Frederick had vowed to go on the Fifth Crusade, but although he sent a number of troops, he never actually reached the Holy Land himself and eventually was excommunicated by the pope for

failing to uphold his sacred pledge. Long after the undistin-
guished end of the Fifth Crusade, however, Frederick
headed to Outremer without papal authority. His primary
motivation seems to have been to add Jerusalem to his empire. In 1225, Frederick had married Queen Yolanda of
Jerusalem, and although she had died young, she had left
him a son through whom he planned to claim the right to
the throne of the Kingdom of Jerusalem.

Frederick arrived in Outremer in September 1228, at a
time when Muslim leaders were fighting among themselves.
The sultan of Egypt was more than willing to come to terms
with Frederick and they commenced peaceful negotiations.
On February 18, 1229, they signed an agreement in which
Jerusalem, Bethlehem, Nazareth, and other cities and territories were restored to the Christians. Exactly a month later,
Frederick was crowned king of Jerusalem at the Church of
the Holy Sepulchre. He left for Europe shortly thereafter,
never to return to his kingdom in the Holy Land.

The treaty signed by Frederick and the Egyptian sultan
had also guaranteed ten years of peace between the Franks
and the Muslims. Regrettably, the Franks spent these ten
years mired in civil war. Then in 1244 another nomadic
group of Muslim Turks known as the Khorezmians swept
down onto Jerusalem and sacked the city, leaving few survivors. The Franks quickly formed a coalition with the Syrian Muslims, but this combined army was shattered by the
Khorezmians and the Egyptian forces at the Battle of Harbiyah in October.

These events triggered the Seventh Crusade, led by the
pious King Louis IX of France. Louis and his army arrived
in Outremer in 1249 and speedily captured Damietta, but
then they proceeded to Mansourah, which was to doom the
Seventh Crusade as surely as it had sealed the fate of the
Fifth Crusade. To Louis's credit, he waited to advance on
Mansourah until the annual flooding of the Nile had sub-
sided, and his siege of the city almost succeeded. But after a
fierce battle on February 8, 1250, the Egyptians were able to
cut off the crusaders' supply routes. Louis held out for a
while, hoping for a turn of events, but by April famine and

disease had so weakened his troops that he attempted to retreat. The Muslims followed in hot pursuit, and Louis, himself so ill that he could barely stand, was forced to surrender his entire army. Although Louis and many of his knights were eventually ransomed and allowed to return to Europe, the Seventh Crusade had utterly failed.

The Mamluk Threat

The Christians of Outremer soon faced a new threat to their existence. In 1261 a Mamluk Turk named Baybars was declared the sultan of Egypt. According to Payne, Baybars "provided Islam with something it had not possessed since the time of Saladin: a core of iron, a relentless determination." And Baybars was determined to rid Muslim lands of the Franks once and for all. He began to attack the crusader kingdoms, steadily conquering fortress after fortress, town after town. Baybars also had a reputation for ruthlessness; unlike Saladin, he rarely showed mercy to the Franks whom he captured.

King Louis IX of France was now an old man, but he had never forgiven himself for his failure in the Seventh Crusade. When he heard of the atrocities committed against the Christians in the Holy Land, he raised an army and rode out once more on a Crusade. Nevertheless, Louis was not fated to succeed; in fact, he never even reached Outremer. His army had reached only as far as Tunisia when it was struck by an epidemic, and Louis was among the many who died. A few months after Louis's death, Prince Edward of England and a small contingent of crusaders arrived at Acre, but they were no match for Baybars's mighty army. In May 1272 the city of Acre signed a ten-year truce with Baybars, and Edward returned home.

Despite the truce, Pope Gregory X was concerned about the precarious standing of the crusader kingdoms and tried to drum up interest in a new Crusade. Runciman writes that Gregory's "appeals for men to take the Cross and fight in the East were circulated throughout Europe, as far as Finland and Iceland. It is possible that they even reached Greenland and the coast of North America. But there was no response."

Gregory was right to be worried. In 1277, while the truce was still in effect, Baybars died and was succeeded by Qalawun, who was even more determined to eliminate the Franks. Starting in 1285, Qalawun systematically eradicated all but a few of the remaining Frankish settlements.

The Fall of Acre

By 1289, except for a few minor towns, Acre was the Franks' sole stronghold. The truce between Acre and the Mamluks still held, but the increasingly nervous inhabitants of Acre sent messengers to Europe, asking for help. As it turned out, they would have been better off without the small group of Italian crusaders who arrived in the summer of 1290. According to Runciman:

> From the moment of their landing they proved an embarrassment to the authorities. They were disorderly, drunken and debauched. Their commanders, who were unable to give them their regular pay, had no control over them. They had come, they thought, to fight the infidel, so they began to attack the peaceful Moslem merchants and peasants.

Less than a month after they arrived, the Italian crusaders started a riot and ran through the streets of the city, killing every Muslim they encountered.

For Qalawun, this was the last straw. He resolved to destroy Acre, vowing that he would not leave a single Christian alive in that wretched city. On November 4 he marched out of Cairo with his army, but within days he suddenly fell sick and died. At first, the Franks were heartened by this news; they assumed the danger was past. However, Qalawun had a son, Al-Ashraf Khalil, who promised his dying father that he would carry out the destruction of Acre.

In April 1291, Al-Ashraf and his vast army positioned themselves outside the gates of Acre and lay siege to the city. The Franks fought bravely, but they were greatly outnumbered, and the city fell on May 18. The massacre that followed was almost as bloody as the fall of Jerusalem to the First Crusaders. Some Franks managed to escape; others were spared only to become slaves. Most, however, died that day. As news of the slaughter at Acre spread, the residents of the last Frankish towns quickly surrendered and fled Outremer forever.

Although there would be more papal calls for holy wars and intermittent crusading movements over the decades that followed, for all intents and purposes the Crusades ended at Acre. Never again would the Latin Christians rule in Outremer; never again would the knights and nobles of Europe fight the caliphs and sultans of the East in the streets of Jerusalem. For centuries, the conquest of Jerusalem remained a dream for popes and kings alike, but with the crushing defeat at Acre, the spirit and drive that had spurred the crusaders to war simply faded away. The dream of a Christian Jerusalem would remain just that—only a dream.

Chapter 1

The Origins of the Holy Wars

Turning|Points

IN WORLD HISTORY

An Upheaval of Empires

Alfred Duggan

The roots of the political situation that led to the First
Crusade of 1096 can be traced back several hundred years.
In the following selection, Alfred Duggan examines some
of the key events, many of which involved the rise and fall
of empires in Europe and Asia Minor.

The adoption of Christianity in the fourth century as
the official religion of the Roman Empire gave the religion more strength at the same time that the Empire was
weakening, Duggan writes. Shortly thereafter, the Empire
was divided into eastern and western sections. Duggan explains that the eastern section (the Byzantine Empire)
flourished, while the western region was invaded by pagan
barbarians. In the seventh century, the new religion of
Islam became predominant in Arabia, and the Muslims
went on to conquer a large portion of the known world,
invading parts of both Western and Eastern Europe. Further incursions by Turkish Muslims into the Byzantine
Empire led the emperor to request assistance from the
western pope, setting the stage for the military campaigns
that came to be known as the Crusades.

A prolific author, Alfred Duggan is known foremost as
a historical novelist. However, he also wrote biographies
and historical nonfiction, including *The Story of the Crusades*, from which this selection is excerpted.

Ever since the Church was founded at the first Pentecost
there have been Christians in Jerusalem; though sometimes
they took refuge in the countryside while the Holy City was
attacked by hostile armies. In particular two Jewish revolts
against Rome brought terrible retribution. In A.D. 71 the

Excerpted from *The Story of the Crusades, 1097–1291*, by Alfred Duggan. Copyright
©1963 by Alfred Duggan. Reprinted by permission of Pantheon Books, a division
of Random House, Inc.

Temple was destroyed after a bitter and destructive siege; in A.D. 135 the Emperor Hadrian rebuilt captured Jerusalem as a normal Roman town, with temples in which the usual Roman gods were worshipped. But the Church endured. There has always been a Bishop, successor to St James; and a congregation, however small, for him to rule.

Therefore when the Emperor Constantine recognised Christianity as the official religion of the Roman Empire, some 300 years after the Passion [Christ's crucifixion], the sites of the main Holy Places were still remembered; just as we can still identify the sites burned in the Great Fire of London, 300 years ago. Constantine's mother, St Helena, could go straight to Calvary, where she dug up the True Cross. The well-remembered tomb where the Body of God had lain for three days is so near the place of Crucifixion that she was able to include both under the roof of a mighty Roman basilica, the Church of the Holy Sepulchre. A new city-wall was built out to the north to include this great shrine; for Calvary, like most places of execution, was originally outside the city. About the same time the Church of the Nativity was built at Bethlehem; and other Holy Places, some of less certain authenticity, were worthily commemorated. Pilgrims came to Jerusalem from all parts of the Roman Empire, as they have come ever since to this day.

The Eastern Empire

The Emperor Constantine also founded a new capital at the city of Byzantium, renamed Constantinople in his honour. But by about the year 400 it was recognised that the troubles of the time were too grave to be dealt with by one sovereign, and the Empire was divided. The lands west of the Adriatic were ruled by an Emperor whose capital was nominally Rome, though in fact he lived at Ravenna; the Balkans and Asia Minor were ruled by the Emperor in Constantinople.

The western Empire was overrun by warlike barbarians, our ancestors. But the eastern Empire flourished until by the year 600 Constantinople ruled all the Greek lands of Europe and Asia, and in addition southern Italy and the north African coast right up to Morocco. The Emperor of Constantinople was by far the most powerful monarch in the known world; his only rival was the Emperor of pagan Persia, on his eastern frontier.

The east-Romans were devout Christians; though in Egypt and Syria the natives supported heretical sects because they disliked being ruled by Bishops sent from Constantinople. But the organisation of the eastern Church, whose liturgy was said in Greek, differed greatly from that of the west, whose Mass was said in Latin. In the west all Christians obeyed the Pope, who represented among other things the vanished civilisation of Rome; in Constantinople the unquestioned head of the Church was the Emperor, who bore among his official titles that of Isapostolos, Equal to the Apostles. He appointed the Patriarchs of Jerusalem, Antioch, Alexandria and Constantinople, and might dismiss them at his whim. The Greeks agreed that the Pope was the senior Patriarch, but they would not take orders from him alone. They held that doctrine should be settled by a General Council, or at least by an agreement of the five Patriarchs; and that in matters of discipline their Emperor was supreme. Unfortunately the Empire was not hereditary. In theory the Emperor was elected by the people and the army; in practice he was often a successful soldier who had seized power by murdering his superior officer. Fear of rebellion might make him a cruel tyrant; and the more competent soldier-Emperors knew little of Church affairs.

In 610 the Persians invaded the Empire. In 614 they captured Jerusalem, with help from the large Jewish community within the city. Sixty-five thousand Christians were massacred, and the thirty-five thousand survivors sold into slavery. The Persians burned the Church of the Holy Sepulchre, and carried off the True Cross as a trophy of victory. In 630, after years of bitter fighting, the Emperor Heraclius defeated them and forced them to return the True Cross. A large part of it was sent back to Jerusalem; though to avoid another such disaster portions were sent to Constantinople and Rome. From these fragments many tiny splinters have been taken, the relics now venerated in churches all over the world.

For his liberation of Jerusalem Heraclius was reverenced

by posterity as the first Crusader. But the war had continued for nineteen years, with appalling devastation from the Bosphorus right up to Mesopotamia. Both Persia and the Empire were greatly weakened.

The Rise of Islam

Meanwhile, in 622, Mahomet [Muhammad] began to preach among the Arabs. When he died ten years later Islam was supreme in Arabia. The Moslems appointed as the successor of Mahomet a Caliph, a supreme temporal and religious ruler, and under his guidance set out to conquer the world.

They met with amazing success. Both the east-Romans and the Persians were too war-weary to undertake another long struggle. In 638 Jerusalem surrendered to the Caliph Omar. By 717 the Moslems had conquered the whole northern coastline of Africa, southern Spain, the Persian Empire and the eastern lands as far as India. But after the Moslem invasion had reached the very walls of Constantinople the east-Romans rallied; in Asia Minor the frontier of Christendom was fixed at the Taurus Mountains. Though the Caliph was now the most powerful ruler in the world the Emperor in Constantinople was still the most powerful Christian ruler.

In Jerusalem the Church survived. As well as a creed, Mahomet had laid down a code of laws for his followers, and in it he made provision for conquered peoples who would not accept Islam. For idolaters there was no mercy; conversion or death were the alternatives. But those who worshipped One God, the Peoples of the Book—Zoroastrians, Jews, and Christians—might live in peace under Moslem masters. Of course they must accept certain disabilities. They must pay an annual tax for the privilege of being left alive; they might never ride a horse nor carry a weapon; they might not convert a Moslem nor marry a Moslem girl, though Moslems might take Christian girls by force into their harems. Existing churches, including the Church of the Holy Sepulchre, remained Christian, but no new ones might be built. (This rule could be dodged by judicious bribery.) Disputes between Christians were judged by their own clergy, who were held responsible for the good behaviour of the laity and hanged if their flock rebelled. Such a life was not intolerable, and the Christians of Syria tolerated it; except for the mountaineers of Lebanon who became defiant Christian rebels. But these mountaineers had usually been in rebellion against the tax-collector from the plain.

The Christians of Syria and Palestine still regarded the Emperor in Constantinople as the head of their church. The Caliphs respected his military power, and heeded his protests on behalf of his fellow-Christians. Pilgrims continued to visit Jerusalem, welcomed by the Moslem rulers for the money they brought into the country.

Changes Throughout the Region

In 800 the Pope crowned Charlemagne as Emperor. This new Empire naturally annoyed the Greeks, as we may now call the east-Romans. So Charlemagne negotiated directly with the Caliph Haroun al Raschid, who recognised him as protector of Latin pilgrims and allowed him to set up Latin hostels in Jerusalem for their convenience.

In the 10th century the Greeks grew stronger. They reconquered Cilicia and in 969 took the great city of Antioch. By this time there was no single Caliph ruling the whole Moslem world. A Caliph in Baghdad reigned over Mesopotamia and the east, while a Caliph in Cairo was obeyed by Africa; but both these Caliphs were spiritual figureheads whose power was wielded by the commanders of their armies.

In 1004 the Caliph of Cairo, Hakim, went mad. In an effort to extirpate Christianity he ordered the destruction of the Church of the Holy Sepulchre. But soon after he proclaimed himself to be God, and his Moslem subjects got rid of him. The Greek Emperor was permitted to rebuild the Holy Sepulchre and all went on as before; except that the Druze community among the mountains of Syria still worship Hakim and wait for him to come again.

By 1050 western pilgrims were visiting Jerusalem in large numbers. The journey was reasonably safe, by the standards of those days. The Hungarians and the Poles had been recently converted. A German had only to travel down the Danube, among Christians, until he entered the Greek Empire at Belgrade; then the Emperor's police would guard him until he reached Antioch. At the Syrian frontier he bought a safe-conduct from the officials of the Egyptian Caliph, who policed the road as far as the Holy Places. From France or England the normal route was by way of Rome to Bari, the capital of the Greek province of Italy, and then across the Adriatic to Durazzo at the head of the great road to Constantinople. Of course such a long journey had its hazards, and the expense was very great. A pilgrimage to Jerusalem, imposed as a penance, got rid of a disturber of the peace for at least a couple of years; and by the time he came back he would be too poor to make trouble. Sweyn Godwinsson [brother of Harold, King of England] was ordered to make the journey as a penance for his many crimes; in 1052, on his way back, he died of exposure among the mountains of Asia. But Nature was the most dangerous enemy; both Greeks and Moslems welcomed Latin pilgrims.

The Normans and the Turks

Two migrations broke up this peaceful arrangement. The Normans had a particular devotion to the warrior-angel St Michael, whose most famous shrine is on Monte Gargano in southern Italy. They went there in great numbers and presently intervened in the struggle between the Italian cities and their Greek governors. By 1059 the Pope had recognised the Norman leader Robert Guiscard as Duke of Apulia and Calabria, and Robert's brother Roger was campaigning against the Moslem rulers of Sicily.

Later the Normans crossed the Adriatic to pursue the war against the Emperor from whom they had conquered southern Italy. In Greece they won no permanent foothold, but they showed themselves to be dangerous neighbours. In Constantinople, where no one had hitherto bothered about barbarous Latins, the Normans were feared.

About the same time, the 1050s, the Turks appeared in Asia Minor. They were nomads from the steppe, moving south to pillage civilisation. They had recently become Moslems, though they were not yet strongly attached to their faith; they could sometimes be converted to Christianity, which could never be done with genuine Arab Moslems.

These uncouth Turks were awed by the superior culture of Baghdad. They could have overthrown the Caliph, but they preferred to be his servants; so long, of course, as the Caliph did what his servants told him. A Caliph who annoyed his Turkish advisers would be put away, and another Caliph chosen from the correct Arab family.

Turkish raids into the Greek Empire became more and more serious. All the raiders were mounted, usually driving a herd of spare horses, and the excellent Greek regular army seldom caught them before they had done grave damage. At last the Emperor Romanus Diogenes made up his mind that the only thing to do was to march east and fight a decisive battle with the Sultan of all the Turks wherever he might find him. In August 1071 the two armies met at Manzikert on the eastern frontier of the Empire near Lake Van.

The Battle of Manzikert

The Emperor brought all the soldiers he could scrape together, perhaps as many as 100,000 horse. About half were drilled and disciplined heavy cavalry; the other half were the private retainers of noble families. The great weakness of the Empire was the lack of a true royal house, so that any famous general might snatch at the crown. Romanus, himself a famous general, had married the widow of the last Emperor; his young stepson Michael Ducas would share the throne when he came of age, unless in the meantime Romanus won such a great victory that his subjects begged him to reign alone. That was one reason why he wanted to fight a decisive battle. His second in command was Andronicus Ducas, a noble so powerful that the Emperor dared not leave him behind in Constantinople, and so well born that if he were present with the army he must hold a high command.

After a morning of hard fighting the Greeks began to give ground. They might have got away in good order, but Andronicus thought more of the interests of the house of Ducas than of the well-being of the Empire. He ordered the second line to retire, leaving the Emperor and his regular cavalry surrounded by the Turks. Romanus was wounded and captured.

The Empire never recovered from Manzikert. The regular army had been destroyed, and every surviving senior officer tried to win the throne for himself. Romanus bought his freedom, which made things worse by increasing the number of pretenders. Turkish bands roamed through Asia Minor, destroying the farms and killing the peasants until the richest and most populous part of the Empire had become a desert. For a time the great walled cities held out; but their garrisons no longer took orders from Constantinople, where rival Emperors continually rose and fell. The Turks entered Nicaea as mercenaries of a pretender; after he had been defeated they remained. Another Turkish chieftain gained possession of Smyrna and began to build a pirate fleet. The great fortress of Antioch was ruled by an Armenian general in the Greek army, who to keep it paid tribute to the Turks. In 1085 his son sold the city to the infidel. Other Armenian princes moved into the mountains of Taurus and took over the fortresses of Cilicia. The Armenians, a warlike race, were Christian heretics. The King of Armenia had established Christianity in his realm a few years before it became the religion of the Roman Empire, and the Armenians have never forgotten that theirs was the first Christian state. They would rather pay tribute to the infidel and keep their ancient creed than obey the Greek Orthodox Patriarch of Constantinople.

During all this chaos and destruction there occurred an odd little incident. Before Manzikert, Romanus had hired a band of Norman mercenaries from Italy, led by a knight named Roussel de Balliol. They escaped the battle because they were besieging a nearby fortress. After the disaster Roussel established himself as independent ruler of the city of Amasia in Pontus. His government was so just, orderly and cheap that his Greek subjects preferred him to their own Emperor. A young Greek noble, Alexius Comnenus, was sent to suppress him. Alexius had to give out that he had blinded his prisoner to stop the Amasians continuing to fight for their Norman lord. Roussel was not in fact blinded, because Alexius also admired and liked him. It seemed that Latins, especially Normans, might be a grave danger to the Empire. Given the choice, Greeks of the Orthodox faith would rather be ruled by Latin Normans than by their own extortionate governors.

Schism and Turmoil

In 1054 the Pope excommunicated the Patriarch of Constantinople, and the Orthodox Church has remained in schism ever since. At the time it was seen as a personal quarrel between two angry prelates, a quarrel that would soon be healed. It did not affect the other Patriarchates, Jerusalem, Antioch and Alexandria, whose subjects remained in communion with both Rome and Constantinople.

Asia Minor was infested with Turkish bands. In Syria every city was ruled by a different Arab or Turkish chieftain. The mountains were held by Armenian nobles. Each of these rulers was at war with all the others. Jerusalem was fairly well governed by the officers of the Egyptian Caliph, but it was impossible for a pilgrim to get there from the west.

In 1081 Alexius Comnenus became Emperor of Constantinople. He had no soldiers except foreign mercenaries; in Asia Minor he held nothing but a few scattered seaports; the Normans of Italy menaced his European possessions. But he still had a great deal of money, and he was a very intelligent statesman. Above all, he was a patriot, who thought first of the welfare of his Empire. He was not interested in the fate of the Holy Places, save in so far as they might be useful to his own country.

In the spring of 1095 Pope Urban II held a council at Piacenza in northern Italy. . . .

A Plea for Help

Now that the mighty Turkish horde had split up into numerous bands the Emperor Alexius hoped to go over to the offensive. But he lacked soldiers. The trained regular army which had been destroyed 25 years ago at Manzikert had never been replaced; because its recruits came from Asia Minor, now devastated by the Turks. Alexius, who had plenty of money, relied on foreign mercenaries, either heathen Patzinak horse-bowmen from the steppe, or the Varangian Guard of Scandinavians and English who fought on foot with two-handed axes. He had no heavy cavalry, and perhaps he remembered how formidable had been the Norman knights who followed Roussel de Balliol. He asked the Pope to proclaim to the council that knights would be serving God if they took service with the Greek army in defence of the oppressed Christians of Asia Minor. Alexius did not forget that he was the head of a church which had broken away from the Pope. He explained that he could not now heal the schism, for if he ordered his subjects to submit to Rome they would overthrow him. Of course after he had conquered the Turks he would be more powerful, able to compel even his bishops to do as he said. In the meantime his Latin mercenaries might bring their own priests . . . Alexius was always quite willing to heal the schism if the Pope would meet him halfway. No Greek understood that the Pope cannot go halfway to compromise with error.

Urban promised to ask for recruits at a convenient opportunity. He was all the more willing because he feared that Constantinople was not so strong as its Emperor supposed. At any moment the Turks might break in; and then they would be on the borders of the Latin west, his own responsibility.

The Feudal System and Church Reform

Sidney Painter

In the following article, Sidney Painter maintains that two crucial developments in the society of medieval Europe enabled the Crusades to occur. First, Painter maintains, the growth of the feudal system laid the groundwork for the massive armies that the Crusades would require. He writes that under the feudal system, knights owed allegiance to their lords, who in turn were subject to the authority of higher-ranking lords, who had pledged loyalty to the king. The most important aspect of the feudal system was the military aid that vassals owed to their lords, Painter explains, which allowed lords and kings to raise large armies with little trouble.

Painter also describes significant reforms that occurred in the church prior to the Crusades. Many of these reforms were designed to free the church of secular influences and control while simultaneously strengthening the church's authority, he points out. These changes would ultimately allow the pope to call upon the great lords of Europe to fight in the Crusades.

Sidney Painter was a professor of history at Johns Hopkins University in Baltimore, Maryland. His books include *A History of the Middle Ages: 284–1500*, *French Chivalry: Chivalric Ideas and Practices in Mediaeval France*, *Mediaeval Society*, and *The Rise of the Feudal Monarchies*.

The crusades had their origin in eleventh-century western Europe and to understand them one must know something of the environment in which they emerged. No mere static

Excerpted from Sidney Painter, "Western Europe on the Eve of the Crusades," in *A History of the Crusades*, vol. 1, edited by Marshall W. Baldwin; ©1969 by the Regents of the University of Wisconsin. Reprinted by permission of The University of Wisconsin Press.

description of the land and its people can serve this purpose. The picture must be a moving one that shows the basic forces that were slowly molding medieval civilization, for the crusades were a natural product of these forces. The eleventh was the first of the three great creative centuries of the Middle Ages—an era of pioneers, soldiers, and statesmen. During its span the political and economic institutions that had been gradually taking shape since the sixth century were firmly cemented together to form the foundations of medieval civilization. While many of those who were to make the twelfth century an age of saints, scholars, artists, and creative literary men were born before the first crusaders set out for Palestine, their day lay in the future. The great lay figures of the eleventh century, William the Conqueror, the emperors Henry III and Henry IV, Roger I of Sicily, and Alfonso VI of Castile, were soldier-statesmen, and their ecclesiastical counterparts, pope Gregory VII, the early abbots of Cluny, and archbishop Lanfranc, were priestly statesmen. They sought essentially power, order, and efficiency. Even the chief monastic order of the period, that of Cluny, represented administrative rather more than spiritual reform. The hardy peasants who cleared forests and drained marshes to bring new land under cultivation and the Genoese and Pisan seamen who swept the Moslems from the coasts of Europe must have been moved by the same vigorous spirit as their conquering lords. In short, both expansion and organization marked the eleventh century. The crusades were a part of the former and were made possible by the latter. . . .

Expanding the Feudal System

One of the most important features of the eleventh century was the crystallization and extension of the feudal system. Feudal institutions had been developing since the eighth century. Charles Martel had given benefices [landed estates] to men who swore loyalty to him and were ready to serve him as soldiers. By the time of Charles the Bald benefices were becoming hereditary in practice if not in theory and the same tendency was affecting the countships and other royal offices. In eleventh-century France the benefice had become the hereditary fief. Although the office of count was not absolutely hereditary, a competent heir was practically certain of the inheritance. When an office changed hands, this was less likely to be the result of royal action than of the successful aggression of a powerful rival. Moreover, during the ninth and tenth centuries when civil war combined with Viking raids to keep France in a state of anarchy, the land-holders had but two practical alternatives. One could obtain military support and protection by becoming the vassal of a powerful neighbor or one could sink into the category of an unfree villager. Almost every landholder whose resources permitted him to equip himself as a soldier chose the former course. Only the most powerful and most stubborn could stay outside the feudal system. Although eleventh-century France contained *allods*, that is, lands held from no lord, they were quite rare and most of them disappeared in the twelfth century. In short, eleventh-century France, especially in the north, was almost completely feudalized and the principle so dear to feudal lawyers of "no land without a lord" was nearly true of it.

As the feudal system spread over France its members became arranged in a hierarchy. At the head stood the Capetian king, who was suzerain [the sovereign] of the great lords of the land. Below him came a group of feudal potentates who may best be described as feudal princes—the men whom a later age called the "peers of France". According to the theory developed in the twelfth century, there were six lay peers—the count of Flanders, the duke of Normandy, the count of Champagne, the duke of Aquitaine, the count of Toulouse, and the duke of Burgundy. The powerful counts of Anjou were not called peers because they were considered vassals of the Capetian king in his capacity of duke of France, the title held by the family before its elevation to the throne, but they were far more important than the vassals of the royal demesne [lands] in the Île de France such as the lords of Coucy and Montmorency. Each of these great lords who held directly of the king had his own vassals, many of whom were counts or had usurped that title. It was by no means un-

common for a vigorous lord to wake up some bright morning and decide he was a count, and usually no one bothered
to dispute the claim. These secondary vassals in turn had
their own vassals and rear-vassals, and the hierarchy continued down to the simple knight who had just enough land and
peasant labor to support him. This minimum unit of the feudal system, the resources that would enable a man to be a
knight, was called the knight's fief or fee. . . .

Warfare

The fundamental purpose of the feudal system was coöperation in war. Every lord was bound to protect his vassal from
enemies outside the fief and every vassal owed military service to his lord. In some cases the vassal owed only his own
personal service; in others he was bound to lead a certain
number of knights to his lord's army. By the thirteenth century the military service owed by vassals was carefully defined and limited, but this process was not complete in the
eleventh century. In most fiefs a distinction was made between offensive and defensive campaigns and the length of
time a vassal had to serve in the former was limited—forty
days was usual in the thirteenth century. When the fief was
in danger, obviously the vassals were bound to stay in service
as long as they were needed. . . .

As a form of government feudalism had both advantages
and disadvantages. It supplied a military force of heavy cavalry at every stage in the hierarchy. Thus each barony, each
county, and each kingdom had its army. It also furnished vigorous and interested local government. The extensive recla-
mation of land and the founding of towns were largely the
result of the desire of feudal lords to increase their resources.
It is highly doubtful that mere agents working for the benefit of a central government could have accomplished so
much. But as a means of keeping peace and order the feudal
system was no great success, for it was based on the assumption that there would be continual warfare. In theory, quarrels between lords and vassals and between vassals of the
same lord were settled in the feudal courts. Actually when
two vassals of a lord quarreled, they went to war and the lord

did not intervene unless he thought one might be so seriously weakened that he could not perform his service. And no spirited vassal accepted an unfavorable decision by his lord's court until he was coerced with armed force. Between vassals of different lords there was no hindrance to war. In short, in eleventh-century France, feudal warfare was endemic and it was a fortunate region that saw peace throughout an entire summer. . . .

At the beginning of the eleventh century France was the only feudal state in Europe. . . .

During the course of the eleventh century feudalism expanded rapidly. The conquest of England by duke William of Normandy created a new feudal state. . . .

At about the same time that William of Normandy established a feudal state in England a group of Norman adventurers were doing the same thing in southern Italy and Sicily. . . .

Church Reform

While . . . the knights were developing and extending feudal institutions, the churchmen were making similar progress. The local administration of the church was clarified and strengthened and an effective central government was created. At the same time missionaries converted the Scandinavian lands and labored among the Slavs. Christian Europe was both strengthened and extended. . . .

During the ninth and tenth centuries the church had become deeply involved in secular affairs. The extensive lands of the bishops and abbots were held of lay lords by feudal services, and the prelates had to perform the functions of vassals either personally or by deputy. Some doughty bishops led their troops in battle wielding a mace, which they insisted did not violate canon law as it drew no blood, but most had secular agents called advocates to head their levies. But the prelates were appointed by the secular lords and invested by them with the insignia of their holy office. They served the lords as counselors and administrators. . . . This situation was harmful to the spiritual functions of the church. A bishop should be primarily devoted to his episcopal duties rather than to the service of a lay prince, and an abbot who was essentially a baron was unlikely to be an effective father to his monks.

The Abbey of Cluny

As early as the tenth century this situation had alarmed many devout men. In the hope of improving the monastic system duke William of Aquitaine had in 911 founded the abbey of Cluny. Cluny was forbidden to hold lands by feudal service. A donor to this foundation had to make his gift in free alms—that is, the only service owed was prayers for his soul. Cluny adopted a modified form of the Benedictine rule. St. Benedict had directed his monks to spend long hours at manual labor, but once a monastery grew rich in land and peasant labor, it was impossible to get the monks to work in the fields. The Cluniac rule greatly extended the hours to be devoted to performing the services of the church in the hope of keeping the monks occupied in that way. By the eleventh century Cluny had many daughter houses. Some were new foundations while others were old monasteries that were more or less willingly reformed by Cluniac monks. The order also developed a highly centralized administration. There was only one abbot—the abbot of Cluny. Each daughter house was headed by a prior who was subject to the abbot of Cluny, who was supposed to visit regularly and in-spect every house of the order. In the eleventh century Cluny had enormous influence. With the support of the em-peror Henry III Cluniac monks reformed many German monasteries and men inspired by Cluny revived English monasticism. All enthusiastic and devout churchmen tended to gravitate toward Cluny.

These enthusiasts were not willing to limit their reforms to the monasteries. They were anxious to remedy the abuses that were common among the secular clergy. The most seri-ous of these was lay appointment of ecclesiastics. The great lords appointed bishops and abbots, and the lords of villages appointed the parish priests. Closely related to this was the sin of simony, the payment of money to obtain church offices. The lay lords were extremely inclined to bestow offices on the highest bidder. Another abuse that seriously troubled conscientious churchmen was the marriage of priests. To some extent this was a moral question—canon law required priests to be celibate. But it also vitally concerned the material interests of the church. A married priest was inclined to think of his family before his priestly duty and was most likely to use church property to endow his children even if he did not succeed in making his office hereditary. There were, of course, other abuses that interested the reformers, but these were the ones on which they concentrated their attention.

Strengthening the Papacy

The reformers realized that there was but one way to achieve their ends. Even if the bishops of Europe could be made enthusiastic supporters of reform, they were as individuals helpless before the power of the lay princes. Only a strongly organized church with an effective central government could hope to make much progress. Hence their eyes turned toward the papacy. The pope was elected by the clergy and people of Rome, which meant in practice by the dominant faction of the Roman nobility. But when a strong monarch occupied the imperial throne, his influence could be decisive. Neither of these methods of choice pleased the reformers. If the papacy was to lead in the reform of the church, it had to be removed from lay control. The emperor Henry III was a pious as well as an efficient ruler, and he gladly supported the reformers by appointing popes favorable to their aims. The first important step was the creation of the college of cardinals. The six bishops who were suffragans [subordinates] of the pope as bishop of Rome, the pastors of the more important Roman churches, and some of the deacons of the Roman church were formed into a corporation. When a pope died, these men were to meet and elect his successor. If outside pressure was put upon them, the election was to be void. . . .

In all the varied phases of civilization the eleventh century was a period of vital growth and energetic development. The twelfth and thirteenth centuries were to see the flowering of medieval civilization, but the plant matured and the buds were formed in the eleventh. The men of western Europe had faith in God and in their own strong arms. They also had a willingness to adventure, to innovate, and to organize. The two great complexes of institutions, the church and the feudal system, had achieved the strength of maturity without losing their capacity for further development and expansion. And it was the church and the feudal system that made the crusades possible.

The Importance
of Pope Urban II

Robert Payne

The crusading movement did not arise spontaneously—
most Crusades, including the first one, began when the
pope issued a call for an army to go to the Holy Land. For
example, Pope Urban II's famous speech at Clermont,
France, in 1095, in which he exhorted his listeners to aid
the Byzantine Empire against Muslim invaders, sparked
the First Crusade. In the following selection, Robert
Payne argues that Urban II was the right person at the
right time: a charismatic yet practical pope who knew how
to appeal to the hearts of the knights and nobles who
would fight in the Crusade. Furthermore, Payne writes,
Urban II had other motives for preaching the Crusade,
such as distracting the battle-eager French lords from
warring among themselves.

Robert Payne was a prolific writer who published more
than one hundred books in his lifetime. He wrote nonfiction, biographies, fiction, and poetry, as well as edited anthologies and translated Chinese and Russian works. His
nonfiction books include *The Holy Fire: The Story of the
Fathers of the Eastern Church* and *The Holy Sword: The Story
of Islam from Muhammad to the Present*. The following selection is excerpted from Payne's last book, *The Dream and
the Tomb: A History of the Crusades*, which was published
after his death.

Between A.D. 896 and A.D. 904 eight popes succeeded one
another. But the monk Hildebrand, who reigned as Pope
Gregory VII from 1073–1086, restored the papacy to full

Excerpted from Robert Payne, *The Dream and the Tomb: A History of the Crusades*
(London: Robert Hale, 1986). Reprinted by permission of David Higham Associates as agents for the author's estate.

authority. He received appeals from Constantinople to mount a Crusade against the Turks, but he was too busy reorganizing the Church to spend his energy on Byzantine affairs. The time was not yet ripe for the Crusade.

Pope Urban II

Then, with the coming of Urban II to the throne in 1088, the Crusade became eminently possible. The new pope was practical, and he possessed a peculiarly French sense of reaching to the heart of a problem. He was by birth a French nobleman. His original name was Eudes de Lagery, and he was born in the family castle near Châtillon-sur-Marne in about A.D. 1042. He rose rapidly in the church hierarchy to become a canon of St. John Lateran in Rome. Suddenly he abandoned Rome, and we next see him wearing the habit of a simple monk at Cluny, then the intellectual center of French Catholicism. The abbot of Cluny made him a prior and sent him on missions to Rome. Gregory VII admired him, made him bishop of Ostia, and then a cardinal. Cardinal Eudes was sent as a papal legate to Germany, where he acquitted himself well. An ancient portrait shows him in his cardinal's robes, bald except for tufts of hair above his ears but with a long beard and an unusually heavy mustache. He looks singularly robust and determined. This was the man who would become Pope Urban II. This was the man who would call the Crusade into existence.

It was not by any means a sudden call based upon an emotional sympathy for the Christians who had suffered in Asia Minor and the Holy Land. It was more, and it was less. Urban II was asserting the pope's leadership in the West, he was attempting to dominate the quarreling princes of Europe by declaring a holy war in the East and the Truce of God in the West, and he was trying to give direction to a divided Europe at a time when the quarrels were becoming dangerous not only to the papacy but to the very survival of Christendom. Although Charles Martel had effectively stopped the advance of the Muslims into France, the possibility of a Muslim breakthrough from Spain was very real. To ensure that France remained free of Muslim influence,

Urban II called upon the French nobility to arm themselves and attack Islam in the Near East. In the most limited sense he was concerned that French noblemen should give a good account of themselves, for he was himself a French nobleman and his chief sympathies were with France.

Thus, the character of the pope gave color to the Cru-

Incentives for the Crusades

Barbara N. Sargent-Baur is a professor of French and the director of the Medieval and Renaissance Studies Program at the University of Pittsburgh in Pennsylvania. The following excerpt is taken from the introduction of her anthology, Journeys Toward God: Pilgrimage and Crusade.

When Pope Urban II summoned the French chivalry in 1095 to cease fighting among themselves and direct their energies against the Turkish conquerors of the Holy Land, he founded his appeal on a multiplicity of long-maturing phenomena. Among these were the establishment, by the late eleventh century, of the authority of the Catholic Church as centered in the papacy; the veneration of holy places and especially the Holy Land; the conviction that sin could be expunged and salvation achieved through "works"; the tradition of long-distance pilgrimages in large groups; the existence of a professional fighting caste whose *raison d'être* [reason for existing] was, precisely, fighting; the protracted struggle against the Moors in Spain; and the formation of various peace movements intended to limit warfare within Christendom (with the consequent appeal of carrying combat beyond its borders). Specific events combined to channel these developments. The Turkish encroachments in the Christian East, the appeal of the Byzantine Emperor for help against the infidel, the perceived threat to the pilgrimage routes in Palestine, and, not least, the inducements of adventure and enrichment—all of these constituted powerful incentives to the Church-sanctioned military expeditions to the Holy Land.

Barbara N. Sargent-Baur, *Journeys Toward God: Pilgrimage and Crusade,* 1992.

sade, which remained essentially French and aristocratic throughout its two-hundred-year history. When he proclaimed the necessity of the Crusade at a general gathering of the clergy and the laity at Clermont on November 27, 1095, he was speaking as a Frenchman to Frenchmen concerning a matter of peculiar relevance to France. . . .

The pope spoke in French, standing on a podium in the midst of an immense field crowded with people of all classes from poor peasants to princes, and around the podium stood an army of archbishops, bishops, abbots, prelates and priests. He had already spent many days in council, discussing a host of important matters concerning the machinery of the Church, the morals of princes, the right of sanctuary, and that Truce of God which was very close to his heart. By the Truce of God he meant to outlaw fighting of any kind from Sunday to Wednesday, and to put an absolute ban on fighting involving priests, monks, women, laborers, and merchants on any day of the week. At Clermont the pope was able to impose a further ban on fighting on certain religious holidays. There was some irony in the fact that the pope who called so strenuously for peace in France was also calling for a holy war in the Holy Land.

In fact, the two ideas were closely, even intimately, connected. He was aware that a war against the Turks would divert the energies expended by Christians in killing other Christians. It was a time when the princes and princelings of France were bristling with new-found powers, invading each other's territory, sacking towns, relentlessly skirmishing. There were endless dynastic disputes, and to become a prince or count meant waging war against one's own relatives. Urban II hoped to establish the principle that the Church was the supreme arbiter over earthly kingdoms with the power to authorize wars and to prevent wars, especially the wars in France. . . .

"God Wills It!"

Near him, in that vast audience, were the princes who had come to him because he had summoned them, and now he addressed them with a special vehemence. They were the men who commanded armies and were continually fighting against other Frenchmen, and he was determined that their fighting should cease in the Truce of God. He did not mince his words. . . .

His words were intended to shock, and also to heal. Christ's words sustained his argument. In the mythology he was developing throughout his sermon, he was relying on all those cryptic and well-known words where Christ demands that his followers should abandon their fathers, mothers, wives, and children, and for this abandonment they would be rewarded a hundredfold and enter eternal life. Significantly, it was when he was reciting these words that the crowd suddenly roared back at him: "God wills it!" *"Dieu li volt!"* cried the northerners, and the southerners cried, *"Diex le volt!"* It was at that very moment that the Crusade came into existence.

The Pilgrimage Origins of the Crusades

Marcus Bull

For centuries prior to the Crusades, thousands of European Christians made pilgrimages to places in the Middle East that were considered holy, especially the city of Jerusalem. Although many other Europeans were not wealthy enough to undertake such a long and difficult journey, the concept of making a pilgrimage to the Holy Land would have been familiar to them.

Pope Urban II and other promoters of the First Crusade made explicit links between pilgrimages and the idea of a Crusade, Marcus Bull writes in the following article. Bull explains that in calling for the First Crusade, Urban II stressed the hardships faced by European pilgrims who sought to travel in a region controlled by Muslims. In addition, Bull notes, Europeans often perceived the Crusades as armed pilgrimages: religious wars in which the soldier-pilgrims liberated the sacred shrines of the Holy Land from the hands of infidels.

Marcus Bull teaches medieval history at the University of Bristol in Great Britain. He is the author of *Knightly Piety and the Lay Response to the First Crusade*.

On November 27th, 1095, at Clermont in central France, Pope Urban II delivered the sermon which launched the expedition now known as the First Crusade. He called on the faithful, in particular the lords and knights who formed society's military élites, to relieve the oppression of Eastern Christians and to liberate the Holy Places by means of an armed pilgrimage, participation in which would earn remission of

Excerpted from Marcus Bull, "The Pilgrimage Origins of the First Crusade," *History Today*, March 1997. Reprinted with permission.

one's penances because of the great hardships which would be faced. The pope's message was bold and challenging, and it received an enthusiastic response; according to Robert the Monk, one of the chroniclers who described the scene, everyone shouted 'God wills it!' once Urban stopped speaking.

A Defining Moment

Why was this speech important? Urban was a good communicator, but what he said was as much a briefing as a piece of oratory. His audience mostly comprised bishops and abbots who had assembled some days earlier for a church council. Not many lay people were present, and only a small minority of those who went on the crusade could claim that they had heard the Clermont speech. Nor was Urban's message a one-off, for it was repeated many times in the following months by the pope himself and by other churchmen. Many people learned about the crusade from popular preachers and through other unofficial channels. So the pope's initial speech was just one small part of a much wider recruitment effort. None the less, contemporaries soon came to remember Urban's sermon as a great defining moment; the myriad complexities of the preaching and organisation of an expedition which involved tens of thousands of people from many parts of Europe could be understood more easily by focusing on the rousing events at Clermont and the emotions they released.

This makes it all the more frustrating for historians that it is impossible to know precisely what Urban said. A number of accounts of his speech survive, some of them by members of his audience, but they were written a decade or more later and were influenced by the authors' knowledge of how events unfolded after Clermont, in particular how the crusaders captured Jerusalem in 1099 after a remarkable three-year campaign. The best way to reconstruct Urban's message, therefore, is to examine the ideas and images which he used to excite his audience. After all, the crusade needed careful presentation. Urban was proposing a novel idea to a generally conservative society. He was also asking people to volunteer to do something which was very expensive, time-consuming, arduous and dangerous. What he told them, then, had to be direct and vivid.

Horror Stories

Two ways to win over an audience are to conjure up bold, easily visualised images and to tap into deep-seated emotions. Urban used both techniques skilfully. He described a state of crisis in the eastern Mediterranean: the Byzantine Empire was in retreat; churches were being defiled and polluted by infidels; Christians were being subjected to horrible persecutions including rape, torture, mutilation and murder. The Muslim aggressors were portrayed as wantonly cruel: according to Robert the Monk, Urban claimed that Christians were being tied to stakes so that they could be used for archery target practice. The particular villains of the piece were the Turks, nomadic warrior bands with roots in central Asia who had been extending their power into Asia Minor, Syria and Palestine since the 1070s. Of particular concern was their treatment of Jerusalem, which Urban reminded his listeners was the holiest place known to Christians.

Urban had almost certainly never been to the Holy Land himself, and what he said owed more to rhetoric than reality. His depiction of the sufferings of Christians, with its lurid details of torture and pain, resembled contemporary ideas about what it was like to suffer in Hell. It is possible that the Turks, as newcomers to the western Fertile Crescent and its complicated religious history, were sometimes hostile to the Christians living in their domains. But their treatment seldom, if ever, amounted to the sort of horror stories which Urban recounted. Nor was the composition of the Muslim world as straightforward as the pope's message implied. In fact the Turks lost control of Jerusalem to the Egyptians in 1098, a year before the crusaders arrived: it is a curious irony that the enemies faced at the climax of the crusade were not those whom Urban had originally envisaged.

Most Westerners' understanding of the politics and peoples of the Middle East was vague at best, and Urban exploited this. His aim was to instil the feeling that there was something gravely wrong, dirty and dishonourable about the plight of the

Holy Land. This was a substantial achievement: such a sense of urgency comes through in the accounts of Urban's speech that it is easy to lose sight of the fact that Christians had not controlled Jerusalem since the Arabs captured it from the Byzantines in 638. Yet Urban was able to present a long-term fact—457 years of uninterrupted Muslim rule—in terms of a pressing injustice against God and His people. This was the key reason for the success of his message. Why?

Linking Crusades and Pilgrimages

An important clue is contained in the version of Urban's speech written by the contemporary chronicler Guibert of Nogent. Having described at length the important role which Jerusalem had played in history and would play at the Last Judgement, the pope asked his audience to consider the plight of those who went on pilgrimage to the Holy Land. The richer among them, Guibert has Urban say, were subjected to violence at the hands of infidels; they were also forced to pay heavy tolls, taxes, entry fees to get into churches, and bribes. The poorer pilgrims were badly mistreated by locals trying to get money off them at any cost. 'Remember, I urge you', the pope said, 'the thousands of people who have died horribly and take action for the Holy Places'. This is rhetorical exaggeration, but there is also an underlying idea that Jerusalem meant something very real to Western Europeans.

Perhaps Urban did not actually dwell on the troubles of Westerners going to the Holy Land as much as this—other accounts of the speech focus more on Eastern Christians—but Guibert was right to suppose that mentioning pilgrimage was an excellent way to evoke a sympathetic response in an audience. Jerusalem was a distant, exotic place, but it was also within the bounds of many people's experience. Monks sang about it daily in their psalms. Relics of the True Cross and other physical reminders of the Holy Places were to be found in many European churches. And significant numbers of people had been to the East themselves. Jerusalem was, paradoxically, both far away and familiar.

By linking his crusade message with Jerusalem pilgrimage

Urban was cleverly tapping into a long-established feature of Christian religious practice. Some churchmen had reservations about the value of pilgrimage, doubting whether the faithful could earn greater spiritual merit in some places rather than others. It was also argued that travelling to the actual Jerusalem was less important than striving through prayer and good works to enter the celestial Jerusalem, the community of the blessed in Heaven. But such detached attitudes were a minority view. Enthusiasm for relics and sites associated with saints was widespread among both clergy and lay people. More specifically, interest in the humanity of Christ—an emerging feature of eleventh-century spirituality and devotion—focused attention on the Holy Land, which was in a sense one huge relic sanctified by Christ's presence.

The emotional appeal of Jerusalem in particular could be enormous. This is clearly illustrated by the behaviour of Richard of Saint-Vanne, an abbot who arrived on pilgrimage on Palm Sunday 1027. Throughout Holy Week he busied himself visiting places associated with Christ's life, Passion and Resurrection. He would regularly throw himself on the ground in prayer, sobbing and crying. According to his biographer, seeing the pillar where Christ was scourged and Calvary where he was crucified reduced Richard to floods of tears. So strong was his attachment to the Holy Sepulchre that when an Arab threw a stone which bounced into the shrine, Richard kept it as a treasured relic.

Christian Activities in Jerusalem

Richard was able to find and be moved by the scenes of the Passion and other holy places largely because of building work done by the Byzantines many centuries earlier. Interest in Jerusalem had blossomed in the fourth century, when Constantine the Great (306–37) recognised Christianity as an official religion of the Roman Empire. Sites familiar from the Gospels were identified by drawing on the traditions of Christian communities in Palestine and through architectural detective work: for example, Christ's tomb was reckoned to be beneath a pagan temple built in the second century by Emperor Hadrian.

A Pilgrimage for Warriors

Carl Erdmann was a promising young teacher at the University of Berlin in Germany when he published The Origin of the Idea of Crusade *in 1935. However, Erdmann was also a vocal critic of the Nazi regime, which significantly hampered his career. He was drafted into the German army as a translator and died during World War II. Erdmann's book is still considered to be one of the most important works on the history of the Crusades. The following excerpt is taken from the 1977 English translation.*

Several different elements prepared the ground that allowed the general idea of crusade and of war upon the heathen to assume the special form of a Jerusalem crusade. . . . It is well established that pilgrimages to Jerusalem had been popular long before the crusades and had attained great size in the eleventh century. Neither does it need to be proved that these peaceful pilgrimages had at least a superficial relation to the crusades to Jerusalem. . . .

That these phenomena were interrelated seems to be beyond doubt. . . . Both pilgrimage and crusade show that the ecclesiastical ideal of life had spread beyond clerics and monks and had strongly affected the lay world; both had a special impact upon knights, by withdrawing them from everyday, secular fighting and subordinating their activity to a spiritual idea. . . .

From the standpoint of the ethic of knighthood, a pilgrimage was far less attractive than a crusade. It meant suspending one's martial profession, since the pilgrim stopped being a warrior for the duration of his travels. In its early development, the popular form of the idea of crusade did not at all coincide with the idea of a pilgrimage: its focus was war upon heathens. Pope Urban II was the first to unite pilgrimage and crusade in a synthesis—a synthesis that simultaneously renounced the application of the idea of crusade to hierarchical ends.

Carl Erdmann, *The Origin of the Idea of Crusade*, translated by Marshall W. Baldwin and Walter Goffart, 1977.

As the holy topography of Jerusalem became established, Constantine began an ambitious construction programme, the centre piece of which was a collection of buildings containing Calvary and the Holy Sepulchre. To these was later added the site of where Constantine's mother Helena was believed to have found the cross used at the Crucifixion. Over the next 300 years emperors and other rich benefactors continued Constantine's work, turning the city and nearby places into an impressive complex of churches, monuments and shrines. Jerusalem was not an important mercantile or industrial centre, and its agricultural hinterland was not particularly rich. Much like Rome in later centuries, its prosperity came to be based largely on its churches and the visitors attracted by them, among whom were Western Europeans.

The flow of Western pilgrims to the Holy Land was disrupted by the Arab conquests in the seventh century and later by unsettled conditions within Europe as political conflicts and the depredations of Vikings, Arabs and Magyars made long-distance travel difficult. But interest in Jerusalem survived, and the journey there was still made by some hardy souls such as the Anglo-Saxon St Willibald in the 720s and a Breton monk named Bernard in about 870. The fact that Jerusalem was never forgotten was important, because it meant that the numbers of pilgrims grew quickly once conditions became more favourable in the years either side of 1000.

Hungary was converted to Christianity, and the Byzantines extended their power in the Balkans and Asia Minor. This meant that travelling to Jerusalem entirely by land, slower than going some of the way by sea, but cheaper and open to more people, became a practicable proposition. What had earlier been a pious adventure for an élite few could now exert a wider appeal. This important change is memorably described by the Burgundian chronicler Ralph Glaber. Writing of the time around the millennium of the Passion (1033), Glaber reports that an 'innumerable multitude from all over the world began to flock to the Saviour's sepulchre in Jerusalem': swept up in the excitement, he says, were men and women, lowly people, those of middling status and also nobles and bishops.

By the time that Glaber's pilgrims were going to Jerusalem, the city had changed a great deal from its Byzantine heyday. In 1009 the Fatimid caliph al-Hakim, who was possibly mad, ordered that the church of the Holy Sepulchre and other Christian places in and around Jerusalem be razed to the ground. There was widespread destruction: when the crusaders arrived ninety years later they found many churches still deserted or ruinous. But the worst of the damage was eventually halted. After al-Hakim died in 1021 his successors were more moderate. . . .

A Difficult Undertaking

Long-distance pilgrimage was a grim business in the eleventh century. Its physical and mental rigours made it effective as a penance. A cemetery just outside Jerusalem, Akeldama, contained the bodies of many pilgrims who died there. And the accounts of pilgrims like Richard of Saint-Vanne being swept up in outpourings of emotion on their arrival in the Holy City read like the explosive release of tension and anticipation after months of suffering.

One way to cope with the dangers and stresses was to seek safety in numbers. Groups of pilgrims sometimes formed around a prominent noble or prelate. Richard of Saint-Vanne, for example, is reported to have had 700 companions whom he supported with money given him by Duke Richard II of Normandy (Robert I's father). The most remarkable instance of a mass pilgrimage was that undertaken by a group of Germans in 1064–65 under the leadership of a team of bishops and nobles. Figures of 7,000 and 12,000 are given by chroniclers; even the lower number is probably inflated, but even so this was the largest movement of Western Europeans to Jerusalem before the First Crusade. Interest seems to have been generated by the fact that in 1065, for the first time in over seventy years, Easter Sunday fell on March 27th, the date commonly ascribed to the historical Resurrection. The large numbers may also have been encouraged by the leaders because in recent years some pilgrims had found their journeys disrupted by unsettled conditions in the Holy Land. In 1055, for example, Bishop Lietbert of Cambrai had been refused permission to proceed by the governor of Latakia, the Byzantines' border outpost in northern Syria, because of fears for his safety. The pilgrims of 1064–65 must have hoped to overcome any problems by sheer weight of numbers.

With large numbers, however, came a problem which was to dog the whole enterprise. The leaders had to provide substantial amounts of supplies. One of the most practicable ways to do this was to carry, in addition to cash, luxury items which could be sold or exchanged en route. Contemporary chronicles describe the bishops' lavish tent hangings and gold and silver vessels: these represented good forward planning as well as aristocratic display. But so much wealth slowly on the move made the pilgrims very vulnerable. Robbery began to be a serious problem as the party passed through the Balkans, and it became worse in Palestine. About two days' journey from Jerusalem they were ambushed by Arab bandits. Some of the pilgrims fled to a deserted village, organised resistance and managed to keep their attackers at bay. The Arab leaders were lured into a parley, where they were overpowered by followers of Gunther of Bamberg, the most dynamic of the bishops. Soon afterwards there arrived a relief force sent by the Fatimid authorities, mindful of the value of keeping the pilgrimage route open. A fortnight later the remnants of the party were taken under armed escort to Jerusalem.

This remarkable episode has often caught the imagination of historians looking for precursors of the First Crusade. In particular attention has focused on the fact that some of the pilgrims fought back even though this was contrary to the centuries-old principle that pilgrims should renounce violence. The willingness of the German pilgrims to break this powerful taboo has seemed to anticipate the First Crusade, which was conceived as a fusion of warfare and pilgrimage. But perhaps historians have exaggerated the significance of what happened. The pilgrims did not set out from Germany armed. When they were attacked they at first fought back with stones and whatever else was to hand before using weapons snatched off their opponents. The fighting was an exceptional episode born of desperation and intense pressure, and it was only made possible by the unusually large numbers involved.

Crusading's Debt to Pilgrimage

What is more significant about the 1064–65 pilgrimage is what it demonstrates about the conditions faced by pilgrims generally in the years before Urban's speech at Clermont: the great expense, the physical effort, the constant dangers, and the fact that poorer travellers relied heavily on the resources and leadership of nobles and senior clergy. All these features are also to be found, magnified, in the story of the First Crusade.

It is clear that crusading owed a great debt to pilgrimage, and Urban II realised this when he set about creating his crusade appeal. His use of scare stories, exaggerations, and stereotyping of the enemy was effective because he knew that Western European society had formed a strong attachment to Jerusalem. Pilgrimage to the Holy Land was an important reason for that sense of attachment, and it was one of the firm foundations upon which the popularity of crusading came to be built.

Economic Factors

Hans Eberhard Mayer

In the following selection, Hans Eberhard Mayer maintains that economic conditions in Western Europe were an important factor in the origin of the Crusades. During the Middle Ages, he writes, agricultural production was not able to keep pace with population growth.

This problem was caused in part by the custom of dividing inherited land among all the children in a family, he notes. In some areas of Europe, especially northern France, this system of dividing land was gradually eliminated in favor of primogeniture, in which the eldest son in a family inherited all the property. In other areas of Europe, Mayer states, families continued to hold land in common, but they kept a tight control on how many family members married and had children in order to keep the number of possible heirs low. Mayer concludes that both systems of inheritance left little opportunity for many young men, who may have seen the Crusades as their best chance for worldly success.

Mayer is a professor of history at the University of Kiel in Germany. He is the author of *The Crusades*, from which this selection is excerpted.

In the historical discussion about the origins of the crusades it seems probable that too much attention has been paid to the eleventh-century developments in the Church's concept of a holy war. . . .

Despite everything that has been said about pilgrimages and holy war, it would be wrong to hope to explain the big part played in the crusade by the knights only in terms of religion, group psychology, and a professional ethos. Dry eco-

Excerpted from Hans Eberhard Mayer, *The Crusades*, trans. by John Gillingham (Oxford: Oxford University Press, 1988). Reprinted by permission of the publisher.

nomic and social factors were also significant, more so indeed than is commonly allowed today. Frequently specialists have tended to ignore this side of the problem, important though it clearly is. Instead a great deal has been said about the knight's love of adventure and his lust for booty. In the East he had the chance of making a quick fortune and of rising to a much higher position than he could ever have hoped for in his native country. . . . Doubtless some of the leaders of the First Crusade thought in such terms, especially the Normans from south Italy, Tancred and Bohemund of Taranto, and perhaps Robert of Normandy as well. After all, at Clermont Pope Urban II himself had promised that all those who went on crusade would enjoy undisturbed possession of the lands they conquered.

An Agricultural Crisis

Love of adventure, lust for booty—these are characteristics of individuals. But thanks to the work of G. Duby and D. Herlihy we know of economic and social problems which touched the knightly class as a whole and taught it to look upon the crusade as a way out. Herlihy has argued that there was a crisis in the agrarian economy of south France and Italy beginning in about 850 and becoming steadily worse until its climax was reached in about 1000. For the years after 1000 we have vivid chronicle descriptions of recurring famines which can be explained in terms of the failure of agricultural production to keep pace with the rising population. The still prevalent Carolingian custom of dividing an inheritance between all the heirs tended to hinder efforts to increase production. After 1000 the position began to improve, slowly at first, but then with gathering momentum. This was achieved mainly by doing away with the custom of splitting up the land into ever smaller holdings. There was no relaxation of population pressure. The Church and the nobility began to buy out small landholders in order to build up efficient economic units. Care was taken to ensure that land, once gathered together, should not again be dispersed. The knightly classes—the crusading classes par excellence— did this in various ways. In north France they developed the system of primogeniture, the right of the eldest son to succeed to the inheritance. Younger sons had to look after themselves, whether by entering the Church or by going in for a military career. Obviously the crusade acted as a kind of safety valve for a knightly class which was constantly growing in numbers. It is within this context that we must see an individual's love of adventure or hunger for loot.

In Italy and in France south of the Loire, above all in Burgundy, fragmentation of land was avoided by various forms of shared possession. We are particularly well informed about conditions in the Mâconnais, where there was a very strong tie binding the individual to the family. Here allodial land, i.e. land which was freely owned, was almost always held in common by the members of the family. This was a legal form known as *frérêche (fraternitia)*. It usually remained effective up until the second generation and prevented the splitting up of allods. Control of an inheritance passed to the brothers in common, or sometimes it might be shared with uncles, nephews, and even legal persons. Even if the individual's stake in the whole was only a small one, the community remained rich enough to equip one or two mounted knights. In this way the family's social status was preserved and at the same time provision was made for the uninterrupted administration of the estate by those who stayed at home. But this was an institution which worked only when the individual submitted to a tight discipline—the control exercised by the head of the family, a control which seems to have been extraordinarily strict at the end of the eleventh century. This was particularly so in matters of marriage, since, for economic reasons, the success of the *frérêche* depended upon an upper limit to the number of share-holders being enforced. Against the tide of a generally rising population the number of children had to be kept roughly constant. At that time there was only one really effective way of doing this: by a deliberate restriction of marriage. If, despite this, there were still too many potential heirs, some of them would have to be provided for in monasteries or in cathedral chapters. It is in fact possible to trace the outlines of such policies being pursued by the families of the Mâconnais.

The Crusade as a Safety Valve

Thus the maintenance of the family's economic and social position, in other words its standard of living, involved considerable sacrifices on the part of the individual. Men of an independent outlook may well have been frustrated by such strict family authority; not all were prepared to bow to the harsh requirements of the community, to renounce marriage even. One way out was to enter the Church but that was to exchange one community for another. The other great safety valve of the twelfth century, the crusade, offered a real chance of escaping from the tutelage of the *frérêche*, a real chance for the individual to become independent. But if there were some men who went on crusade in order to break away from the forced community of the family and to make a freer life for themselves, there were also others who chose to go in order to serve the best interests of the family, particularly in a situation where there were too many heirs and where fragmentation seemed inevitable unless some of them left home. An example of this occurred in the Mâconnais family of La Hongre. In 1096 it consisted of five men. Two of them were monks; two went to Jerusalem and did not return. This left Humbert who remained behind as the sole heir of their allodial possessions. In 1147 one of Humbert's grandsons went on the Second Crusade, leaving the whole inheritance to his brother. Thus the La Hongre family was still well-off at the beginning of the thirteenth century when others of their class were already beginning to feel the pinch of new economic developments. It is also worth noting that the early legislation of the crusader kingdom of Jerusalem was clearly appropriate to the needs of men with strong family ties like those of the *frérêche*. The estates held by the knightly families of Jerusalem could be inherited not only by daughters but also by collateral relatives [i.e., nephews, cousins, uncles, etc.]. Not until *c.* 1150 was the right to succeed limited to direct descendants. The earlier custom was clearly designed to persuade knights to settle down in the Holy Land; thus it had to accept the requirements of the *frérêche*. If the crusader died then the family back home in Europe could choose another member to take over the

Palestinian inheritance, in this way further easing conditions within the *frérêche* itself. It is not accidental that the Mâconnais has bulked large in this discussion. In this region Urban II's appeal met with a notable response. We know the names of many crusaders who came from this part of Europe in the first half of the twelfth century. This is not just the result of chance survival of evidence. It reflects clearly the social and economic situation of a class which looked upon the crusade as a way of solving its material problems or—to say the very least—which was, owing to this situation, all the more ready to consider going on a crusade.

Chapter 2

Why Participants Went on the Crusades

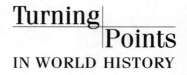

Turning Points
IN WORLD HISTORY

A Variety of Reasons for Crusading

Ronald C. Finucane

People went on the Crusades for a variety of reasons, both spiritual and worldly. According to Ronald C. Finucane, most crusaders were strongly motivated by religious factors, including the heavenly rewards promised by the pope and an earnest desire to help their fellow Christians in the East. However, Finucane points out, they were also attracted by the prospect of gaining riches through conquest and by the many practical privileges granted to crusaders. In some cases, crusaders had no choice: Murderers and other wrongdoers could be sent to the Crusades as part of their punishment for their crimes. On the other hand, the author writes, many robbers and highwaymen viewed crusading as a rich opportunity for plying their trade. Finucane concludes that although some crusaders did have questionable motives, the majority were at least partly impelled by sincere religious convictions.

Ronald C. Finucane is a professor of history and the chair of the history department at Oakland University in Rochester, Michigan. He has written *Miracles and Pilgrims: Popular Beliefs in Medieval England*, *The Rescue of the Innocents: Endangered Children in Medieval Miracles*, and *Soldiers of the Faith: Crusaders and Moslems at War*, from which the following selection is excerpted.

From 1095 to the end of the Middle Ages, the call to the Holy Land resounded across Europe as preachers harangued crowds amidst the green valleys and mountains of Wales, or from wooden platforms erected in the golden fields of

Excerpted from Ronald C. Finucane, *Soldiers of the Faith: Crusaders and Moslems at War* (London: J.M. Dent, 1983). Reprinted by permission of the publisher.

France, or in the echoing, dark naves of Rhenish cathedrals. Enthusiastic priests, prelates and popes exercised all the tricks of the orator's trade, cajoling, threatening, promising. . . .

Responding to the Call

People responded to the call for many different reasons. Some made their crusade vows because they were moved by the rumoured plight of their fellow-Christians, the so-called desecration of the Holy Land and atrocities allegedly committed by the infidels. Undoubtedly these wild tales infuriated many people, but it is unlikely that righteous indignation alone could have sustained the majority over the long trek east. Though the question of motivation is complex, . . . one easily identifiable motive for the Jerusalem trip was the crusade indulgence promised by preachers and guaranteed by popes. There can be no doubt that the indulgence was a much-prized benefit, or that it prompted hordes of peasants and nobles alike to take their vows to rescue Jerusalem. What was said of an indulgence offered for the ill-fated Fourth Crusade was generally true in all recruitment campaigns: 'The hearts of the people were greatly moved by the generous terms of this indulgence,' the contemporary author Geoffroy de Villehardouin reported in his chronicle of the Fourth Crusade, 'and many, *on that account*, were moved to take the cross' (emphasis added). Basically the indulgence was thought to lighten the burden of punishment for sin. Beyond this general statement not much had been formulated. . . . For the potential crusader, the important thing was what *he* thought the preacher meant by 'indulgence'. When the pope himself promised crusaders full remission of sins and 'an increase of eternal salvation', for example (the words of Innocent III at the Fourth Lateran Council, 1215), this filtered down to the ordinary man in the crowd as a promise of instant heaven, if he died on crusade—or while travelling to the Holy Land. Everyone, whatever his evil past, might thereby wipe the slate clean and perhaps even qualify for martyrdom. . . .

Popes, wise in the ways of the world, also offered more concrete, practical rewards for crusaders, and kings usually assisted in their implementation. These temporal privileges began to appear as early as the First Crusade and were well-developed by the early thirteenth century. Generally speaking, the protection that ordinary pilgrims were supposed to enjoy was augmented for crusaders, all of whom were in theory under papal direction: whoever insulted or injured them insulted or injured the pope. The well-organized crusader double-checking his gear before departure would be wise to obtain a papal or episcopal 'passport', just to make certain that his protected status was recorded in black and white. English crusaders also sought royal assistance, as did the Welsh, like Griffith son of Rutherik to whom King Henry III gave (or sold) a letter of protection and safe-conduct on crusade in 1233. The Church also promised to look after crusaders' lands and families left behind, that is, to put them under the protection of the Apostolic See, to use Clement III's terminology of 1191. Innocent III repeated these guarantees in 1215. In England four years later, the Archbishop of Canterbury wrote to the royal justiciar to remind him of this, and to ask him to restore the lands of a certain crusader which were *sub protectione Dei* [under God's protection]. Attorneys could be appointed to administer the property of an absent crusader and to look after the welfare and marriage of his heirs should he die on his holy mission. There were also other inducements. If a man wished to terminate bothersome lawsuits before his departure, the law was speeded up for him. No one could sue him during his absence; this even applied to accusations of homicide. For example, it was suggested that a certain Luke, a constable, may have killed someone unjustly. But since the constable was preparing to go on crusade, according to the anonymous scribal bureaucrat who recorded the case,

> The king, compassionating the pious vow of the said Luke . . . to save him harmless, as far as he can of right, grants that if he or any of his household going to the Holy Land, be charged with the deaths, they shall not be outlawed by reason of their absence, nor suffer any injury of their lands or possessions.

Any accusations were to be lodged with King Henry III, who would look into the matter when the constable returned. Alternatively, attorneys were allowed to prolong lawsuits already begun—an activity in which they have always excelled—by pleading crusader status for the absent defendant. An even greater benefit for many Christians was the suspension of interest payable on debts and an exemption from the crusader taxes that non-crusaders had to pay. Naturally there were complaints that some took the cross just to enjoy these privileges, having no intention of going off to risk their necks in some sandy waste.

There were many reasons for going on crusade in addition to spiritual and temporal perquisites. . . . Some men were involuntary members of these armed expeditions, for instance, having been sent there as penance for their sins. An obvious example is King Henry II: as part of the price of his implication in Archbishop of Canterbury Thomas Becket's murder in 1170, he was to support 200 knights for a year in the Levant, and to serve on crusade for three years. Henry, defending his lands from his wife, his sons and the French king, understandably never went. But seventeen years later, the money he had sent was used (unavailingly) to bolster the Christian forces in the face of a new threat from Saladin. By the thirteenth century the enforced crusade or its equivalent was a customary penance. In 1291, for example, John Cleymund of Boston whacked a local priest not once but twice across the tonsured pate with his sword, causing bruises but no bloodshed. For this outrage he was to finance a suitable warrior on the next expedition. In a more serious case, a London cleric involved in the murder of Bishop Stapleton of Exeter was ordered, in 1329, personally to go on the next crusade.

Wicked Men and Ruthless Plunderers

The old concept of a penitential pilgrimage was therefore easily extended to the penitential crusade. There were, however, some who went on crusade whom the Church would have preferred to see remain at home. Take this assorted unsavoury bunch, for instance, the criminals and pestilent men, wicked and impious, sacrilegious, thieves and robbers, homicides, parricides, perjurers, adulterers, and traitors, pirates, whore-mongers, drunkards, minstrels, dice-players, mimes and actors, apostate monks, nuns that are common harlots, and women who have left their husbands to live in brothels, or men who have run away from their true wives and taken others in their stead.

Such wicked people, Jacques de Vitry lamented, crossed the Mediterranean to take refuge in the Holy Land, only to continue plying their nefarious trades and committing their horrible sins. This was a thirteenth-century criticism, but the problem was hardly novel. During a recruitment campaign at Regensburg in 1147, the historian Otto of Freising—who was there—noted somewhat naively how 'so great a throng of highwaymen and robbers (strange to say) came hurrying forward' to take the cross. Some forty years later, . . . Gerald of Wales observed that some of the most notorious criminals of the area, highwaymen, robbers and murderers, were among the volunteers. There is probably some justification in questioning the sincerity of such people, though a few among them may truly have seen the crusade as a means to wipe away their crimes. The uncharitable, but perhaps more realistic, view is that such people saw the Holy Land and all lands en route as new fields in which to ply their trades, fresh pickings courtesy of the Church. Certainly the behaviour of even some of the crusade leaders suggests this. Stephen of Blois wrote to his wife from Antioch in 1098 that he had gained twice as much silver, gold and other riches as he had started out with; at the fall of Antioch, the crusade leaders boasted to the pope that they had killed the city tyrant and his soldiers, but had kept their wives, children, servants, gold, silver and all other goods. An often-quoted passage from the anonymous *Gesta Francorum et Aliorum Hierosolimitanorum* [The Deeds of the Franks and Other Jerusalemers] sums up this attitude: 'Let us all unite in Christ's faith and the victory of the Holy Cross, for, God willing, today we shall all be made rich.' The Byzantine historian Anna Comnena, writing her famous description of the western barbarians of the First Crusade, claimed that the simple folk were sincere, whereas the leaders were villains out to capture Constantinople itself. Alongside these motives which reflect the seamier side of the crusade, one can as easily cite examples of unselfish devotion to the cause, a willingness to give one's life for the recovery of Jerusalem. As one Moslem historian wrote of the Third Crusade,

> A Frankish prisoner told me that he was his mother's only son, and their house was their sole possession, but she had sold it and used the money . . . to equip him to go and free Jerusalem. There he had been taken prisoner. Such were the religious and personal motives that drove the Franks on.

. . . Though the crusaders may have been impelled by a mixture of motives, the 'religious' impulse was still the most visible. Many rushed forward to accept their cloth crosses in the sincere belief that Jerusalem cried out to be liberated from the infidel, that their armed pilgrimage would win them the blessings of the Church in this life and the companionship of the saints in the next.

Taking the Cross: Responsibilities and Rewards

Jonathan Riley-Smith

Jonathan Riley-Smith is the Dixie Professor of Ecclesiastical History at Cambridge University in England. He has also taught at the University of St. Andrews in Scotland and the University of London in England. Riley-Smith has written numerous articles and books on the Middle Ages. His books about the Crusades include *The Crusades: A Short History*, *What Were the Crusades?*, *The First Crusade and the Idea of Crusading*, *The First Crusaders: 1095–1131*, *The Knights of St. John in Jerusalem and Cyprus*, and *The Feudal Nobility and the Kingdom of Jerusalem*.

In the following article, Riley-Smith describes the ceremony surrounding the "taking of the cross," in which crusaders vowed to go to the Holy Land and received cloth crosses to sew onto their garments as a symbol of their vow. According to the author, these crusaders knew that fulfilling their vows would expose them to many dangers and hardships. However, he writes, crusaders were also entitled to many appealing privileges and rewards. For example, those who took the cross could earn indulgences, which would absolve them of most or all of their sins. Such spiritual rewards motivated many of the Europeans who chose to fight in the Crusades, Riley-Smith concludes.

Crusaders 'took the cross', which involved making a vow of a particular kind, often at emotional public gatherings under the influence of preachers whose business it was to whip their audiences up into a frenzy. It has been suggested that by the third quarter of the twelfth century the taking of the cross

Excerpted from Jonathan Riley-Smith, "The State of Mind of Crusaders to the East, 1095–1300," in *The Illustrated History of the Crusades*, edited by Jonathan Riley-Smith (Oxford: Oxford University Press, 1995). Reprinted by permission of the publisher.

and the rite granting the pilgrimage symbols of purse and staff were being merged into a single ceremony. This may be so, but originally the rituals were distinct. King Louis VII of France went through two of them, separated in time and space, when he was preparing for the Second Crusade. He made his vow to crusade on 31 March 1146 at Vézelay, where a large gathering had assembled. Louis and the greater nobles took the cross at a semi-private ceremony, at which the king was given a cross sent by the pope. He joined the preacher, St Bernard of Clairvaux, for the public meeting and stood on a platform with him wearing his cross, obviously to encourage the audience. Such was the enthusiasm with which Bernard's sermon was greeted that the packet of cloth crosses which had been prepared for distribution was used up and Bernard had to tear his monastic habit into strips to provide more. Then, over a year later on 11 June 1147 at St Denis, Louis received from the hands of the pope the symbols of pilgrimage, the purse and the oriflamme, the battle-standard of the French crown, given presumably in place of the staff.

These procedures were paralleled everywhere in the early decades of crusading. After nobles and knights had taken the cross, they would make private arrangements to receive the purse and staff, and perhaps also the blessing which appears in the later rites, from a local bishop, abbot, or prior. This second ceremony was sometimes associated with a financial arrangement with, or a donation for, the religious community concerned. For instance, on 22 May 1096 in the chapter house of Lérins, Fulk Doon of Châteaurenard donated quite a lot of property to the abbey. He was handed a napkin (in place of the pilgrim's purse) and a staff by the abbot, who enjoined the crusade on him as a penance and also gave him a mule. Ceremonies of this type may have continued long after the two rites had been joined together: in 1248 John of Joinville received the symbols of pilgrimage, and apparently them alone, from the abbot of Cheminon.

A Powerful Symbol

Introducing the cross as a visible symbol of the vow of commitment, Urban associated the taking and wearing of it in a highly-charged way with Christ's precepts, 'Every one that hath left house or brethren or sisters or father or mother or wife or children or lands, for my name's sake, shall receive an hundredfold and shall possess life everlasting' (Matthew 19:29) and 'If any man will come after me, let him deny himself and take up his cross and follow me' (Matthew 16:24 or Luke 14:27). From Syria the crusade leaders wrote to him as 'You who by your sermons made us all leave our lands and whatever was in them and ordered us to follow Christ by taking up our crosses'.

Some men responded hysterically, branding crosses on their bodies, but the sight of the ordinary cloth crosses must have been striking enough. An early twelfth-century sculpture from the priory of Belval in Lorraine shows a crusader wearing on his chest a cross made from 5 cm wide strips of cloth; the cross looks as though it measured 15 by 15 cm. Contingents soon came to distinguish themselves by the style or colour of the crosses they wore—this practice seems to have been introduced in the late 1140s for the Wendish crusaders, who wore a badge of a cross superimposed on a ball—and at a planning meeting for the Third Crusade it was decided that the French participants would wear red crosses, the English white ones, and the Flemish green.

Crusaders were expected to wear their crosses on their clothing at all times until they came home with their vows fulfilled: in 1123 the bishops at the First Lateran Council referred to those 'who had taken their crosses off' without departing. It should, therefore, have been possible to tell who was a crusader and it was important to do so. The leaders of the First Crusade were convinced that there was a reservoir of additional manpower in the West which could be deployed if only the Church would force laggards to fulfil their vows. Demands of this sort were made throughout the history of the crusading movement and attempts were periodically made to establish just how large the reservoir of 'false crusaders' was. But it was a lot easier to rail against those who had had second thoughts than to make them do what they had promised.

Another reason why it was important to know who had

taken the cross was that crusaders enjoyed special rights. At first there was confusion, even among the higher clergy, about at least one of the privileges granted them by the Council of Clermont, the commitment by the Church to protect their families and properties while they were away. Hugh II of Le Puiset, who had taken the cross for the crusade of 1107, felt threatened by a castle thrown up on a farm in his viscounty by Count Rotrou of Mortagne, who had, incidentally, been on the First Crusade. Hugh's bishop, Ivo of Chartres, although one of the greatest canonists of the age, passed the matter over to a secular court. Violence ensued and Hugh appealed to the pope who reallocated the case. Ivo pointed out that churchmen could not agree what to do, because 'this law of the Church protecting the goods of knights going to Jerusalem was new. They did not know whether the protection applied only to the crusaders' possessions, or also to their fortifications.'

By the thirteenth century, however, the privileges had become clearly defined, giving crusaders an advantage in law, because so many of them had legal implications. Besides the indulgence, about which more below, and protection, they included a delay in the performance of feudal service or in judicial proceedings until return, or alternatively a speedy settlement of a court case before departure; a moratorium on the repayment of debt or the payment of interest; exemption from tolls and taxes; freedom for a cleric to enjoy a benefice *in absentia* [in his absence] and for a knight to sell or pledge fiefs or inalienable property to raise money; release from excommunication; licence to have dealings with excommunicates and freedom from the consequences of interdict; the ability to use the crusade vow as a substitute for another not yet fulfilled; and the right to have a personal confessor with wide powers of absolution.

Honor and Infamy

Crusaders obviously had a high profile. No one has yet made a study of the effects on their social standing of engaging in such a prestigious activity, but there can be little doubt that the title *Jerosolimitanus* [those who have gone to Jerusalem]

adopted by them gained them honour in their neighbour-
hoods and even internationally. When Bohemond of Taranto
toured France in 1106, in a triumph which culminated in his
marriage to the king of France's daughter in Chartres cathedral, many French nobles wanted him to be godfather to
their children. He lectured about his adventures to large audiences and his experiences as a prisoner of the Muslims became incorporated in the *Miracula* [*Miracles*] of St Leonard,
whose shrine he ostentatiously visited. Two or three generations after the First Crusade families were still proud of ancestors who had fought in it.

A much less welcome consequence of taking the cross was
often obloquy. No group of people in the central Middle Ages
brought down on their heads such venomous criticism as did
crusaders. The reason was that failure in God's own war
fought at his bidding could not possibly be attributed to him,
but only, as it had been in the Old Testament, to the unwor-
thiness of the instruments at his disposal, in this case the soldiers of Christ. Because it was ideologically necessary to blame
them for every failure, crusaders were subjected to torrents of
abuse from reactions at home to the disasters of 1101 onwards.

The Motivations of the Crusaders

But whether a crusade was a success or a failure, every crusader risked death, injury, or financial ruin, and apprehension
shrouded the charters issued before departure like a cloud. . . .

Crusading was so unpleasant, dangerous, and expensive
that the more one considers crusaders the more astonishing
their motivation becomes. What did they think they were
doing? And why did catastrophes, which might be expected
to induce cynicism, indifference, and despair, only heighten
their enthusiasm? What was in their minds?

Over the last sixty years the theology of Christian violence has been intensively studied, and the ways it contributed, at an intellectual level, to ideas of Christian holy
war in general and to crusading thought in particular, have
become reasonably clear. The reactions of men and women
to the call to crusade are beginning to be explained as responses to the popularization of that ideology, presented to

them by preachers in ways which related to their day-to-day religious concerns. But even in terms of the history of theories of Christian violence crusading was a startling development. The First Crusade was the culminating surge towards the Holy Land of a cult of the Holy Sepulchre which had regularly spawned mass pilgrimages to Jerusalem throughout the eleventh century, but it was not only much the largest of these pilgrimages; it also differed from the others in being at the same time a war. Two Provençal brothers, Geoffrey and Guy of Signes, took the cross 'on the one hand for the grace of the pilgrimage and on the other, under the protection of God, to wipe out the defilement of the pagans and the immoderate madness through which innumerable Christians have already been oppressed, made captive, and killed with barbaric fury'. And in the Limousin Aimery Brunus 'was mindful of my sins and desired to go to fight the Muslims with the Christian people, and to visit the Sepulchre of the Lord which is in Jerusalem'.

Making a pilgrimage is a penitential, devotional act, requiring a frame of mind which is traditionally at the opposite end of the spectrum from that of a warrior. The intentions of eleventh-century pilgrims from the arms-bearing classes, who could certainly travel with splendour and panache, had been generally purely peaceful. The crusaders, on the other hand, intended war to be an integral part of their penitential exercise. It was officially described as an expression of their love for their Christian brothers and sisters and for their God, and commitment to it was considered to be a 'true oblation', a sacrificial surrender of self. In spite of its often flamboyant trappings, crusading was as much a devotional as a military activity, and the notion of a devotional war suggests a form of war-service which can be compared to saying a prayer.

War as an Act of Penance

In preaching the First Crusade, therefore, Pope Urban had made a revolutionary appeal. The notion that making war could be penitential seems to have evolved in the 1070s and 1080s out of a dialogue between Pope Gregory VII and a circle of reform theorists which had gathered around his supporter Mathilda of Tuscany. Urban took the idea, which was without precedent, and made it intellectually justifiable by associating warfare with pilgrimage to Jerusalem. The writer of the Monte Cassino Chronicle, probably a curial official who had accompanied the pope on his journey to France, described his initiative as a pastoral move, giving armsbearers the chance of contributing to their own salvation by undertaking an act of severe penance which did not entail the abandonment of their profession of arms or the humiliating loss of status involved in pilgrimaging without weapons, equipment, and horses. . . .

So radical was the notion of a devotional war that it is surprising that there seem to have been no protests from senior churchmen. If the First Crusade had failed, there would surely have been criticism of the association of war with pilgrimage, but its triumph confirmed for participants and observers alike that it really was a manifestation of God's will. 'The Lord has certainly revived his miracles of old', wrote Pope Paschal II. One of the most striking features of the letters from crusaders and the eyewitness narratives is the growing feeling of astonishment that prevailed in the army which crossed into Syria in 1097 and proceeded to Antioch and eventually to Jerusalem, with the heavens glittering with coincidental but actual pyrotechnics—comets, auroras, shooting stars—and the nights disturbed by visitations: Christ, the saints, and ghosts of crusading dead who returned to assure the living of the validity of relics or the certainty of heavenly rewards. The crusaders became convinced that the only explanation for their victorious progress was that God's hand was intervening to help them physically and that God did approve of holy war's association with penance and pilgrimage. The eyewitness reporters of the crusade came to use of it phrases which until then had been usually applied only to the monastic profession—the knighthood of Christ, the way of the cross, the heavenly Jerusalem, spiritual warfare—and most of these were taken up and refined by commentators, who dwelt on the crusade's penitential character and stressed the unique way its course had demonstrated divine approval. . . .

Indulgences

The Council of Clermont and Pope Urban had summarized the benefits this penitential act would bring in the indulgence. As we have seen, Urban seems to have intended this to be an authoritative statement that the penance the crusaders were going to undertake was likely to be so severe that it would be fully satisfactory, paying back to God not only the debts of punishment owed on account of their recent sins, for which penances had not yet been performed, but also any residue left over from earlier penances which had not been satisfactory enough. . . .

St Bernard presented the Second Crusade as a special opportunity for salvation open to those who took the cross: '[God] puts himself into a position of necessity, or pretends to be in one, while all the time he wants to help you in your need. He wants to be thought of as the debtor, so that he can award to those fighting for him wages: the remission of their sins and everlasting glory. It is because of this that I have called you a blessed generation, you who have been caught up in a time so rich in remission and are found living in this year so pleasing to the Lord, truly a year of jubilee.' Bernard's oratorical treatment of the indulgence was magnificent: 'Take the sign of the cross and you will obtain in equal measure remission of all the sins you have confessed with a contrite heart. The cloth [of the cloth cross] does not fetch much if it is sold; if it is worn on a faithful shoulder it is certain to be worth the kingdom of God.'

The Military Orders

Henry Treece

One of the most unique developments of the Crusades was the founding of the Christian military orders in the European-controlled Kingdom of Jerusalem. These orders combined the religious tradition of the monastery with the warrior ethic of Western Europe. Members of the military orders typically took vows of poverty, chastity, and obedience; they lived a communal and contemplative life, disdaining most worldly entertainments or concerns. Unlike other religious communities, however, the military orders combined this way of life with fighting the Muslims and defending the European settlements in the Holy Land. In the following selection, Henry Treece examines the two primary military orders: the Knights Hospitallers and the Knights Templar.

Henry Treece was a versatile British author, editor, and lecturer who wrote novels, verse, literary criticism, stage and radio plays, and television scripts. Treece's specialty was historical fiction and nonfiction.

In 1100 was founded a Christian military order. Its institution came about in this way: poor pilgrims to Jerusalem needed shelter, so a hostel was provided for them—by permission of the enlightened Egyptian governor of the city—and dedicated to St. John the Almsgiver, an early Patriarch of Alexandria. The staff of this hostel were mainly from Amalfi in Italy. They took monastic vows of a Benedictine sort and worked under the direction of a master. By the time the Christians had taken Jerusalem the Hospitallers had grown in power, since they had a knowledge both of Christian and Moslem customs and, moreover, were well informed

Excerpted from *The Crusades*, by Henry Treece. Copyright ©1962 by Henry Treece. Reprinted by permission of Random House, Inc., and John Johnson, Ltd.

as to Moslem military dispositions and strengths. Soon the master of the hostel, or hospital, had persuaded the Frankish conquerors of Jerusalem to make impressive donations to their enterprise. The staff of the hospital was increased by pilgrims, who saw in it the beginnings of a new sort of power. The next step was for the Hospitallers to withdraw from their subservience to the Benedictines and to flower as an order themselves, offering allegiance only to the Pope.

By 1118, such was the wealth and the power of the Hospitallers that they decided to throw aside their simple function as guides and feeders of pilgrims, and to become such a military force as would beat back the Moslem if needs be and so keep open a permanent route to the holy places. The order still contained brothers whose duty it was to tend the hungry and sick, but the main striking force was an army of knights, at first bound by vows of poverty and chastity, whose constant dream was the destruction of Islam. They wore a white cross on their tunics and, to mark their new and independent status, took as their patron St. John the Evangelist.

The Knights Templar

At the same time, in 1123, another similar order evolved— that of the Knights Templar, probably founded by a knight from Champagne, Hugh of Payens. Hugh persuaded King Baldwin I of Jerusalem to give him a wing in the royal palace, which had once been a mosque and was situated in the area of the Temple. The Templars, though at first under Benedictine control, soon became independent and established themselves as a tight-knit community. With the active support of the king, they recruited far and wide, and formed themselves into three classes: first, the knights, who were often of noble birth and who wore a red cross on a white tunic; then the sergeants, solid middle-class men, who wore a red cross on a black tunic. These sergeants, besides being warriors, also acted as grooms, and bailiffs to the Templars. The third degree of this order consisted of clerics, whose duties were religious, medical and non-military. Though the declared intention of the Templars was to keep open the pilgrim-routes to Jerusalem, it soon became obvious that the

The Rule of the Templars

Marie Luise Bulst-Thiele has taught at the University of Heidelberg and the University of Kiel, both in Germany. In the following excerpt, Bulst-Thiele depicts the lifestyle of the Knights Templar.

The Order of the Templars . . . was designated as sacred and sanctified from the beginning. It had been founded for the praise and glory of God, to defend the faithful and to liberate the church of God. Though they were only one of several orders founded c. 1100, the Templars were different. While the Cistercians and the Augustinians aligned themselves with the doctrine of the Church Fathers, the aims of the Order of the Templars were startlingly new. The Templars combined monastic discipline with a fighting vocation. Only in the fervor of their vows did they resemble other orders. . . .

The rule of St. Benedict of Nursia was the model for the Templars' rule, from which many phrases were adopted. Members of the order shared simple meals of meat and wine and slept together in one room, fully clothed and belted, with a candle burning. The ban on personal property was only one of the many edicts the Templars followed with unswerving obedience; they had to live together amicably and to care for the old and the sick. . . .

The rule of the Templars governed all aspects of life. It began by outlining their religious service and the canonical hours of prayers and Paternosters. It detailed the type of alms and prayers to be said for the dead. Frugality and plainness of dress and weapons were required. The knights were allowed three horses and one shield-bearer. No worldly pleasures were permitted: no chess, hunting, or hawking. . . .

Their militia was holy and secure. They lived by the rule: brotherly love, voluntary poverty, asceticism, abstention from amusement and respectful submission to the grand master and the Chapter.

Marie Luise Bulst-Thiele, "The Influence of St. Bernard of Clairvaux on the Formation of the Order of the Knights Templar," in *The Second Crusade and the Cistercians*, ed. Michael Gervers, 1992.

knights were men of military ambition who eagerly sought any opportunity of defending the Kingdom of Jerusalem and of gaining favour with its king.

It must be said here, however, that the Templars in their pride did not bow the knee to the king—their only master being the Pope—even though he and his lords endowed them lavishly with money and vast estates. Baldwin I was shrewd enough to see that in the Templars he had a permanent standing army, on whom he could call with confidence at any time: which was more than could be said of the great mass of crusaders, whose desire only too often was simply to get rich without delay and then to sail back to their castles in France or Germany.

Soon the glamour and fighting-fame of the Templars rapidly spread through Europe; and it became the ambition of many a young lord to leave his impoverished estate and to enlist in an order whose temporal power and wealth were increasing yearly. One day, it was thought—and rightly—these arrogant horsemen in the white tunics would become the most powerful Christians in the Arab world. One day they might even challenge the Christian King of Jerusalem himself. . . .

Growing in Power and Prestige

As the years went on, the Christian military orders, composed as they were of so many European peoples, assumed the status of a permanent standing army. The average crusading lords, and even kings, were in a sense mere migrants, sometimes idealistic and often predatory *visitors*, who would come and go as soon as their immediate purpose was fulfilled: but the Templars and the Hospitallers were dedicated and disciplined *residents*. Furthermore, the Grand Masters of both orders were no longer the mere heads of military contingents but became more and more elevated until they sat at the treaty table even with kings, patriarchs and great barons. In the field, the two orders generally provided half the Christian striking-force.

Of the "sergeants," or armed troopers of Frankish origin, there were perhaps 5,000, supplemented by half-caste mercenaries and "Turcopoles" of native origin. While the nobility tended to marry into other European, Greek or Armenian families, the sergeants and mercenaries were less discriminating, and found wives where they could, many of them Turks or Arabs. Nevertheless, the dominant language used for common intercourse was probably northern French, though of course Greek, Italian and German would be heard here and there. . . .

The political system in the Kingdom of Jerusalem was basically a feudal one, each community tied to the land and paying a proportion of its produce to the overlord so as to feed his standing army of "sergeants" and "Turcopoles." Of the great landholders the Templars and Hospitallers were among the most powerful, and, long before the twelfth century had ended, they overshadowed most aspects of life in the Middle East, largely because there was about them the air of a permanent institution in what otherwise was a seasonally-changing world.

Wealthy enough to build and maintain great fortresses at strategic points, and now constantly supplied from Europe by idealistic young recruits of good family, they made themselves increasingly necessary in the social system of Palestine and elsewhere. No king, however misguided, would care to offend them for fear of losing his own kingdom to the watchful Saracens who surrounded the crusading states.

As "policemen" of the routes leading to holy places, they were undoubtedly superb. The rich Hospitallers, always more concerned with charitable acts than the military Templars, housed and tended upwards of a thousand sick and needy pilgrims in Jerusalem alone. The Templars, though giving alms on a less generous scale, were esteemed both as an offensive striking-force and as bankers. No doubt the rate of interest on all loans would be very high, although usury was forbidden by the Church, but the bankers of the Temple had their secret methods of collecting payment.

A Force to Be Reckoned With

In all the feudal world there can have been nothing quite like these two military orders, who could disregard the word of the king, who held their lands for ever, whose tenants were not required to pay church-tithes and who fought only when they chose to do so. Their Grand Masters, or their representatives, sat in judgement in the High Courts of Jerusalem, Antioch and Tripoli, and often gave their verdicts as it suited them and not as it suited justice or kings and princes. They made their own diplomatic advances and treaties with the Saracen rulers, irrespective of the official policy of any feudal monarchs in Outremer. Both to Hospitallers and Templars, the military order came first, the Kingdom of Jerusalem a poor second. . . .

Yet, though these orders might at first seem disruptive elements in the Holy Land, it is possible that seen against the corruption of the Venetian and Genoese merchant princes and the weak indecisions of the barons and lordlings freshly out from Europe, they were points of stability—headstrong, spiritually arrogant and unscrupulous—but solid. This unscrupulousness was mainly seen among the Templars, who as bankers were as willing to oblige Moslem as Christian clients, and who retained a large staff of Saracens intimate with all Islamic affairs and requirements. The spy-system of the Templars seems to have been the most efficient in Outremer and after a while most of the Knights of the Temple spoke Arabic as well as they did their own native language. In many ways they seem to have anticipated both the political princes of the Renaissance and the fighting Jesuits of the Catholic Church.

Religious Hysteria Led to Participation

Norman P. Zacour

Europeans in the Middle Ages were prone to periodic outbreaks of mass hysteria that frequently were religious in nature and sometimes resulted in violence. In the following article, Norman P. Zacour links the tradition of mass religious hysteria to the formation of the Children's Crusade in 1212. Zacour compares the religious enthusiasm surrounding the Children's Crusade to that of other mass uprisings during the crusading period. Although the Children's Crusade was not as violent as some of the other mass movements of the Middle Ages, it was still a tragic event, ending in defeat and disintegrating only after many of the young participants had died.

Zacour was a professor of history at the University of Toronto in Ontario, Canada, for many years. His books include *An Introduction to Medieval Institutions* and *Jews and Saracens in the Consilia of Oldradus de Ponte*. He is also the coeditor of the fifth and sixth volumes of *A History of the Crusades*.

The great masses of common people were often bewitched by thoughts of liberating the Holy Land. With each successive proclamation of a crusade, the preachers aroused an excitement shared alike by men and women, the old and the young, all eager to redeem past failures and to drive out the "infidel" from the holy places. Within each crusading army the low-born regarded themselves as the elect of God. This was a cliché of the Middle Ages, but one which never failed to find a response, especially among the poor and the op-

Excerpted from Norman P. Zacour, "The Children's Crusade," in *A History of the Crusades*, vol. 2, edited by Robert Lee Wolff and Harry W. Hazard; ©1969 by the Regents of the University of Wisconsin. Reprinted by permission of The University of Wisconsin Press.

pressed (to say nothing of the unbalanced) always looking for the millennium. . . . As time passed, with the obvious failure of knightly arms to free Jerusalem, the idea that the meek might do what the proud and mighty had been unable to do all the more possessed the minds of lesser folk. . . .

Episodes of Temporary Insanity

It was easy to release the religious enthusiasm of the Middle Ages, always close to the surface; it was far more difficult, however, to keep it within bounds when once aroused. Especially was this so in areas of great social ferment such as the Rhine valley and the Lowlands, where old social forms were breaking down in the face of increased industrial and urban development, where population was growing rapidly, and where economic insecurity was becoming chronic. The sustained excitement of crusade preaching acted on the people of such areas with explosive force. One could never be certain what form their enthusiasm might take. It was sure to enhance the irritability of those for whom relief from anxiety was often to be obtained only in giving free rein to their passions, and who found in sudden violent action a release from the unbearable insecurity of their dreary lives. But it was a release to be found, then as now, in the crowd, defined by Everett Dean Martin as "a device for indulging ourselves in a kind of temporary insanity by all going crazy together." "Around this time," it is reported in contemporary annals, "naked women ran through the towns and cities, saying nothing." There was always a touch of madness in the air.

There were many examples of the kind of mass psychosis that might develop when religious enthusiasm ran riot. . . .

[For] example, [in] the year 1182, in south central France, . . . an obscure carpenter, Durand of Le Puy, had a vision in which the Virgin ordered him to exhort the people to peace. She gave him a scrap of parchment upon which was the figure of Mary bearing the infant Jesus in her arms, and the prayer: "Lamb of God, who taketh away the sins of the world, give us peace." There quickly grew up around Durand a large movement, dedicated to the destruction of the brigands of the region, and almost as quickly a "rule" was drawn up. The new confraternity briefly enjoyed the support of all classes of society. Soon, however, it also turned on the established authorities, lost the support of nobility and church, became an outcast and undisciplined mob, and was hunted down and finally destroyed. Later writers would express horror and disgust at this "dangerous presumption", this "rebellion against their betters", in which there was shown "no fear, no reverence, of their superiors".

In the remarkable movement which grew up around the carpenter of Le Puy there is evident the same emotionalism which was to nourish the Children's Crusade. . . .

The Children's Crusade Begins

The movement which boiled up for a brief moment in 1212 was never, despite the convictions of those who took part in it, a crusade in any legal sense, blessed by the church and encouraged by indulgences. On the contrary, it was deplored by all responsible authority. What has often been looked upon as its "French phase" may not have been considered a crusade even by the participants. In June 1212, it is said, a shepherd boy named Stephen, from Cloyes near Vendôme, beheld a vision of Jesus, who appeared to him in the guise of a poor pilgrim, received some bread from him, and then gave him a letter for the king of France. Soon many of his fellow shepherds gathered about Stephen and accompanied him to St. Denis, and then to Paris to see the king. Meanwhile, a sort of mass hysteria seems to have gripped much of the countryside round about. Many other children were being held in great reverence by the simple crowds, and around these there gathered larger and larger followings of yet more children whose purpose it apparently was to join the "sanctus puer" [holy youth], Stephen. Another source tells of processions of children, and some adults too, carrying banners and candles, crosses and censers, passing through towns and hamlets and chanting in the vulgar tongue, "Lord God, exalt Christianity! Lord God, restore to us the true cross," and other chants also, since there were many such groups, each singing its own variation. . . . From Jumièges on the lower Seine comes a brief notice that the children claimed to be "seeking God". Aside from this vague aspiration, however, there seems to be no contemporary evidence that the children who followed Stephen had any idea of going to the Holy Land.

"Going to God"

There is little wonder, however, that in the later accounts of this movement Stephen and his shepherd boys came to be connected with the Children's Crusade. The strange excitement in which they were caught up during that summer of 1212 had already raced swiftly through the region of old Lotharingia between the Rhine and France. There other crowds, young and old, were going far beyond mere processions and chants. To the north and east, in the Benedictine monastery of Andres, near Guines, the monk William was noting the remarkable "peregrinatio" [migration], as he called it, of an infinite number of children from various cities and towns, castles and villages, making their way toward the Mediterranean. When asked by their parents and others whither they were going, they too replied as though moved by a single spirit, "to God!" Did they have some notion of going to the Holy Land? It seems almost certain.

Farther east, in the Benedictine house of St. James at Liége, the monk Reiner witnessed a local outbreak of this same movement. He reports that it embraced not only French but also German children, especially young shepherds and shepherdesses. Those whose parents would not allow them to go wept bitterly. Here at Liége the purpose was clear enough: the children wished to do what princes and kings had failed to do—cross the sea and recover the Sepulcher of Christ. . . .

South of Liége, at Trier, it was much the same story, though here only German and not French children are mentioned. Their leader was a certain Nicholas, a young boy whose home was Cologne. . . .

Farther east again, there are additional reports and a few more details. One contemporary, writing in Cologne, provides dates for what he calls "a remarkable, indeed a more-than-remarkable, affair"—around Easter and Pentecost,

March 25 and May 13. This is considerably earlier than the date recorded for Stephen's procession in France, and suggests that the movement may have had its origins in the Lowlands and the Rhine valley, and only its outer fringes on the Seine. Many thousands of children ranging from six years to the age of discretion came together, despite the opposition of their parents, relatives, and friends. Some left their plows, others the flocks and herds which had been in their care, and rushed to take the cross. They moved off in groups of twenty, fifty, or a hundred, with Jerusalem their goal. It was unbelievable. How, they were asked, could they expect to do what kings, dukes, and so many others had failed to do. They replied with simplicity that they would obey the divine command and bear with willing spirit whatever God placed upon them. Another Cologne chronicle, quite independently, confirms that French as well as German children were involved, of various ages and conditions. There is the additional note, hardly surprising in view of the circumstances and the times, that some "maligni homines" [evil men] joined the pilgrimage, pilfered the contributions made to the children by the faithful, and then secretly stole away. One of them was caught and hanged in Cologne. . . .

The Route of the Journey

The route of the various bands which seem to have gathered and formed in or around Cologne lay up the Rhine and eventually, for most of them, over the Alps into Lombardy. Some of the children were turned back at Mainz; the heat was excessive, and the weak began to fall by the wayside. From Speyer we have a brief notice of their passing—not contemporary, it is true, but of some interest since it preserves the date they went through the town, July 25. At Ebersheim, on a little island in the Ill not far from Schlettstadt, they made a striking impression on the chronicler of the monastery. Nicholas is again named as the leader of this "infinite number" from Germany and France, all convinced that once they reached the sea they could walk across the tops of the waves without wetting their feet.

The expedition passed near Marbach, southwest of Colmar. There the chronicler of the Augustinian house grumbled over the indiscretion and uselessness of such a business, and moralized on the inevitable failure of any such venture undertaken "without the balance of reason or the force of counsel." From Marbach, the multitude swarmed through the Alps and into Italy. . . . There they broke up into groups and dispersed among the various towns of Lombardy where they were despoiled by the natives. A notice from Salzburg indicates that some reached Treviso; possibly they hoped to take ship at Venice. But the main body seems to have gone in the other direction, reaching Piacenza on August 20. Nicholas was still the leader of what, despite losses, must even yet have been an impressive pilgrimage, a "great and innumerable multitude of German children, babes at the breast, women and girls," according to a contemporary chronicle, all hastening down to the sea to fulfil the prophecy of an angel of God that they would recover the Holy Sepulcher from the hands of the iniquitous Saracens. Nearby, at Cremona, bishop Sicard also recorded their passage, in drier tones perhaps, but with the authentic note that the company had come from Cologne.

The Crusade Falls Apart

From the valley of the Po, Nicholas and his followers pressed on to the south and the sea. They were in Genoa by Saturday, August 25, bearing crosses, with their pilgrim staves and leathern wallets—more than seven thousand, so it was estimated. They obviously received no encouragement, no offer of sea transportation to the Holy Land, for the very next day most of them were gone again, although many of their number dropped out and remained behind. From Genoa there is no longer any clear trail to follow. The "crusade" had been breaking up all the way from Germany to Italy; many had died, many others had returned home discouraged, or stopped at places such as Genoa and gone no further. A late source reports that two boat-loads sailed from Pisa, of whom nothing more was heard. There are reports that a body of the crusaders went to Rome, where Innocent III relieved of their crusading oaths those who were too young and those weighed down by too many years. He is said to have remarked: "These children put us to shame. They rush to recover the Holy Land while we sleep." The chronicler of Trier puts some crusaders ultimately in Brindisi, where the archbishop refused them permission to sail. There are two conflicting accounts of what happened to their leader, Nicholas. One has him going on the Fifth Crusade and fighting at the siege of Damietta, finally returning home safe; the other states that he died in Italy and that his father, who had been guilty of selling some of the children as slaves, committed suicide after returning to Cologne. From these vague and conflicting accounts we may assume that much of the Children's Crusade melted away in Italy. The footsore and deluded crusaders, greatly reduced in number, now began the long trek back over the Alps. They had marched south proudly in great singing crowds. Now, with no dream to sustain them any longer, they made their painful way homeward, barefoot, hungry, objects of scorn and derision to those who had so recently held them in awe and reverence. . . .

Medieval Children and Mass Hysteria

There would be other examples of mass hysteria of children, not always, to be sure, connected with the crusade. For instance, in 1237 some thousand or so children danced and leaped their way from Erfurt to Arnstadt. Although their parents went out and brought them home the next day, some of the children continued ill for some time, suffering from trembling of the limbs. From the slight notices we have of the matter, it seems to have been an early form of St. Vitus' dance.

This episode has a certain affinity with the legendary case of the children of Hameln, in the diocese of Minden. On the day of Sts. John and Paul, June 26, 1284, there came over the bridge and in through the Weser gate a young man of thirty years, whose beauty and fine dress everyone admired. He had a silver flute, and when he played it all the boys who heard him, to the number of 130, followed him out through the Eastgate to the place where beheadings were held, called "Calvary" by the villagers. There they all disappeared. The mothers of the missing children ran from town to town, but could find no trace of them. And, so the tale goes, as one would ordinarily reckon the date according to the birth of the Lord, or as such and such a year after a jubilee, in Hameln it is done according to the year of the disappearance of the children.

Here is the earliest surviving version of the well known story of the Pied Piper of Hamelin—without, as yet, any rats. It comes from a fifteenth-century manuscript, but reports an older tradition: "These things I have found in an ancient book. And deacon John of Lügde's mother saw the children go off." What really happened to these children we do not know. The actual event is obscured by the later legend, and there is no contemporary evidence. But it can hardly be doubted that we are in the presence of yet another of the sudden and inexplicable seizures from which juveniles in the mass suffer from time to time—a phenomenon not unknown in our own day.

The Shepherds' Crusade

Even more important than these examples, however, is the rising of the shepherds in France in 1251. They planned to go to the Holy Land to rescue their king, Louis IX. Here again are all the confused elements of restlessness, religious hysteria, and blind violence generally to be feared in movements of this kind. The "Master of Hungary", as the leader was called, had . . . a command from the Virgin to preach the crusade to the lowly shepherds, since the military pride of the Franks was displeasing to God. The movement is thus akin to the Children's Crusade, all the more so because of the area of its origins . . . and its heterogeneous composition of men, women, and children. Matthew Paris even accuses the Master of being an old leader of the Children's Crusade "around forty years ago". Though at first favored by the queen, Blanche of Castile, the movement quickly degenerated into a lawless rabble. Everywhere they went there were scenes of terror and bloodshed: at Rouen, where they ejected archbishop Odo and his clergy from the cathedral; at Orléans, where they clashed with the scholars and killed or threw into the Loire some twenty-five of them, wounding many more; at Tours, where they assaulted the Dominican convent, profaned the churches, even mutilated a statue of the Virgin. Later the Master, with the greater number of his followers, occupied Bourges, where one of the citizens, an "executioner with a two-edged sword," says Matthew, "sent him headless to hell"; his body was left to be eaten at the crossroads, while his followers were dispersed "and were everywhere cut down like mad dogs".

The Children's Crusade . . . never went so far as to invite this kind of destruction. Though opposed by responsible elements of society, it was nevertheless tolerated since it retained the form and appearance of a crusade and did not challenge established authority so far as we know. Seen in its historical setting, however, it remains one of a series of social explosions through which medieval men and women—and children, too, wonderfully sympathetic to the agitations of their elders—found release.

Chapter 3

Social Changes and Cultural Influences of the Crusades

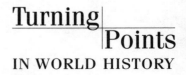

Turning Points
IN WORLD HISTORY

Life in the Crusader Kingdoms

Antony Bridge

After the first crusaders conquered Jerusalem, they established a kingdom there and in other Middle Eastern cities. Those crusaders who chose to remain in the East discovered a new way of life, vastly different from that of Western Europe. Antony Bridge describes the world of the crusader kingdoms in the following excerpt from his book *The Crusades*.

Bridge points out that although the European settlers never completely assimilated, they adopted many aspects of the eastern way of life. Furthermore, he stresses, most of the changes were positive ones, with the result that the Europeans who remained in the East typically enjoyed a much higher standard of living than those who returned home. Over time, they adopted diets, clothing, and personal habits more suited to the desert environment in which they now lived, Bridge writes. While the Europeans were often at odds with the Muslims and the Greek-speaking Christians who inhabited the region before their arrival, at other times the groups coincided peacefully and even intermarried.

A professional painter and an ordained minister, Antony Bridge has written several books, including *Richard the Lionheart*, a biography of England's crusading king.

Many of the original Crusaders went home, but others settled down to spend the rest of their lives in Outremer. Many of the minor knights and most of the rank and file had little or no incentive to make the return journey. But perhaps the words 'settled down' are misleading, for life in the Crusader kingdoms throughout their history was turbulent and unset-

Excerpted from Antony Bridge, *The Crusades* (New York: Franklin Watts, 1982). Reprinted by permission of HarperCollins Publishers Ltd.

tled. Internally it was beset by dynastic quarrels between the great ruling families, who were violently jealous of one another and chronically incapable of living in peace together, while externally it was lived against a background of almost perpetual war with the Moslems. . . .

Becoming Middle Easterners

The first Crusaders were nearly all either Norman or French, and the states they founded were unmistakably created by Frenchmen; everyone spoke French, and the feudal structure of contemporary French society was faithfully reproduced in Outremer, while the Orthodox Church and its Greek liturgy was ousted by the Catholic Church and its Latin rite. During the two centuries of their existence, the Crusader kingdoms did not change in these respects. In all sorts of other ways, however, the way of life there was profoundly changed by the climate, the physical conditions and the natural resources of the land, and as the years went by the Franks of Outremer succumbed to a slow process of orientalisation, the results of which regularly shocked newcomers from the West. Perhaps if they had been more numerous, more of their western ways and customs might have remained unchanged over the years, but during the whole course of their history they were a tiny minority both racially and socially in the lands which they ruled. It has been estimated that there were never as many as a thousand knights resident in the Kingdom of Jerusalem, although their numbers were swollen by visitors from time to time; and much the same was true of the entire knightly population of the Principality of Antioch and the Counties of Edessa and Tripoli taken together. The rank and file were more numerous, but even they were vastly outnumbered by the local people. These consisted of Greek-speaking Christians alongside Armenians, Jews, Egyptians and Arabs, some of whom were Christians and some Moslem, but there was not much social contact between the Franks and those whom they ruled. Intermarriage was exceedingly rare; in aristocratic circles members of the ruling families tended to marry only members of similar families, although a few of them married well-bred Armenians or Byzantines, all of them Christian. Any kind of sexual intercourse with a Moslem, in marriage or in concubinage, was strictly outlawed; indeed, the Council of Nablus in 1120 decreed that a man found guilty of going to bed with a Moslem woman should both be castrated and have his nose cut off. But members of less exalted Frankish families felt free to marry the daughters of local Christians, whatever their ethnic origins might have been; and the result was that, as time went by, their descendants, who were known as *poulains*, were often difficult to distinguish from other members of the native population. In contrast, the Venetians, the Pisans and the Genoese, who as time went by were to be found acting as merchants and *entrepreneurs* in almost every city, kept their identity better than most of the Franks, partly because they lived together in streets allocated to them by the various princes with whom they had made treaties, and partly because they travelled to and from Italy on their mercantile occasions, and so never lost touch with their native cities.

Everyday Life

Life in the villages was much the same as it had been in Old Testament times, so little had it changed, but very few Franks settled in them. Wherever it was possible, they were built on the tops of hills, both because such sites were more easily defended than more accessible settings, and also because they were windier and thus both cooler in summer and better suited for winnowing at harvest time. Those Franks who did live in the villages had to endure the primitive conditions endured by the native villagers, and this was one reason why they were unpopular. Those who lived in the towns enjoyed much better amenities. Some lived in simple, single-storeyed houses, but most had homes with two floors, and the rich lived in much grander abodes, which they called 'palaces'; these were built in a style inherited from Graeco-Roman days, as much else had been by Arab civilisation in that part of the world. Usually they consisted of a square of rooms on two floors surrounding a central *patio;* apart from the main entrance, all the doors and windows opened onto the central court, as did a row of verandas in the more luxurious houses, and their roofs were flat. People slept upstairs, while the living-rooms, dining-rooms and kitchens were on the ground floor. Unlike their oriental subjects, who reclined to eat their meals as the Romans had before them, the Franks sat around a table when they ate together; the table was covered with a cloth, lit by candles or oil lamps at night and, as the years went by and old prejudices slowly died, it was furnished with just such luxuries as knives, spoons and forks, glass decanters and goblets, elegant dishes and plates, as had aroused the angry derision of the first Crusaders to pass through Constantinople and observe the 'effeminate' table manners of Emperor Alexius' court.

Changes in Personal Habits

The Franks' personal habits changed in many ways too, although not in all. The men continued to wear their hair long to their shoulders and to shave their chins, although a few grew beards like those of the Greeks and Syrians. In Jerusalem there was a barbers' quarter near the Church of the Holy Sepulchre, to which many people went to be shaved once or twice a week, while others were shaved by attendants at the public baths; and presumably other cities had similar amenities. The women wore their hair in two long plaits, painted their faces and dressed superbly. A Spanish traveller who was in the Kingdom of Jerusalem in 1181, a man named Ibn Jubayr, was dazzled by a Frankish bride whom he saw on her wedding day in Tyre. 'She was most elegantly arrayed in a beautiful dress,' he wrote, 'from which there floated, according to their traditional style, a long train of silk. On her head she wore a golden diadem covered by a net of woven gold, and on her breast there was a similar ornament.' The men were scarcely less splendid; for some time they continued to wear European clothes, which consisted of long stockings, a shirt with long tight sleeves, and over it a short jacket with short sleeves, but whether these garments were made of fine wool, cotton, linen or silk, invariably they were brilliantly coloured and embroidered with gold or silver thread. But as the years passed most of the knights abandoned Western fashions altogether and, returning from whatever battlefield happened to have been claiming their professional attention at the time, removed their armour and put on a silk burnous in summer and furs in winter.

But perhaps the single biggest change in their habits took place in their attitude to personal hygiene. In Europe, washing had been despised, but in the climate of Outremer they began to patronise the public baths, to be found in every city. They were similar to the Turkish baths of today or the Roman baths of antiquity; the bather first undressed, and then donned a towel and sandals, although apparently some of the Franks sometimes dispensed with the towel; the Prince Usamah, a member of an independent dynasty of Munqidhite Arabs with a castle at Shaizar near Hama, who travelled widely through Outremer, made many Frankish friends, and wrote his *Memoirs*, complained that some people did not bother with a towel but bathed naked. But whether clothed or not, the bather entered a heated room, where he began to sweat; then, when he had sweated enough, he called an attendant, who soaped him all over, rubbed him down, and dried him with another towel. Before leaving he rested in an ante-room where couches were provided on which he could lie in comfort. Bathing became so much a part of everyone's way of life that it was even required on certain occasions; for instance, young men seeking admission as novices to one or other of the Military Orders were obliged to bathe in a communal bath-house before they were formally admitted. Women bathed as frequently as men, going to the baths two or three times a week, although needless to say they bathed separately from the men.

If the Franks were cleaner in Outremer than they had been at home in Europe, they were much better fed too; for not only was their food rich and varied, but it was cooked by local people who were artists in the kitchen. Chicken, crane, quail, pigeon and partridge were plentiful; mutton, beef, wild boar, ibex, roebuck and hare were cooked with garlic and herbs and seasoned with mustard and pepper, or served with delicious sauces; there was an abundance of freshwater fish, and eels were much prized as delicacies; cooked vegetables included such things as beans, peas, artichokes, asparagus and rice, while lettuces and cucumbers were eaten raw. When they first arrived, the Franks were astonished by the novelty and variety of the various kinds of fruit which they found growing everywhere, many of which they had never even heard of let alone seen or eaten; there were bananas, oranges, lemons, dates, carobs, the fruit of the sycamore tree which they named 'Pharaoh's figs', grapes, peaches, plums, quinces and ordinary figs, and with them various nuts including almonds. Since wine was forbidden to Moslems, there were no vineyards, but that was a deficiency soon remedied, and after the first few years wine was plentiful and much of it was good. In the heat of summer it was chilled with snow from the mountains of Lebanon, which was brought south protected from the heat of the sun by straw, and it was drunk both in private houses and in taverns. Beer brewed from barley was also popular, and fruit juices were cheap and easily available.

Trades and Pastimes

In the intervals between wars, some of the Franks practised trades of various kinds. They were great builders, as both their churches and their castles still testify, and although much of the work of building them must have been done by local Arabs and other native people, the masons' marks to be found on some of their stones proves that Frankish craftsmen were also active. The area around Tyre was famous for its pottery and glass, and a Frankish glass-smelting furnace has been found at Samariya near Acre, so some of the Crusaders must have learned how to blow glass from their Arab neighbours, who had been manufacturing it since Roman days and before; the Venetians, who held large parts of Tyre and the country round it, seem to have learned to be glassmakers there. There was a thriving textile industry in Outremer too, and probably some Franks were employed in the manufacture of silk and cotton fabrics. But then as now the most thriving industry was the manufacture of religious souvenirs for the pilgrims who came in large numbers to visit the holy places of the Christian faith, and the resident Franks must have been involved in this highly lucrative trade.

But if involvement in trade was not beneath the dignity of some of the less aristocratic Frankish citizens of Outremer, the knights scorned it as unworthy of their nobility; war was their profession, and when they were not fighting one another or their Moslem neighbours, they spent most of their time hunting. Mounted and armed with spears, they pursued such beasts of prey as lions, leopards, bears and wolves for the sheer enjoyment of the chase, while they also hunted wild boar, deer, ibex and hares for the pot. Needless to say, there were accidents from time to time and men were hurt or even killed; but this deterred no one. . . .

Luxurious Homes

When they were not enjoying themselves out of doors, the Franks spent their time at home or visiting their friends, and as the years passed some of their houses became astonishingly luxurious: so luxurious indeed that they shocked newcomers from the West. Like the houses of wealthy Byzantines, the palaces of some of the richer Franks were adorned with Persian carpets, damask hangings, mosaic floors, inlaid marble walls, carved furniture of ivory or rare wood and dinner services of silver or Chinese porcelain brought by caravan from the East. Their owners slept in comfortable beds between fine linen sheets, and in some of the northern cities, where water was abundant the biggest houses had their own private bathrooms with running water. People played dice a great deal, and such games as chess were also played; they drank a lot, both at home and in taverns, and drunkenness was common. Musicians, strolling players and mimes performed in the squares of the cities and in other open spaces; their performances were popular and well attended, but the performers themselves were regarded as the lowest of the low, little better than prostitutes. These, too, were to be found on the streets of every city.

Most of these pursuits were, however, masculine preserves; it is difficult to discover what the Frankish women did in their spare time. No doubt the greater part of their lives was spent either preparing to be married or, after their marriages, bearing children, even if desperately few of their babies survived to the age of five. But everyone was used to the fact that in the midst of life they were in death, and they took the deaths of many of their children as much for granted as they took the way in which their marriages were arranged for them. It was not at all unusual for the children of the upper classes to be married when they were five or six years old in the hope that one day they might grow up to consummate their union and produce some dynastically desirable children, while on other occasions a child might be married to a much older adult in order to join two dynasties in a desirable political union; for instance, Baldwin III of Jerusalem married a little Byzantine princess named Theodora when she was thirteen years old and he was twenty-seven. . . .

Just as the standard of living of the Franks in Outremer was much higher than anything they had ever known at home in Europe, so they enjoyed a much higher standard of medical care too. The skill of their physicians was borrowed over the years from the Arabs, who were far in advance of doctors in the West. Indeed during the early years of the Crusader kingdoms everyone consulted local physicians in preference to men of their own race; the chronicler, William of Tyre, noticed how his contemporaries 'scorned the medicines and practice of our Latin physicians and believed only in the Jews, Samaritans, Syrians, and Saracens'. At the height of their prosperity and power, the Crusader kingdoms probably had more hospitals than any other countries of comparable size; in Jerusalem alone there were four, and Acre, Nablus, Ascalon, Jaffa and Tyre each had its own. . . .

A Higher Standard of Living

Throughout their whole history the Franks in Outremer remained a conquering race. Rather like the British in India, . . . they found themselves far better off in their new home than they had ever been in Europe, and so there was a fairly constant stream of new arrivals from the West. Fulcher of Chartres described the situation. 'Every day our dependents and our relatives follow us, leaving behind, unwillingly perhaps, all their belongings. For he who was poor there now finds that God has made him rich here. He who had little money now possesses countless gold coins. He who did not hold even a village over there now enjoys a town which God has given him. Why should anyone return to the West, who has found an Orient like this?' Why indeed! Moreover, as time went by, in many little ways the Franks learned to live on friendly terms with their Moslem neighbours, and as the process of orientalisation continued to change their habits, the superficial differences between them diminished, and an ever firmer *modus vivendi* [way of life] was established by the two sides. 'We who had been occidentals have become orientals,' wrote Fulcher of Chartres; 'the man who had been a Roman or a Frank has here become a Galilean or a Palestinian; and the man who used to live in Rheims or Chartres now finds himself a citizen of Tyre or Acre. We have already forgotten the places where we were born; already many of us know them not, or at any rate no longer hear them spoken of. Some among us already possess in this country houses and servants which belong to them as of hereditary right. Another has married a wife who is not his compatriot: a Syrian or an Armenian woman perhaps, or even a Saracen, who has received the grace of baptism. He who was once a stranger here now a native.'

Hindrances to Full Assimilation

But two things prevented this process of slow assimilation from resulting in a full acceptance of the Franks by their non-Christian neighbours: the Moslems never forgot the massacres of their compatriots by the Christians in Antioch and Jerusalem; and during the whole history of the Crusader kingdoms there was a steady influx of newcomers from the West, whose first question on arrival was, 'Where are some Moslems that I may kill them?' Again and again, enthusiastic knights would arrive bursting with determination to do God service by slaughtering some of the enemies of Christ, with whom the citizens of Outremer might just have made a treaty or concluded a truce, which was not only necessary to their own welfare but sometimes essential to their survival. But such political arrangements seemed almost blasphemous to the less sophisticated Christians from the West, and usually nothing deterred them from charging out of Christian held territory in a fine flurry and fury of faith, hell-bent on a little godly bloodshed. The fact that they often got themselves killed in the process was little consolation to the long-suffering Franks, who had to live with the consequences of their aggression, which often included renewed warfare with their neighbours when they least wished it. Yet they could not afford to discourage immigrants from the West, for they were perennially short of manpower, and only reinforcements from overseas made up for the twin evils of a chronically low birth rate and a chronically high rate of infant mortality, which between them crippled Outremer. It was a dilemma which was destined never to be solved except by the eventual extinction of the kingdoms founded by the first Crusaders; for while recruits from the West could still be found who were willing to fight for the triumph of the Cross, as they understood it, Moslem hostility was inevitably replenished; and when their enthusiasm eventually faded, and no more recruits were forthcoming, the fate of the Crusader kingdoms was sealed.

Relations Between Eastern and Western Christians

R.C. Smail

Although the Muslims ruled the Holy Land before the First Crusade, there were also numerous Christians living in the area. These Christians were not Catholics; rather, they were members of the Greek Church or other churches of the Eastern Orthodox or Coptic traditions. They held no allegiance to the Roman pope and disagreed with the Catholic Church on many theological points.

In the following selection, R.C. Smail examines the relations between Eastern and Western Christians in the crusader kingdoms. For the most part, Smail writes, the two groups coexisted peacefully. The European conquerors generally respected the traditions and laws of the Eastern Christians, and the Easterners often aided the crusaders in fighting the Muslims. On the other hand, Smail notes, problems between the two groups did arise periodically and created instability in the politics of the region.

R.C. Smail taught at Cambridge University in England, where he served as the director of Studies in History for several years. The following selection is taken from his book *The Crusaders in Syria and the Holy Land*. He also wrote *Crusading Warfare: 1097–1193* and many scholarly articles on the Crusades.

Western Europeans were able to control Syria for nearly two centuries because they devised forms of government which were sufficiently strong and workable, and sufficiently acceptable to the majority of the inhabitants. Such government was monarchic, even though in a limited sense, in that

one man was recognized as its head and principal director—
a king in Jerusalem, a prince in Antioch, a count in Tripoli
and in Edessa. . . .

The principal European groups in the crusader states
[were] the secular government, the major and minor feudatories, the established Latin Church, the Frankish laity who
were neither feudatories nor serfs, the Military Orders, the
exempt merchant communities. All these were always a minority of the population; what were their relations with the
majority?

These indigenous communities had been established in
that country too long for their customs and institutions to be
easily changed, and the Franks were too small a group to
bring such changes about. To do so by force was certainly
beyond them, the more so because all the force they could
muster was too often needed against the external enemy.
There is no evidence, except perhaps in the very earliest
years, that they ever contemplated such a solution. They
showed the normal medieval respect for what was customary
and established. . . .

The Christian Churches of the East

The Franks thought of their subjects in terms of religious
communities, Christians, Moslems, Jews and Samaritans.
The first-named were not of one Church, but of many. Centuries before the crusades the Christians of Asia and North
Africa had fallen apart on a number of theological and meta-
physical problems of great complexity, and especially on that
of the relation between the human and divine elements in
Christ's nature. Religious and political unity were so closely
associated that the East Roman emperors had a particular
interest in averting doctrinal schism. From the fourth century into the eighth a series of General Councils of the
Church were held so that orthodoxy might be declared and
preserved; . . . but these efforts were not enough to keep
Christians within one fold. Among the individuals who were
unreconcilable dissidents from official policy, some attracted
followers who formed a Church; such were Nestorius and
Jacob Baradaeus [founders, respectively, of the Nestorians

and the Jacobites]. Sometimes regional or ethnic groups rejected the authority of Council and emperor and went their own way, again as a separate Church—Armenians, Copts, Georgians, the Maronites in the Lebanon.

Down to the seventh century, when Syria and the Holy Land were still Byzantine provinces, all the inhabitants were Christian and were members either of one of the dissident Churches, or still maintained their religious allegiance to Constantinople and to the supreme ecclesiastical authority of its emperor and patriarch. During the centuries following the Arab conquests there were two gradual developments: large-scale conversion to Islam and the spread of Arabic as the prevailing colloquial language. There remained, and remain, a multiplicity of liturgical languages: just as Europeans, whatever their vernacular language, then heard Latin in church, so Arabic-speaking Syrian Christians heard Syriac or Greek.

Cordial Interactions

Although the leaders of the First Crusade initially regarded all eastern Christians as heretics, the western settlers never attempted persecution or coercion. The Church over which they probably exercised the greatest degree of control was the Greek. Many Latins regarded the Greeks as Christians who ought rightfully to be in communion with, and therefore subject to, the Roman Church. Certainly many Greek hierarchs were replaced by Latin; the patriarchs of Antioch and Jerusalem provide the principal examples, and in many places and at many times Greek clergy and laity must have been subordinated to the Latin hierarchy. The picture is far from clear, however, because Greek bishops are sometimes mentioned in the records of the crusader states; we hear, for example, of the Greek bishops of Gaza, Sidon and Acre. Was there an unbroken succession of such prelates, or could they establish themselves only when the crusaders' relations with Byzantium were particularly friendly, as in the time of Amalric I, or when Byzantine pressure on the crusader states was particularly severe, as it was on Antioch in 1138 and 1158? We need to know more in detail about the status of the

Greek clergy and their congregations in the crusader states, and their relationship with the Latin rulers. We know in general that, though there were difficulties, the relationship worked well enough. . . .

As for the other eastern Churches, their members were subject to Frankish government, and therefore their clergy were in a sense subordinate to the Latin; at the same time the crusaders recognized that they were separate and autonomous, and soon came to accept them as facts in their new life. Armenians, Jacobites and the rest were fellow Christians among whom the western settlers lived and with whom they freely intermarried for nearly two hundred years. Hereditary succession in the royal house of Jerusalem was first secured by an Armenian, and later continued by a Greek, marriage. It is no surprise to find in the records, therefore, many examples of harmonious relations between Latin and eastern Christians. Michael the Syrian, historian and Jacobite Patriarch, was cordially received in Jerusalem by Latin king and clergy; Meletos the Syrian, described in a charter as 'Archbishop of the Syrians and Greeks' in the region of Gaza and Beit Jibrin, and who is associated with the Hospitallers as a confrater, received a gift from the Master of that Order; on the intervention of Queen Melisende, judgement in a property dispute was made in favour of the Jacobite Metropolitan. Greek monasteries continued to flourish on Mount Carmel, Mount Tabor and in the Judean desert. Masons and sculptors were busy in twelfth-century Jerusalem not only at the Church of the Holy Sepulchre but at the Armenian Cathedral of St James the Great.

Religious Mergers and Secular Cooperation

Friendly co-existence was no mere superficiality. It could raise hopes of reunion which in the 1180's were shown to be more than a Utopian dream when the Maronites, some 40,000 in number, entered into communion with Rome, and so remain. In 1198 the Armenian Church followed the same course although, as a calculated move in an unstable international political situation, it did not last. The Jacobites considered the possibility, and in the 1230's their patriarch made a profession of obedience to the Pope; but he could not carry his fellow hierarchs with him, much less his Church as a whole.

In the sphere of secular activity, some eastern Christians gave important military assistance in establishing and maintaining the crusader states. The fame of the Maronites as archers may well have played its part in drawing them closer to the Franks and Rome. The first Baldwin's creation of the county of Edessa at the head of so small a Frankish retinue is to be explained only by the strong Armenian support he received, and the same is true, though to a lesser extent, of the principality of Antioch. And throughout the crusader occupation there were no doubt many Syrian Christians who served the Franks among the infantry or the Turcopoles [light-armed horsemen]. It is known that many of these were Syrians, or were born of one Syrian and one Frankish parent.

Friction and Prejudice

Between eastern and western Christians in the crusader states there came to be bonds of many kinds. But there could also be serious friction. This was particularly the case in the early days when the eastern Churches were deprived of buildings and sources of income by their new masters; it was circumstances such as these that caused relationships to become strained and the native Syrians to think of the Franks as aliens, heretics and oppressors. There were also westerners, especially newcomers (a few exist still) who were antipathetic to Levantine men and manners, to whom the eastern Mediterranean peoples were supple, untrustworthy opportunists, effeminate, unprincipled, militarily useless. Such sentiments might well reflect the exasperation of Europeans outwitted in the market place, or unable to understand why foreigners whom they ruled should be less than enthusiastic in fighting their battles; but they were repeatedly expressed, and not only by excitable writers with a taste for invective like James of Vitry; they are not entirely absent from the pages of so sober an observer as William of Tyre, who was himself a native of Latin Syria.

When community relations deteriorated, the consequences for the Franks could be serious because all eastern

Christians had centres of loyalty outside the crusader states. In the Taurus ranges Armenian leaders established principalities beyond crusader control. By the end of the twelfth century these had become a kingdom, whose history in the thirteenth was much involved with that of crusader Antioch, but which was independent of it. Armenians under Frankish rule could look to an Armenian king, just as Greek Christians could look to a Byzantine emperor in Constantinople or Nicæa. The communities of Nestorians, Jacobites and Copts outside the crusader states were more numerous and important than those inside. Their primates and patriarchs usually lived in lands under Moslem rule, and were more experienced in dealing with Moslem governments and in securing concessions from them than with any other.

This is a point of major importance which connects with another. Not only had Syrian Christians lived under tolerant Moslem rule for centuries, they had lived among Moslems as well. Though a common Christianity might link them with the Franks, they were at one with their non-Christian neighbours of long standing in everything else—habits, customs, common memories, language. Throughout the Christian era, and for centuries before that, they had lived under a succession of imperial masters, of whom the most recent had been Moslems, and they could contemplate with equanimity the prospect of doing so again. They lived peaceably enough under crusader rule, and many of them assisted it; but they were not as a whole fully committed to it, and would certainly not risk everything in its defence.

The Crusades' Impact on Women and Jews

Ronald C. Finucane

Ronald C. Finucane is a professor of history at Oakland University in Rochester, Michigan, where he has served as the history department's chairperson since 1991. His books include *Miracles and Pilgrims: Popular Beliefs in Medieval England* and *The Rescue of the Innocents: Endangered Children in Medieval Miracles*. The following selection is excerpted from Finucane's *Soldiers of the Faith: Crusaders and Moslems at War*.

Finucane writes that the Crusades greatly affected the status and well-being of European women and Jews. He explains that whether women accompanied the crusaders or remained at home, they frequently found themselves in insecure—even dangerous—positions. While these women were sometimes able to turn this to their advantage and break away from established societal roles, they did so at significant risk to themselves. The Jews of Europe faced even greater dangers: It was not uncommon for crusaders to attack Jewish populations on their routes through Europe, mercilessly killing those Jews who refused to convert to Christianity. Finucane argues that the hatred that flared up against the Jews during the Crusades had a lasting impact on Europeans' attitudes toward and treatment of the Jewish populations in their midst.

The crusades grew out of far-reaching social and psychological currents which deepened and broadened throughout the eleventh century. Similarly, the consequences of the movement involved much more than armed pilgrimage to the

Excerpted from Ronald C. Finucane, *Soldiers of the Faith: Crusaders and Moslems at War* (London: J.M. Dent, 1983). Reprinted by permission of the publisher.

Holy Land, impinged upon a variety of other aspects of contemporary European society and affected many who fell outside the qualification of Christian crusader or Moslem enemy. Though many others could be considered from this point of view, here we briefly examine the general effects of the crusades upon only two groups, women and Jews.

Women Who Went on the Crusades

Though generations of historians and popularizers have fixed the archetype, the crusading knight, firmly in the public mind, it is less easy to picture the women who went along on these ventures. Women followed the pilgrimage routes of medieval Europe as avidly as men, and the reports left by some of them, like Etheria of Aquitaine (who went to Palestine in the fourth century) and Margery Kempe (an English raving mystic-cum-tourist who accompanied and disrupted many a fifteenth-century pilgrimage by her pious howling) contribute a great deal to our knowledge of medieval pilgrimage in general. But the crusades, though they are often called pilgrimage in the medieval sources, were, as contemporaries knew, very special kinds of pilgrimage. Women suffered while on ordinary pilgrimage to the Holy Land, and they could hardly expect lighter treatment on the crusades. And yet they went. It seems to have been common enough for the nobility to bring their wives and, sometimes, families. The case of Eleanor of Aquitaine, who accompanied her husband Louis VII of France on the Second Crusade, is a well-known . . . example. . . .

Other well-known ladies accompanied their husbands on these dangerous journeys, for example the wives of Baldwin of Boulogne and Raymond of Toulouse, leaders in the First Crusade, and the wife of Richard the Lion-heart, who married him in the course of the Third Crusade. . . .

The Risks They Took

Most of the women who accompanied the crusaders were the wives of ordinary pilgrim-warriors, or independent but respectable females, or the usual crowd of whores and hangers-on to be found near any army camp, as well as the do-

mestics who looked after the other needs of the crusaders.
. . . Sometimes the proportion of women must have been relatively high, considering the dangerous nature of the expeditions. On the First Crusade the armies were held up at Antioch on their way to take Jerusalem when a pestilence
struck: it was reported, incredibly, that 'nearly fifty thousand' women died within a few days. Even though medieval
statistics are untrustworthy, in this case the writer is clearly
saying that a great many women died; their overall numbers
may well have been quite high. Whenever a fight was in the
offing, women and other non-combatants (the clergy, the
sick, the old and children) were usually herded together in
some secure position while the infantry, knights and their
leaders formed up for action. But there were bound to be fa-
talities. Some non-combatants, including women, were
killed by enemy action while on the march or in camp, regardless of security measures taken by the crusaders. When
security was faulty, the results were correspondingly more
serious. As a prelude to the First Crusade, Peter the Hermit's
band was wiped out just beyond Constantinople, in the
course of which the Turks invaded the base-camp of the
Christians, as described by Albert of Aix:

> And going within the tents, they destroyed with the sword
> whomever they found, the weak and the feeble, clerics,
> monks, old women, nursing children, persons of every age.
> But they led away young girls whose face and form was pleas-
> ing in their eyes, and beardless youths of comely countenance.

Moslem girls and boys were likewise often spared by the
Christians, sometimes for baptism when this could be ef-
fected, but basically because they were a useful and valuable
commodity. . . .

Sexual abuse of prisoners—male as well as female, according to some historians—was common enough in these
encounters. Among the rabble who accompanied the First
Crusade, the Tafurs [peasants] were supposedly habituated
to raping women of whatever religious disposition. . . . In ac-
cordance with the received prejudices concerning the
Moslems, their men were assumed by the Christians to be

over-sexed, and consequently all female Christian captives almost certainly condemned to a fate worse than death. . . .

Women Warriors

The role of most non-combatant women was passive, but there are clear indications that women sometimes took a more active part in the fighting. This might be as elementary as bringing water to the fighting men, as the women of Bohemond's camp did at a skirmish beyond Nicaea and at the siege of Jerusalem, in addition to cheering and encouraging the men as best they could. At Damietta during the so-called Fifth Crusade in the early thirteenth century, they brought water, wine and bread, as well as stones to use as projectiles, to the warriors. Others assisted the fighters in more positive ways, like the woman helping to fill a moat at Acre during the Third Crusade. After depositing the load she had been carrying, she was shot with an arrow. While she lay dying she asked her husband to use her own body to help fill up the moat, which was done. 'No man', wrote a contemporary, 'ever should forget such [a] woman.' There are also reports of women actually taking up arms and fighting alongside the men. . . .

Women served the crusading armies and pilgrims in yet other ways, much to the regret of Holy Mother Church. The sexual needs of masses of men on the move, perhaps separated from their mates for years, have always presented a problem for the leaders of war. During the Middle Ages it was never easy to draw the line between pilgrims and ordinary camp-followers. Pilgrimage, as a general medieval custom, provided a means for satisfying sexual appetites through casual encounters and mercenary arrangements (and encouraged them, as some churchmen complained). On the extended pilgrimage of a crusade, where women were scattered indiscriminately among armies larger than one usually saw on the battlefields of Europe, the risk of sin was great indeed. It was acknowledged that sin could be a cause of defeat in battle: obviously, God frowned upon a band of sinners who had taken holy vows, and might punish them by giving victory to the Moslems, a chastisement for Christian souls as well as bodies. Fornication, therefore, was a matter of military concern. In the midst of their troubles at Antioch during the First Crusade, army leaders and prelates decided that the troops had displeased the Lord by their dissipation. They therefore expelled the women from the camp, presumably allowing the noble and obviously respectable ladies to remain. . . .

On the Home Front

So far we have considered the women who accompanied the crusaders, but of course a great many women were left behind after those tearful farewells which the chroniclers and poets described so fondly. Although David Herlihy has suggested that the crusades may have helped to raise the general condition of women in the later Middle Ages by throwing responsibility onto their shoulders in their husbands' absence, the opposite is just as evident. The fragile status of most women was made even more apparent when their men went off to battle the infidel. . . . For those wives who remained behind, the Church guaranteed to protect them in their persons and property until their absent spouses should return. Even so, there are enough instances of litigation about parcels of land, for example, to suggest that this protection was not always effective. In the early thirteenth century John came back to his family and lands in Suffolk only to find that during his absence in Jerusalem a certain Thomas had helped himself to thirty acres by the simple expedient of taking it from John's wife, Matilda. Such possibilities must have disturbed the journeys of many ardent pilgrims as they set out on crusade. No wonder that Stephen of Blois wrote to his wife urging her to take care of lands, children and vassals. . . .

Anti-Jewish Riots

Though women were put at risk both when on crusade and when remaining at home and trying to protect hearth and kin, at least the Church openly maintained a policy of protection for the weaker sex. The Christian attitude towards the Jews, on the other hand, was far from protective or consistent. Although crusaders were sometimes victims of nature or their fellow-Christians, they themselves were quite capable of inflicting the worst cruelties on others long before a single Saracen was anywhere to be seen. They were especially liable to indulge their passions for pillage and murder (without the inconvenience of leaving Europe) at the expense of the Jews. Crusader-gangs justified their atrocities by claiming to rid themselves of Christ-murderers in their midst before going off to slay Moslems. The worst, but by no means the only, massacres were carried out by the 'unofficial' peoples' movement in the First Crusade, led by the likes of Fulk, Gottschalk and Emicho of Leiningen. The Jews of Rhineland cities like Speyer, Mainz, Cologne and Worms suffered the most protracted attacks and those of Regensburg and Prague were victims of similar outbursts. Spain, France and England, too, had their own anti-Jewish riots associated with later crusades.

The city of Worms, for example, was the scene of a massacre led by Emicho in May 1096. Worms, home of the famous Jewish scholar Rashi in the 1050s and 1060s, proud of its beautiful Byzantine-style synagogue, contained one of the oldest Jewish communities of the Rhineland. The Jewish cemetery, just outside the line of the medieval city wall to the south-west, is one of the oldest in Europe, with monuments—now mere stumps of stone—going back to the twelfth century. . . . Here too is the synagogue, now an unpretentious building with a plaque stating simply that it was built in 1034 and often destroyed over the past 900 years, the last time in 1938.

The Massacres

In May 1096 when the Worms Jewry heard of some killings at Speyer, some of them rushed down the lanes to the bishop's palace across town. Others, believing in their Christian neighbours who had promised to protect them, and to whom they had entrusted their wealth for safe-keeping, stayed in their homes. It was an empty promise, . . . and soon the little alleys and lanes were littered with men, women and children left dead and naked by the crusader mobs. The Jews' houses were pulled down and plundered, the Torah was trodden on, kicked about in the filth of the road and ripped apart. Many Jews were said to have committed suicide after killing their neighbours and kin. . . . The rabble then attacked the remnant sheltering at the episcopal palace. The sheer numbers of crusaders made resistance impossible. To prevent defilement at the hands of Christians, the trapped Jews chose to kill each other rather than accept Christian baptism. Meschulam bar Isaac snatched up his son, whom God had given to his wife only in her old age, and cried out that he would offer him to the Eternal One. His wife begged him to kill her first so that she would not have to see the deed. He refused. Picking up his knife he said the blessing for an offering, the little boy said 'Amen' and was killed. Isaac, son of Daniel, was captured by crusaders and led to a church with a rope round his neck. There they said to him, 'You can still be saved; will you change your faith?' Since he could not speak he indicated with his finger that they should cut off his head, which they did. By 26 May, just over a week after they had arrived, the Christians swarmed off towards Mainz, leaving some 800 Jewish victims behind.

The most detailed descriptions, written by Jews, were substantiated by Christian writers as well. Even worse tales of atrocity resulted from the attack on Mainz. There the Jews had heard of the slayings at Worms and other places, and had put themselves under the archbishop's protection. Even so, their fate was inescapable. A feeling of helplessness, of resignation to God's will, was reinforced when two Jewish men heard ghosts at prayer inside the synagogue one night—a sure sign of impending doom, according to medieval Jewish folk-beliefs. The Christian mob camped outside the city in their tents. The Jews, hoping to strengthen the bonds with their protectors, handed over a quantity of silver to the archbishop and seven pounds of gold to the local count. It was a waste of money, for a party of Mainz citizens opened the city gates: [the] army . . . attacked and drove the Jews, who fought back, into the archbishop's courtyard and palace. The prelate's men fled, while he himself took refuge in his church. The Jews, trapped in the palace, realized that they were finished. They sharpened their knives—a sacrifice made with a nicked blade was ritually invalid—and prepared to kill each other. As the Christians entered the courtyard and began killing, so, too, Jewish women began to slay their children, the men to slaughter their wives. . . .

In the end more than 900 Jews were said to have perished at Mainz. As a Saxon chronicler wrote, 'it was pitiful to see the great and many heaps of bodies that were carried out of the city of Mainz on carts'. Some Jews, refusing to accept a defeatist attitude, chose to die fighting for their faith, hoping to kill at least a few ungodly Christians before their own lives were lost. Others pretended to accept baptism only to be able to harangue the Christians and tell them what they really thought of their flimsy godling, a creature like any other creature, subject to death and putrefaction, a 'god of nothingness'; Jewish women taunted the Christian mobs, calling Christ the bastard son of a menstruating whore. Naturally, such actions only enraged the crowds and drove them to further acts of cruelty.

When Edessa fell, and then some forty years later Jerusalem, the Second and Third Crusades began like the First with attacks on European Jews. As an abbot of Cluny wrote during the Second Crusade,

> What is the good of going to the end of the world at great loss of men and money to fight the Saracens, when we permit among us other infidels who are a thousand times more guilty towards Christ than the Mohammedans?

In the Rhineland a zealous Cistercian monk urged recruits to the Second Crusade to begin their holy march by killing Jews. . . .

The Legacy of the First Crusade

The slaughter of the First Crusade, however, remained the blackest memory for the Jews of Europe until overshadowed by the even greater slaughter of our own age. In the thirteenth century one Jewish commentator explained the mourning period between Passover and Pentecost as a commemoration of the atrocities of the First Crusade—even though the mourning motif actually went back at least to the eighth century AD in the West. Certainly the bitterness, hatred and aggression of the First Crusade are overwhelmingly clear in Christian writings. One chronicler praised the forcible baptism of 'those impious Jews', some of whom 'returned to Judaism even as dogs to their own vomit'. Many Christians of the First Crusade arrived in the Near East with their anti-judaism as rampant as ever, inflamed by occasional instances of Moslem-Jewish cooperation against the crusaders. . . .

The First Crusade massacres profoundly influenced attitudes towards the Jews. Jews were forced into the role of money-lender during the twelfth century, useful to private individuals as well as to kings, and forced out of a feudal society which ran on Christian oaths and Christian rites. Being pushed to the social peripheries, Jews became an unassimilated category . . . and therefore a threatening source of danger. . . .

Attempting to Help

On the other hand, many kings and princes as well as Church leaders tried to protect the Jews, from both selfish and altruistic motives. A chronicler writing of the First Crusade massacres recognized the dangerous forces at work: even excommunication pronounced by the clergy and the 'menaces of punishment on the part of many of the princes' had little effect in restraining Christians. The historian William of Tyre condemned the 'mad excesses' of the mobs who 'cruelly massacred the Jewish people in the cities and towns through which they passed'. In the Second Crusade Bernard of Clairvaux reprimanded and silenced the Cistercian monk described above, who had stirred up anti-judaism in the Rhineland. Bernard also wrote to the English, urging them to join the crusade, but adding a caution against persecuting Jews. Sometimes Christian protection of Jews went beyond mere words. During the Second Crusade uprisings at Würzburg, according to a Jewish chronicler, a Jewish girl was dragged into a church and—after she spat on a crucifix—was beaten unconscious and left for dead. 'Then a Christian washer-woman came, who dragged her home and there concealed her. So she was saved.' Next day the bishop had the dead Jews collected in a cart, along with their chopped-off parts such as thumbs, hands, feet and limbs. He had them cleaned, anointed with oil and buried in his own garden. Later on, a wealthy Jewish couple bought the garden and established it as a Jewish burial-ground.

Regardless of attempts by some Christians to restrain the animus of their fellows, the massacres continued, the hatreds deepened. Christian anti-judaism, spurred on by the outrages of the First Crusade, itself a result of the Christianization of Europe in the eleventh century, evolved into that now-familiar form, anti-semitism; the stereotypes collected around and were projected against Abraham's people. At the end of the Middle Ages, Franciscan pilgrims were warned by the warden of the convent of Mt Sion in Jerusalem that Jews were not to be trusted. . . . Like Moslems, they were fit only for Christian scorn, an attitude which the crusades helped to define and transmit to our own times.

Expansion of Trade

Hilmar C. Krueger

The Crusades and the establishment of the crusader states in the Middle East presented many economic opportunities to Western Europeans, the most important of which was the expansion of trade. As Hilmar C. Krueger writes in the following article, the Crusades reopened the Mediterranean Sea routes that had been plagued by Arab pirates. Italian merchants took advantage of this situation by securing these routes and extending their trading operations into the Christian settlements in the Middle East. The constant movement of crusaders also spurred commerce and increased the use of credit, Krueger maintains. During this period, he states, European trading gained an international aspect that continued even after the crusading movement ended.

Hilmar C. Krueger was a professor of history at the University of Cincinnati from 1940 to his retirement in 1974; his specialty was twelfth-century Genoese trade and economics. During his career, he was also instrumental in the founding of five junior colleges, including the University College at the University of Cincinnati, where he served as dean. After his retirement, Krueger became an adjunct professor of history at Arizona State University in Tempe, continuing his research in medieval history and publishing several scholarly articles.

The Crusades were part of a pan-European expansionist movement that pushed into all directions, partially under the impetus or guise of Christianity. The conquest of England by Duke William of Normandy, the foundation of another Norman Kingdom in the Two Sicilies, the Spanish campaigns of

Excerpted from Hilmar C. Krueger, "Economic Aspects of Expanding Europe," in *Twelfth-Century Europe and the Foundations of Modern Society*, edited by Marshall Clagett, Gaines Post, and Robert L. Reynolds; ©1961 by the Regents of the University of Wisconsin. Reprinted by permission of The University of Wisconsin Press.

the Christian knights of Spain and France, and the Saxon Crusade across the Elbe, the expeditions of the Scandinavian sailors into the northern seas and the Christian settlements in Iceland and Greenland, the acceptance of Roman Christianity by St. Stephen and his Hungarian subjects were all parts of the same expansionist movement, some antecedent, others contemporary, to the more phenomenal overseas expansion. To a great degree this general development made the Crusades possible and acceptable. In all areas the developments continued beyond the end of the twelfth century.

Economic Motivations for the Crusades

The economic aspects of the Crusades were as varied as the participants. There is little need and no method to weigh and evaluate the varied causes for this overseas expansion. Admittedly, religious, political, and social forces existed in addition to the more material economic factors. Pope Urban II appealed successfully to all interests and by no means did he overlook the economic and material aspects. That these economic interests influenced considerably the activities of some of the crusading elements may be gathered from the denunciations of them when some of the crusades failed to reach the expectations of the more spiritually minded.

In a measure the Crusades were evidence that the Peace of God and the Truce of God had failed. The varied accounts of Pope Urban's speeches refer to bloody strife, plundering and pilfering, homicide and sacrilege, hatreds and dissensions. These actions were economic liabilities for western Europe and any diminution of them was of economic profit to the communities and groups among whom they existed. Urban's references to the actions were couched in terms of religion, humanity, and social conscience, but the economic losses from war and plunder cannot be denied and the gains from their absence cannot be overlooked.

Material Gains

To the feudal barons, "aforetime robbers" who were to become soldiers of Christ, the pope gave promise of material gains. He promised to the overseas crusaders . . . : "The possessions of the enemy will be yours, too, since you will make spoil of his treasures. . . ." "Wrest that land from the wicked race, and subject it to yourselves, that land which, as the scripture says, 'floweth with milk and honey.'" He obviously hoped to gain the support of the landless or land-poor barony, who possessed little property because of the rules of inheritance or the ill fortune of the feudal wars. He knew, too, the inevitable result of increasing population whose

---

Commerce Between East and West

Aziz S. Atiya was born in Egypt and educated in England. He taught at universities in Germany, Switzerland, England, Lebanon, Egypt, and the United States. His books include The Crusades in the Later Middle Ages, The Crusades of Nicopolis, *and* A History of Eastern Christianity. *The following excerpt comes from his book* Crusade, Commerce, and Culture.

Arab ascendancy remained undisputed until the advent of the Normans in Italy and the Mediterranean during the second half of the eleventh century, as well as the outbreak of the First Crusade in 1096. . . .

The impact of these momentous events on the course of medieval commerce was incalculable. It marked the rebirth of European trade with the East, and its gradual growth ultimately reached unparalleled heights in European history. The fleets of Venice, Genoa, and other trade communes and merchant cities in Italy and the southern Mediterranean countries expanded to meet the exigencies of the conveyance of increasing numbers of Crusaders from Europe. Meanwhile, the resumption of the Eastern trade came as a natural consequence to the Crusade, since merchants from Europe accompanied the various expeditions or followed in their steps and opened up fresh markets in every newly conquered seaport in the Levant. Direct contacts between East and West, though begun by the way of the sword, were soon destined to yield to the ways of peace in the fields of commerce and culture.

Aziz S. Atiya, *Crusade, Commerce, and Culture,* 1962.

land "is too narrow. . . . nor does it abound in wealth; and it furnishes scarcely enough food for its cultivators."

The economic gains that were promised to the feudal barons were also obtained by them. The great princes at the head of their feudal levies carved out the largest estates, but lesser barons established themselves as well. As the crusading armies marched southward from Asia Minor into Syria and Palestine, individual leaders conquered and claimed their personal principalities. In that fashion Tancred established himself in Cilicia, Baldwin in the County of Edessa, and Raymond of Toulouse in the County of Tripoli. They often quarreled with one another in complete disregard of the common cause and the Kingdom of Jerusalem and certainly not in the interests of the Holy Sepulcher and the papal see. With them their own personal ambitions ranked first, and they demanded before anything else the establishment of their own political authority along feudal lines which gave them the customary economic returns in fees, services, fines, and products. The lesser barons generally became vassals and enjoyed similar gains, but on a smaller scale. Many of the barons, who had nothing to return to in western Europe, established residence in the Levant and their descendants became part of the Frankish aristocracy of the East. Fulcher of Chartres exclaimed: "He who in Europe owned not so much as a village is lord of a whole city out here. He who was worth no more than a few pence now disposes of a fortune. Why should we return to the West when we have all we desire here?"

Italian Merchants and the Crusades

While the feudal barons formed the majority of the fighting men in the crusading campaigns, the Italian townsmen and merchants were so essential to the whole movement that it would have collapsed without their support. After the First Crusade all western armies travelled eastward, by sea, and even in the First Crusade the naval and military support of Genoa and Pisa was considerable. Pope Urban II recognized the importance of the towns and merchants for the movement and accordingly sent itinerant propagandists into the cities to preach the crusades or had local preachers perform the job.

Since the Italian towns had been fighting the Moslems for several centuries, the papal preachers had no difficulty persuading the Italian merchants to coöperate. The Italians had fought the Arabs for three hundred years before 1095, at first defensively, then offensively. All the great Italian cities, Naples, Rome, Pisa, and Genoa in the west, Bari, Ancona, and Venice on the Adriatic, had been attacked and plundered by the Arabs. In the early tenth century the south Italian cities had wiped out the last Arab base in Italy, and in the early eleventh century Genoa and Pisa had driven the Arabs from the Tyrrhenian Sea. In 1087 a combined force of Italian cities, under the leadership of a papal legate, attacked Mehdia in North Africa, plundered a merchant suburb, gained compensation for damages done to their ships by Arab pirates, and obtained free access to the area for their merchants. The victory cleared the western Mediterranean of Arab pirates and competitors. To the Italian cities the call of Pope Urban II sounded like an invitation to help clear the eastern Mediterranean as well and to obtain similar commercial privileges.

To the Italian merchants the Crusades always appeared to be extraordinary economic opportunities. From the very start the Italians gained financial rewards. Their ships carried the crusaders and their equipment, even their horses, to the Holy Land, and then supplied the crusaders with food, drink, and, on occasion, with timber, manpower, and siege machinery. Genoa and Pisa commandeered all possible ships in their domains for transport purposes and ordered the construction of more and larger vessels. The transport services were a source of immediate income for the communes, merchants, and shipowners. The Fourth Crusade is good evidence that financial return loomed large in the aims of the shipowners and merchants. The Crusades gave to the Italian cities much of the liquid capital that was needed in the capitalistic developments that were just beginning. Furthermore, this capital came from sources unrelated to the Italian towns, from western feudal barons and kings. It was money which the Italians could not have obtained otherwise.

Italian Traders in the Middle East

In addition to these immediate monetary returns Genoa, Pisa, and Venice received promises of quarters in the coastal towns of Syria and Palestine. These promises were generally made in private agreements between the Italian cities and the baronial leaders, the kings of France and England, and the kings of Jerusalem. Often they were made under pressure of the moment and then forgotten when the pressure was lifted. However, the Italians, especially the Genoese, established themselves well enough to enjoy long-term rewards and profits. In at least a dozen coastal towns of the Levant the Italians possessed throughout most of the twelfth century residential and commercial quarters, from which they gained an income from rentals, leases, harbor dues, and court fines. In these centers the Italian merchants carried on their trade with the European colonists and feudal residents, with Arab traders, and with their associates and agents who worked in the area. The Italian quarters of the Levant became the centers of exchange for Oriental and European goods and the markets for the western imports that increased as the century wore on. The Oriental trade was highly profitable and another source of capital in the new money economy of the period. The Crusades were the strongest influence on the development of medieval trade and industry.

Something needs to be said about the Crusades and the general structure of medieval business and capitalism. First of all, the Crusades created a situation in which capital appeared and circulated. Feudal, clerical, and royal participants mortgaged and sold their holdings to obtain money to buy equipment, hire soldiers, and pay for passage. In some instances they melted down their plate and jewelry. Occasionally, the peasants brought out their hoards and bought their freedom from their anxious and hard-pressed lords. Guibert de Nogent wrote: "As everyone hastened to take the road of God, each hurried to change into money everything that was not of use for the journey, and the price was fixed not by the seller, but by the buyer." Generally, as already indicated, this capital went to the Italian merchants and shippers for transportation or other services connected with the venture. Eventually, numerous other people received jobs and wages, including armorers, shipbuilders, ropemakers, and vintners. Obviously, much of the capital paid to the Italians covered the cost of materials and labor, but a considerable part was profit and gain. In turn, much of the profit was reinvested in the Levantine trade, which also was extremely lucrative. The Crusades had promoted the capitalistic cycle of capital, investment, profit, and reinvestment of profit for further profit and capital. The Crusades, cities, and commerce initiated a money economy which threatened and certainly modified the older land economy of western Europe.

Establishing a System of Credit

Another capitalistic instrument given impetus by the Crusades was credit. Credit, after all, was based on the expectancy of income and profit by the borrower. Many participants in the Crusades bought their equipment or obtained loans on credit, expecting to profit from the material rewards which Urban had promised. In the Holy Land many again resorted to loans from the Templars and Hospitallers, hoping to repay from their ventures in the Near East or from their properties in western Europe. The rulers, of course, could expect to pay their loans from tax receipts or new crusade aids. The merchants seemingly did less business with the banking orders, partially because they had capital, primarily because they had their own banking systems and credit arrangements. Nevertheless, the Crusades helped to establish credit on an international scale and gave to credit instruments an international operation between the Italian bases in the Levant and the fairs of Champagne and Flanders in the West.

Similarly, the Crusades gave to commerce an international aspect. They again opened up the entire Mediterranean Sea to Christian ships and trade and provided an entry into the trade with the Near and Far East. The crusaders' acquaintance with Arab and Moslem customs created a demand for Oriental goods in Christian Europe, so that dyes, spices, woods, silk, cotton, precious stones, pearls, and alum became regular western imports from the Italian quarters in the East. Henry of Champagne acknowledged some gifts of Saladin with: "You know that your robes and turbans are far from being held in scorn among us. I will certainly wear your gifts." At the same time the growing industries of the West gave the Italian merchants the chance to carry western goods, especially cloths, eastward to exchange them for the Levantine goods, and the continued residence of westerners in the East created a demand for those western wares. While the Italian quarters served as the *entrepôt* [warehouse] in the Levant, the fairs of Champagne and Flanders served a similar function in the West. The famous fairs of Troyes, Lagny, Provins, and Bar-sur-Aube were instituted in the twelfth century. But between the two distant points the sea merchants of maritime Italy and the land merchants of North Italy and France carried on a regular cycle of purchases and sales, usually on credit. They thrived on a commerce that had become international. Even though the crusader states and the Kingdom of Jerusalem lost heavily to the Moslems toward the end of the twelfth century, the trade relations continued, the coastal cities and the Mediterranean Sea remained open to the European merchants.

An Influx of Knowledge from the East

Martin Erbstösser

After the fall of the Roman Empire, Western Europe lost most of the scientific and philosophical works of the ancient Greeks and Romans. However, the Arabs preserved this knowledge and improved upon it, especially in the areas of mathematics and medicine. The Crusades played an important role in creating the cultural interchange between the East and the West that enabled the Europeans to regain this knowledge from the Arabs. Europeans also borrowed ideas and techniques from Muslim agriculture and craftwork. In the following selection, Martin Erbstösser describes the impact that Arabic culture had on European artisans, scholars, scientists, and merchants.

Martin Erbstösser is a professor at the University of Leipzig in Germany. The following selection is excerpted from the English translation of his book, *The Crusades*. Erbstösser has written several other books on medieval history, of which *Heretics in the Middle Ages* is also available in an English translation.

The influence of Arab Islamic culture, which had come to Europe via the trade routes in the Crusade period, must be considered in connection with the developments of the time.

An indication of the degree to which a specific society is influenced by another can be found in the extent to which its language is enriched by borrowed words. Even a short list is sufficient to show the variety of these words and the objects they describe. It should be noted, however, that this process was not restricted to the period of the Crusades. Words bor-

Excerpted from Martin Erbstösser, *The Crusades*, translated by C.S.V. Salt (New York: Universe Books, 1979). Copyright 1978 by Edition Leipzig. Reprinted by permission of Dornier Medienholding, Berlin.

rowed by English from the Arabic or from Persian and Greek by way of Arabic include lime, lemon, apricot, citrus, sugar, orange and other names denoting fruits hitherto unknown in Europe, the names for spices such as nutmeg, cinnamon, caraway, tarragon and saffron and terms for craft products such as damask (Damascus), muslin (Mosul), atlas, mohair, chiffon, taffeta, satin, carafe, baldachin (Baghdad), pantofle, mattress, divan or sofa. Lilac and azure are likewise names for colours which come from Arabic. Words of Arabic origin are very numerous in the scientific sphere. Almost all the names of constellations and the basic terms of astronomy come from Arabic. Algebra and algorism are distortions of Arab names or book titles. Camphor, benzene, alcohol, alkali, soda, borax and so on also come from the same source. Similar examples could be quoted from other sciences. In the maritime sphere there are the words admiral and corvette and mention can also be made of a series of special terms such as tariff, sequin, arsenal, alcove, bazar, amulet, talisman, elixir and others. . . .

These loan-words can roughly be divided into three main groups: agriculture, trades and crafts, science. . . .

Agricultural Changes

As a result of European expansion in the Orient, Europeans were introduced to a large number of crops and fruits hitherto unknown to them: lemons, oranges, apricots, peaches, plums, cucumbers, melons, maize, rice, saffron, artichokes, sesame, carob, dates, sugar cane and others. Many descriptions of the milieu in the Crusader states are full of praise for the extensive gardens and their tasty fruits. Europe heard about this and many Crusaders and pilgrims brought seeds back with them on their return. However, this had little effect on the spread of these plants since the feudal lords knew little about their cultivation or propagation. From contemporary accounts, it seems that their attempts were regarded more as curious experiments than as serious efforts to bring about changes in European agriculture. The route by which these plants actually came to Europe was via Spain, Sicily and Southern Italy. The Moslem peasants had the necessary knowledge and skills for the cultivation of these crops and it is known that a rapid change took place in the character of agriculture in these areas after the Islamic conquest. In Sicily, for instance, date palms were planted immediately afterwards in a totally systematic manner. They then gradually spread from here to Italy and Southern France in particular. . . . It was during the time of the Crusades that this change was initiated and it continued during the centuries that followed. A second route, which was especially significant for Eastern Europe, was from Byzantium via the Balkans so that it seems likely that many of these crops, such as melons, maize and cucumbers, became known in Central Europe by way of the Balkans.

From the 12th century onwards, the trade with the Orient and Byzantium led to a substantial increase in the consumption of spices, dyes and perfumes and a wide variety of artisan products. Pepper, cloves, nutmeg, amber, incense, saffron, alum, indigo, red sandalwood, lacquer, damask, muslin, silk, velvet, atlas and other products were constantly offered for sale at the great markets of Europe, in addition to splendid apparel and blankets. Oriental carpets were in great demand and high prices were paid for jewellery of pearls and precious stones, enamel work, fine glassware and ceramic articles, ivory carvings and other objets d'art. The same applied to gold and silver work and ornamental weapons of Damascus steel.

To some extent, these and other products were imports obtained through commercial channels. But in the 12th and 13th centuries many of the artisan products in particular had originally been secured as booty or represented gifts from Crusaders. The events of the 4th Crusade provide especially clear evidence of this. Unfortunately, no detailed accounts have survived but many of the collections which still exist in churches and monasteries were originally donated by persons who took part in the Crusades. . . .

A Gradual Influence on Artisans

Although Oriental products were so popular, local artisans were relatively slow in making the change to similar products. Silk production spread to other regions in the course of the 13th century. In the middle of the 12th century, it seems that it was still restricted to Sicily. It was from here that it spread to Central and Northern Italy, Provence and finally to Northern Germany as well. Lucca became the great centre of the silk trade but Bologna, Venice, Augsburg, Ulm and other cities also raised silkworms or produced silk fabrics.

Up to the 13th century, paper was imported from Spain and the Orient but after this date there is evidence that it was manufactured in Europe, too. From this time onwards, merchants made increasing use of paper as a writing material. At the end of the 13th century, it was being made in Genoa and Ravensburg and shortly afterwards in Bologna, Padua, Venice and other cities as well.

The Crusaders and pilgrims had observed the windmills in use in the Orient, and, in this case, it was not long before the first examples appeared in Europe. There is evidence that windmills were in use in various regions of Europe as early as the middle of the 12th century.

There was much indirect influence on the production of high-quality handmade articles, this resulting from attempts to imitate Byzantine and Oriental imports. However, this influence was often nothing more than a stimulus. After the 13th century, the cities of Northern Italy became noted for the production of high-quality woollen fabrics. The raw materials—alum, dyes and wool—were mainly imported from the Orient and Byzantium. Enamel work had been produced in Europe before the expeditions to the Orient but it was only from the 13th century that it achieved real artistic excellence, not least because of the quality of Byzantine enamel work which Europeans had learnt to appreciate. Glass production, especially in Venice, had survived the decline of Antiquity but the art of glass painting by the appropriate fusion process, the making of ground crystal dishes and other techniques date only from after the 12th century. The products of the Orient had a similar influence on the emergence of ivory carving, faience ware and the work of the gold and silversmiths.

The material production of Europe in general and of Italy

in particular was stimulated in numerous ways through the contacts with Islamic Arabic and Byzantine culture. Accumulation from intermediate trade and high productivity in the crafts were two of the essential conditions for the development of that stage of history known as the Renaissance.

A Wealth of Scientific Knowledge

The utilization of the scientific and academic achievements of the Arab Islamic world took a somewhat different form.

From the 13th century, the cultivation of science and learning in Western Europe became centred in schools and universities. The most famous of these included Paris (1174/1200), Oxford (*c*.1170), Cambridge (1209), Naples (1224), Toulouse (1229), Montpellier (1239), Rome (1203) and others. Six universities were founded in Spain during this period and in Northern Italy a series of law schools came into being, centred on Bologna. This resulted from the prosperity of European feudal society and the growing importance of the cities. Under the influence of the Church and with few exceptions, theology and its philosophical consequences was the principal subject studied at the universities. Nevertheless, the natural sciences such as mathematics, physics, biology, medicine, chemistry and others were gaining in importance.

Translations of Scholarly Works

The foundations of this new interest in knowledge were provided by the teachings of Islamic Arabic and Antique authors. Translations from Arabic into Latin of the scientific and philosophical works of Greek Antiquity and the Islamic world had started to appear from the early 12th century. The translation schools were centred in Spain, Sicily and the Crusader states, Spain being the most important. The most favourable conditions existed here on account of the relatively large group of Jews and native Christians who were familiar with Hebraic, Arabic, Greek and Latin and able to make translations. One of the most outstanding of these was John of Seville, also known as John of Spain and Ibn Daud. He was a Jew who had grown up in the cultural tradition of the Omayyad empire in Spain and was a convert to Christianity. He was responsible for a large number of mathematical, astronomical, medical and astrological translations during the first half of the 12th century. A few years later, Gerard of Cremona came to the fore. He was active in Toledo in the years after 1165, probably in association with other native translators. It is said that he was responsible for seventy-one translations. It was mainly Greek authors, such as Aristotle, Euclid and Archimedes, in whom he was interested but he also translated the works of Arab Islamic scholars such as Al-Razi, Ibn Sina, Al-Kindi and others.

There was a similar situation in Southern Italy and Sicily where numerous translations were produced at the court of Frederick II.

In the Crusader states, on the other hand, the native Syrians and Jews were obviously less active in this field; at least there are not many translations which have survived. It is indeed known that pilgrims brought manuscripts back with them but it has been shown that these were translated by priests and Italians who had settled in the Crusader states, such as Stephan of Antioch and Philip of Tripoli who produced translations of medical works.

In Western Europe the number of translators living in Spain and South Italy who were able to make translations of this kind was small. Mention must be made of Adelard of Bath who had learned the Arabian language in Antioch and Toledo, and of Gerard of Cremona. There were constant laments about the difficulties of teaching and studying Arabic, Hebraic and Greek at the universities.

Arabic Influences on European Schools

It is impossible to give even a list of all the translations made and a few examples have to suffice. In the fields of mathematics and astronomy, a series of works were translated which made the Indo-Arabic system of numbers known in Europe. Works by Euclid and other authors of Antiquity attracted interest, as did the works of Arab authors on algebra and trigonometry. The latter included the famous treatise by Al-Khwarizmi (from whose name the term "algorism" was derived): "al-gabr . . ." (hence the term "algebra") which was in use at European universities as a basic textbook on mathematics up till the 16th century. In the field of optics, an outstanding work was the "Book of Optics" by Al-Haitami (Lat. Alhazen) who examined the refraction of light in transparent media and was a source of inspiration for Roger Bacon and others. Chemistry was influenced for a long time by a series of textbooks on alchemy of Arab origin. As early as the 13th century, the works of Al-Biruni on astronomy and the calendar led to suggestions being made in Europe for the reform of the Julian Calendar. Medicine was enriched by what must be described as a flood of translations. . . . It seems that in Toledo the translators specialized in medical texts. The comprehensive work by Ibn Sina, known in Europe as the "Canon of Medicine" remained a standard textbook until the 17th century. The basic compendium of medicine by Al-Razi was translated a number of times. Books on pharmacology and medicaments were widespread.

In philosophy, the translators turned their attention not only to the Antique philosophers and especially Aristotle but also to the philosophical writings of Ibn Sina (Avicenna) and Ibn Rushd (Averroes). These works exercised enduring influence on the discussions of mediaeval scholars.

As early as the middle of the 12th century, the translation of the Koran was commissioned by Petrus Venerabilis, Abbot of Cluny, following a journey to Spain. The Franciscans and Dominicans preparing for missionary work in the Orient no longer went there without a knowledge of Islam. From the 12th century, a great many Islamic Arab manuscripts were translated and many other examples could be quoted.

By way of Spain and the Norman empire in Southern Italy, this mass of learning and scientific knowledge flowed to the universities of Europe. The Crusader states, concentrating only on conquest and later after the rise of Saladin, caught up in a complicated and hopeless military situation and afflicted by major losses of territory, were unable to offer the right atmosphere for scholarly work. In addition, the native population led a separate life, quite different to the situation in Spain and Southern Italy. Nevertheless, the indirect influence of the existence of the Crusader states on the acceptance of Oriental sciences in Europe appears to have been greater than is apparent from the direct evidence.

Western European Scholars in the Orient

The great universities of Southern France and Italy were not only in the vicinity of Spain and Southern Italy but were also the traditional centres of the Crusades and the trade with the Orient. There is evidence that many scholars did not keep to the "contact zone" with the Orient but went further afield. Practitioners took part as personal physicians to kings and princes in the Crusades of the 13th century and used the opportunity to extend their knowledge.

A few instances of individual careers provide an idea of the possible links and influences.

Hugo of Lucca, also known as Hugo of Bologna, was a member of a noble family and took part as a physician in a Crusade in 1218. Returning in 1221, he was appointed municipal surgeon in Bologna and set up a surgical school here, introducing a series of practical innovations. His son, a priest, was the author of a four-volume teaching manual on surgery.

Petrus of Maricourt (Petrus Peregrinus) brought knowledge of magnetism and the compass back to France from the Orient and in 1269 wrote a treatise about magnetism in which an illustration of a compass appears for the first time.

Leonardo Fibonacci, one of the most illustrious mathematicians of the 13th century, was born in Pisa about 1180. His father had been in charge of a Pisan trading station in Bougie (North Africa). It was here that he learnt Arabic and received instruction from an Arab mathematician. He then extended his knowledge of mathematics in the course of commercial journeys to Egypt, Syria, Byzantium, Sicily and Spain. In 1202, he published his "liber abaci" (Book of the Abacus) in which he explained the Arabic numeral system which was soon afterwards introduced in Pisa in actual practice. In other works, he presented the principles of Arab algebra and offered solutions to equations of the first and second degree. However, it was not in Pisa that Fibonacci was held in the greatest esteem but at the Sicilian court of Frederick II where he was a welcome guest.

It is obvious that only few of the men of learning of the 13th century had first-hand experience of the Islamic world. From the 13th century onwards, the principal achievements of Arab Islamic science and of Antique authors who had influenced the Arab scholars were known in Europe. Manuscripts of these works were kept in universities and monasteries. For the following period, there also survives a series of examples of independent interpretations and modifications by scholars from various European countries. . . .

Innovations in Business

In addition to the examples already mentioned, reference must also be made to the stimulus which business activities received from the Orient. Apart from the Arabic system of numbers, this included rationalized calculating methods for book-keeping and the introduction of a simplified system of payment in the shape of cheques and bills of exchange. . . .

All these individual examples were so favourably received in the merchants' own cities that the most important spheres of social life there were given a stimulus which significantly accelerated their historical progress.

Chapter 4

Were the Crusades a Success?

The Crusades Were Successful

T.A. Archer and Charles Lethbridge Kingsford

The following selection is taken from *The Crusades: The Story of the Latin Kingdom of Jerusalem* by T.A. Archer and Charles Lethbridge Kingsford. Both authors taught history at Oxford University in England during the end of the nineteenth century. Archer also edited *The Crusade of Richard I, 1189–92* and published several articles in historical journals. Kingsford wrote numerous books, including *The First English Life of Henry V* and *Prejudice and Promise in Fifteenth-Century England*.

Archer and Kingsford maintain that although individual Crusades may have failed in their objectives, overall the Crusades were a success. In particular, the authors argue, the Crusades served to bolster both the Byzantine Empire and the countries of Western Europe against the incursions of Islam. If the crusaders had not protected Western Europe from Muslim invasions, they assert, the Dark Ages may have continued for centuries more, irrevocably altering the course of history.

The Crusades were the outcome of an enthusiasm more deep and enduring than any other that the world has witnessed. They were no mere popular delusion; for principles of sound reason overruled the ungoverned excitement of the mob. No deep-laid plot of papal policy; for neither Gregory VII when he projected, nor Urban II when he preached the Holy War, could have foretold the purposes to which their successors would, half unconsciously, turn it. Not the savage outbreak of warlike barbarism; for they entailed a patient endurance which only the inspiration of a noble ideal made possible. The Crusades were then primarily wars of an idea, and it is

Excerpted from T.A. Archer and Charles Lethbridge Kingsford, *The Crusades: The Story of the Latin Kingdom of Jerusalem* (New York: Putnam, 1894).

this which sets them apart from all other wars of religion; for into the Crusades proper the spirit of religious intolerance or sectarian jealousy hardly entered. The going on the Crusade was the "Way of God," not to be lightly taken up or lightly laid aside like the common affairs of men. The war was God's warfare, to be waged in His behalf for the recovery of the Heritage of Christ, the land which Our Blessed Lord Himself had trod. If this idea was not present to all when they took the Cross, yet it is safe to say that the great mass of the Crusaders came at some time under its spell. It is hard always for the men of one age to comprehend the enthusiasms of another. We can only marvel at the strange infection which for nearly two centuries ran riot through the West of Europe. It is easier for us to recognise the epic grandeur of the enterprise, in which was concentrated all that was noblest in the mediæval spirit. The Crusades were the first united effort of Western Christendom. They raised mankind above the ignoble sphere of petty ambitions to seek after an ideal that was neither sordid nor selfish. They called forth all that was most heroic in human nature, and filled the world with the inspiration of noble thoughts and noble deeds. Of the manifold consequences that were to spring from this inspiration, the higher ideals of life, the wider range of understanding, enough has been said already to show that the Crusades were as beneficial in their general results as they were undoubtedly sincere in their original undertaking.

Two Main Objectives

From the consideration of ideals which inspired the Crusaders, we pass naturally to the practical purpose which they endeavoured to achieve. Two principal objects presented themselves to the promoters of the First Crusade. The chief was no doubt the restoration of the Holy Places to Christian rule; the secondary object—but to such leaders at least as Gregory VII and Urban II a no less clear one—was the defence of the Eastern Empire against the danger of Turkish conquest. The first was based on a sentiment, but on a sentiment which with some change of form still survives; the second, on an urgent necessity, the pressure of which was yet felt two centuries ago. The first object was within a few years achieved by the establishment of the kingdom of Jerusalem. But the success was barely complete before the process of decay commenced. The causes of that decay [included] the narrow limits and ineffectual frontier of the kingdom, the jealousies of Crusaders for the Syrian Franks and for one another, the rival policies of the military orders and the native baronage, the deterioration of energy amongst those who settled in the East, and the waning enthusiasm amongst those who remained in the West. . . . A failure in this sense the Crusades no doubt were; but with it all we cannot regard as entirely fruitless an enterprise which maintained a fairly vigorous life for one century, and prolonged its death struggle for another.

The success of the second great object of the Crusades is best regarded from a twofold point of view—firstly, as concerns the Empire of the East; and secondly, as concerns the history of the world at large. In the former case, it seems clear that but for the First Crusade the Empire of the Comneni [Byzantines] must have succumbed to the Seljukian Turks. Certainly the twelfth century witnessed a great recovery both of territory and power on the part of the Eastern Empire. But, at the same time, it must be remembered that the constant passage of huge and disorderly hosts was the source of serious harm, and that the destruction of the true Empire of the East was the work of a so-called Crusade. Perhaps it is not too much to say that whatever benefit was wrought by the First Crusade was more than undone by the Fourth. From the time of the latter enterprise there was no strong united power to guard the East, and the success of the Turks was probably due as much to this as to their own prowess. Certainly the political and religious dissensions of East and West were aggravated by the Crusades, but, above all, by the Fourth Crusade, and the power of resistance in Christendom was so far weakened. From this standpoint, therefore, the eventual failure of the Crusades to achieve their second great object was hardly less complete than it was in the case of the first.

Looking at the Crusades, however, from the more general

standpoint of the world's history, we can pass a more favourable judgment. It was an imperative necessity for the welfare of Christendom that the advance of the Turks—which during the eleventh century had made such rapid progress—should be stayed. The First Crusade rolled back the tide of conquest from the walls of Constantinople, and the wars of the next two centuries gave full employment to the superfluous energies of Islam. Even after Acre had fallen, the Latin kingdom of Cyprus, the knights of St. John at Rhodes, and the maritime power of Venice—all creations of the Crusades—combined to delay, if they could not stop, the advance of Mohammedanism [Islam]. The importance of this for Western civilisation cannot be over-estimated. Had the capture of Constantinople by Mohammed II been anticipated by three centuries it is impossible that the Turkish conquests should have been confined to the peninsula of the Balkans and the valley of the Lower Danube. A new influx of barbarism, at the very moment when the gloom of the Dark Ages was breaking, might have been as ruinous to the social and political life of Western Europe as it was to that of Western Asia. At the least it must have put back the progress of civilisation in Europe by centuries, if it had not altered utterly the course of the world's history. . . .

The Crowning Glory

It is easy to contrast the glories of the Renaissance with the wreck of Mediævalism, and to feel that between the two there is a great gulf fixed. But the mediaeval world had had its own glories, which, as they faded, let fall the seeds of future prosperity. The processes of decay and new birth are as natural to the historical as to the physical world, and there is no justice in the taunt of failure; for it is in the failures and half-successes of one age that there are sown the seeds of the glories of another. The Middle Ages were, in their way, as important and fruitful for mankind as any other epoch of the world's history. The Crusades were their crowning glory of political achievement, the central drama to which all other incidents were in some degree subordinate.

The Crusades Were a Partial Success

James A. Brundage

James A. Brundage is the Ahmanson-Murphy Distinguished Professor of History and Courtesy Professor of Law at the University of Kansas in Lawrence. Previously, Brundage taught at the University of Wisconsin at Milwaukee, where he was chair of the history department for four years. He has served as the associate editor of the *Journal of Medieval History* since 1974. His publications include *Medieval Canon Law and the Crusades*, *Richard Lion-Heart: A Biography*, and *Law, Sex, and Christian Society in Medieval Europe*.

The following selection is excerpted from Brundage's *The Crusades: A Documentary Survey*. In it, Brundage contends that the Crusades were a mixed success. On one hand, he writes, the Crusades failed to establish a long-lived kingdom in the Holy Land, set the stage for the fifteenth-century Muslim takeover of the Byzantine Empire, and shattered any hope of reconciling the Eastern and Western Churches. However, he states, the Crusades also contributed profoundly to the political, economic, and intellectual development of Western Europe, laying the groundwork for the achievements of the Renaissance.

The Crusades in their heyday were a manifestation of European idealism, an idealism, however, which to many twentieth-century observers seems hopelessly wrongheaded, incorrigibly vicious, and irretrievably futile.

If the sole outcome of the Crusades had been the establishment of the paltry, short-lived Kingdom of Jerusalem

Excerpted from James A. Brundage, *The Crusades: A Documentary Survey* (Milwaukee: Marquette University Press, 1962). Copyright 1962. Reprinted by permission of the publisher.

and of its smaller, shorter-lived sister states, the movement might justifiably be called "a vast fiasco." Such a judgment, however, does less than justice to the whole enterprise. The Crusades did, after all, have profound and lasting effects upon the political character of Europe. To a very considerable degree, the Crusades conditioned the domestic politics of Europe in the high medieval period. The expeditions to the East enhanced the prestige of the Papacy. In large measure they made possible the emergence, for better or worse, of such a figure as Innocent III. At the same time, the Crusades, by providing an acceptable outlet for the warriors of the West, assisted immeasurably the establishment of a more stable polity in Europe itself. The emergence of the European national monarchies (again, for better or worse) would doubtless have been immeasurably retarded without the Crusades and the existence of the Latin states in the high Middle Ages. Yet these very developments in the West, for which the Crusades were in some measure responsible, to a large extent crippled the Crusading movement in the thirteenth century.

The Fall of Constantinople

The turning point of the whole movement came in 1204, with the sack of Constantinople and the creation of the Latin Empire. This development harmed the other Latin holdings in the East by diverting attention, manpower, and money from them. The founding of the Latin Empire ruined Byzantium and, in the final analysis, did even greater harm to the Crusading movement. Yet, viewed from another angle, the Latin Empire, by crippling Byzantium, virtually assured the fall of Constantinople and the restored Byzantine Empire to the Ottomans in 1453. One result of this was the emigration of Greek scholars, Greek manuscripts, and Greek learning to the West, an emigration which was vitally important in the development of Renaissance learning in Italy.

The commercial importance of the Crusades would be difficult to overestimate. The presence of Genoese, Pisan, and Venetian traders in the Latin States, the influence which these commercial interests exerted upon individual Crusading expeditions: these are obvious examples of the economic involvement of the Italian towns in the Crusades. The end of the fifteenth century saw the end of the Mediterranean's dominance for European trade. By this same token, the importance of the Levant to the West faded, along with the commercial impetus for further Crusades.

Failed Reconciliation of the Churches

One principal aim of the Crusades was the reconciliation of the Eastern and Western Churches. Here, the ultimate result of the whole Crusading venture was to render any permanent reconciliation impossible. The events of 1204 dealt a mortal blow to the dream of Church union. This was, perhaps, inevitable in any event, for the Byzantine and Roman concepts of the Church were diametrically opposed to one another and the Holy War notions in the West, which produced the Crusades, were thoroughly repugnant to Byzantine churchmen. Union between the two Churches, then, was rendered impossible because the events of 1204 dramatically and painfully revealed to the Greeks the consequences of the Roman, West European concepts of the Church militant. When the situation of the Byzantine state became desperate, however, the notion of Church union was revived. In 1439, as a result of lengthy negotiations at the Council of Ferrara-Florence, a union of the two Churches was, in fact, proclaimed. The union, dictated by political exigency, was a total failure. It received little support in the East and, once the Byzantine state had finally fallen to the Ottomans, little more was heard of it. Byzantine Christians, in the light of the Crusades and especially of the Fourth Crusade, found political subjection to the Turks easier to bear than ecclesiastical submission to Rome.

In the short-range view and in terms of the goals which they set for themselves, the Crusades were, beyond any doubt, a disappointment and a failure. In the larger view, taken as a part of the history of the West as a whole, the movement must be judged more generously. There is no second-guessing providence—or fate. Speculation as to what might have been, though fascinating, is futile. The Crusaders failed to achieve their conscious goals and succeeded in attaining goals they had never dreamed of. The national states of the West, the Italian Renaissance, the absolute Papacy, a capitalist economy: all of these are, in part, the heritage and the product of the medieval Crusade.

The Crusades Were a Failure

Steven Runciman

A specialist in medieval and Byzantine history, Steven Runciman has had a wide and varied career. He held diplomatic posts in the Mediterranean and Middle East in the 1940s and served as the president of the British Institute of Archaeology at Ankara, Turkey, from 1960 to 1975. In addition, he has taught at universities in Great Britain, the United States, and Turkey.

Runciman is the author of numerous articles and books, including *Byzantine Civilization*, *The Historic Role of the Christian Arabs of Palestine*, *The First Crusade*, and *The Families of Outremer: The Feudal Nobility of the Crusader Kingdom of Jerusalem, 1099–1291*. His three-volume *History of the Crusades*, published in the 1950s, is still considered to be one of the foremost works on the Crusades.

In the following excerpt from the third volume of *History of the Crusades*, Runciman delivers a devastating assessment of the results of the Crusades. He argues that the Crusades were a disaster for the three primary cultures involved: Western Europe, the Byzantine Empire, and the Islamic Middle East.

The Crusades were launched to save Eastern Christendom from the Moslems. When they ended the whole of Eastern Christendom was under Moslem rule. When Pope Urban II preached his great sermon at Clermont the Turks seemed about to threaten the Bosphorus. When Pope Pius II preached the last Crusade the Turks were crossing the Danube. Of the last fruits of the movement, Rhodes fell to the Turks in 1523, and Cyprus, ruined by its wars with Egypt and Genoa and annexed at last by Venice, passed to them in

Reprinted by permission of Cambridge University Press from Steven Runciman, *The History of the Crusades*, vol. 3 (1954).

1570. All that was left to the conquerors from the West was a handful of Greek islands that Venice continued precariously to hold. The Turkish advance was checked not by any concerted effort of Christendom but by the action of the states most nearly concerned, Venice and the Hapsburg Empire, with France, the old protagonist in the Holy War, persistently supporting the infidel. The Ottoman Empire began to decline through its own failure to maintain an efficient government for its great possessions, till it could no longer oppose the ambition of its neighbours nor crush the nationalist spirit of its Christian subjects, preserved by those Churches whose independence the Crusaders had tried so hard to destroy.

A Vast Fiasco

Seen in the perspective of history the whole Crusading movement was a vast fiasco. The almost miraculous success of the First Crusade set up Frankish states in Outremer; and a century later, when all seemed lost, the gallant effort of the Third Crusade preserved them for another hundred years. But the tenuous kingdom of Jerusalem and its sister principalities were a puny outcome from so much energy and enthusiasm. For three centuries there was hardly a potentate in Europe who did not at some time vow with fervour to go on the Holy War. There was not a country that failed to send soldiers to fight for Christendom in the East. Jerusalem was in the mind of every man and woman. Yet the efforts to hold or to recapture the Holy City were peculiarly capricious and inept. Nor did these efforts have the effect on the general history of the Western Europeans that might have been expected from them. The era of the Crusades is one of the most important in the history of Western civilization. When it began, western Europe was only just emerging from the long period of barbarian invasions that we call the Dark Ages. When it ended, that great burgeoning that we call the Renaissance had just begun. But we cannot assign any direct part in this development to the Crusaders themselves. The Crusades had nothing to do with the new security in the West, which enabled merchants and scholars to travel as they pleased. There was already access to the stored-up learning of the Moslem world through Spain; students, such as Gerbert of Aurillac, had already visited the Spanish centres of education. Throughout the Crusading period itself, it was Sicily rather than the lands of Outremer that provided a meeting-place for Arab, Greek and Western culture. Intellectually, Outremer added next to nothing. It was possible for a man of the calibre of Saint Louis to spend several years there without the slightest effect on his cultural outlook. If the Emperor Frederick II took an interest in Oriental civilization, that was due to his upbringing in Sicily. Nor did Outremer contribute to the progress of Western art, except in the realm of military architecture and, perhaps, in the introduction of the pointed arch. In the art of warfare, apart from castle-building, the West showed again and again that it learned nothing from the Crusades. The same mistakes were made by every expedition from the First Crusade to the Crusade of Nicopolis. The circumstances of warfare in the East differed so greatly from those in Western Europe that it was only the knights resident in Outremer who troubled to remember past experience. It is possible that the general standard of living in the West was raised by the desire of returning soldiers and pilgrims to copy the comforts of Outremer in their homelands. But the commerce between east and west, though it was increased by the Crusades, did not depend on them for its existence.

The Effects on Western Christendom

It was only in some aspects of the political development of western Europe that the Crusades left a mark. One of Pope Urban's expressed aims in preaching the Crusades was to find some useful work for the turbulent and bellicose barons who otherwise spent their energy on civil wars at home; and the removal of large sections of that unruly element to the East undoubtedly helped the rise of monarchical power in the West, to the ultimate detriment of the Papacy. But meanwhile the Papacy itself benefited. The Pope had launched the Crusade as an international Christian movement under his leadership; and its initial success greatly enhanced his power and prestige. The Crusaders all belonged to his flock. Their conquests were his conquests. As, one by one, the ancient Patriarchates of Antioch, Jerusalem and Constantinople fell under his dominion, it seemed that his claim to be the Head of Christendom was justified. In Church affairs his dominion was vastly extended. Congregations in every part of the Christian world acknowledged his spiritual supremacy. His missionaries travelled as far afield as Ethiopia and China. The whole movement stimulated the organization of the Papal Chancery on a far more international basis than before, and it played a great part in the development of Canon Law. Had the Popes been content to reap ecclesiastical benefits alone, they would have had good cause for self-congratulation. But the times were not yet ready for a clear division between ecclesiastical and lay politics; and in lay politics the Papacy overreached itself. The Crusade commanded respect only when it was directed against the infidel. The Fourth Crusade, directed, if not preached, against the Christians of the East, was followed by a Crusade against the heretics of southern France and the nobles that showed them sympathy; and this was succeeded by Crusades preached against the [royal German family of] Hohenstaufen; till at last the Crusade came to mean any war against the enemies of Papal policy, and all the spiritual paraphernalia of indulgences and heavenly rewards was used to support the lay ambitions of the Papal See. The triumph of the Popes in ruining the Emperors both of the East and of the West led them on into the humiliations of the Sicilian war and the captivity at Avignon. The Holy War was warped to become a tragic farce.

Apart from the widening of the spiritual dominion of Rome, the chief benefit obtained by Western Christendom from the Crusades was negative. When they began the main seats of civilization were in the East, at Constantinople and at Cairo. When they ended, civilization had moved its headquarters to Italy and the young countries of the West. The Crusades were not the only cause for the decline of the Moslem world. The invasions of the Turks had already undermined the Abbasid Caliphate of Baghdad and even without the Crusade they might have ultimately brought down the Fatimid Caliphate of Egypt. But had it not been for the incessant irritation of the wars against the Franks, the Turks might well have been integrated into the Arab world and provided for it a new vitality and strength without destroying its basic unity. The Mongol invasions were more destructive still to Arab civilization, and their coming cannot be blamed on the Crusades. But had it not been for the Crusades the Arabs would have been far better able to meet the Mongol aggression. The intrusive Frankish State was a festering sore that the Moslems could never forget. So long as it distracted them they could never wholly concentrate on other problems.

Harm Done to Islam

But the real harm done to Islam by the Crusades was subtler. The Islamic State was a theocracy whose political welfare depended on the Caliphate, the line of priest-kings to whom custom had given a hereditary succession. The Crusading attack came when the Abbasid Caliphate was unable politically or geographically to lead Islam against it; and the Fatimid Caliphs, as heretics, could not command a wide enough allegiance. The leaders who arose to defeat the Christians, men like Nur ed-Din and Saladin, were heroic figures who were given respect and devotion, but they were adventurers. The Ayubites, for all their ability, could never be accepted as the supreme rulers of Islam, because they were not Caliphs; they were not even descended from the Prophet. They had no proper place in the theocracy of Islam. The Mongol destruction of Baghdad in some way eased the Moslem task. The Mameluks were able to found a durable state in Egypt because there was no longer a lawful Caliphate in Baghdad, but only a shadowy and spurious line that was kept in honourable confinement in Cairo. The Ottoman Sultans eventually solved the problem by assuming the Caliphate themselves. Their immense power made the Moslem world accept them, but never wholeheartedly; for they too were usurpers and not of the prophet's line. Christianity allowed from the outset a distinction between the things that are Caesar's and the things that are God's; and so, when the medieval conception of the undivided political City of God broke down, its vitality was unimpaired. But Islam was conceived as a political and religious unity. This unity had been cracked before the Crusades; but the events of those centuries made the cracks too wide to be mended. The great Ottoman Sultans achieved a superficial repair, but only for a time. The cracks have endured to this day.

Even more harmful was the effect of the Holy War on the spirit of Islam. Any religion that is based on an exclusive Revelation is bound to show some contempt for the unbeliever. But Islam was not intolerant in its early days. Mahomet [Muhammad] himself considered that Jews and Christians had received a partial Revelation and were therefore not to be persecuted. Under the early Caliphs the Christians played an honourable part in Arab society. A remarkably large number of the early Arabic thinkers and writers were Christians, who provided a useful intellectual stimulus; for the Moslems,

---

A Costly Mistake

Eighteenth-century author and historian Edward Gibbon is best remembered for his monumental work The Decline and Fall of the Roman Empire. *In the following excerpt, Gibbon maintains that European civilization would have progressed more quickly had the Crusades never been undertaken.*

Great was the success, and rapid the progress, during the two hundred years of the crusades; and some philosophers have applauded the propitious influence of these holy wars, which appear to me to have checked, rather than forwarded, the maturity of Europe. The lives and labours of millions, which were buried in the East, would have been more profitably employed in the improvement of their native country: the accumulated stock of industry and wealth would have overflowed in navigation and trade; and the Latins would have been enriched and enlightened by a pure and friendly correspondence with the climates of the East.

Edward Gibbon, *The Decline and Fall of the Roman Empire*, 1776.

with their reliance on the Word of God, given once and for all time in the Koran, tended to remain static and unenterprising in their thought. Nor was the rivalry of the Caliphate with Christian Byzantium entirely unfriendly. Scholars and technicians passed to and fro between the two Empires to their mutual benefit. The Holy War begun by the Franks ruined these good relations. The savage intolerance shown by the Crusaders was answered by growing intolerance amongst the Moslems. The broad humanity of Saladin and his family were soon to be rare amongst their fellow-believers. By the time of the Mameluks, the Moslems were as narrow as the Franks. Their Christian subjects were amongst the first to suffer from it. They never recovered their old easy acquaintanceship with their Moslem neighbours and masters. Their own intellectual life faded away, and with it the widening influence that it had upon Islam. Except in Persia, with its own disquieting heretic traditions, the Moslems enclosed themselves behind the curtain of their faith; and an intolerant faith is incapable of progress.

Devastating Eastern Christendom

The harm done by the Crusades to Islam was small in comparison with that done by them to Eastern Christendom. Pope Urban II had bidden the Crusaders go forth that the Christians of the East might be helped and rescued. It was a strange rescue; for when the work was over, Eastern Christendom lay under infidel domination and the Crusaders themselves had done all that they could to prevent its recovery. When they set themselves up in the East they treated their Christian subjects no better than the Caliph had done before them. Indeed, they were sterner, for they interfered in the religious practices of the local churches. When they were ejected they left the local Christians unprotected to bear the wrath of the Moslem conquerors. It is true that the native Christians themselves earned a fuller measure of this wrath by their desperate belief that the Mongols would give them the lasting freedom that they had not obtained from the Franks. Their penalty was severe and complete. Weighed down by cruel restrictions and humiliations they dwindled into unimportance. Even their land was punished. The lovely Syrian coastline was ravaged and left desolate. The Holy City itself sank neglected into a long, untranquil decline.

The tragedy of the Syrian Christians was incidental to the failure of the Crusades; but the destruction of Byzantium was the result of deliberate malice. The real disaster of the Crusades was the inability of Western Christendom to comprehend Byzantium. Throughout the ages there have always been hopeful politicians who believe that if only the peoples of the world could come together they would love and understand each other. It is a tragic delusion. So long as Byzantium and the West had little to do with each other their relations were friendly. Western pilgrims and soldiers of fortune were welcomed in the imperial city and went home to tell of its splendours; but there were not enough of them to make friction. There were occasional bones of contention between the Byzantine Emperor and the Western Powers; but either the bone was dropped in time or some tactful formula for its division was devised. There were constant religious issues, exacerbated by the claims of the . . . Papacy. But even there, with good-will on both sides, some working arrangement could have been made. But with the Norman determination to expand into the Eastern Mediterranean a new disquieting era began. Byzantine interests were flung into sharp conflict with those of a Western people. The Normans were checked, and the Crusades were launched as a peace-making move. But there was misunderstanding from the outset. The Emperor thought that it was his Christian duty to restore his frontiers to be a bulwark against the Turks, whom he considered to be the enemy. The Crusaders wished to push on to the Holy Land. They had come to fight the Holy War against the infidels of every race. While their leaders failed to appreciate the Emperor's policy, thousands of soldiers and pilgrims found themselves in a land where the language, the customs and the religion seemed to them strange and incomprehensible and therefore wrong. They expected the peasants and citizens in the territory through which they passed not only to resemble them but also to welcome them. They were doubly disappointed. Quite failing to realize that their thieving and destructive habits could not win them the affection or the respect of their victims, they were hurt, angry and envious. Had it been left to the choice of the ordinary Crusading soldier Constantinople would have been attacked and sacked at a far earlier date. But the leaders of the Crusade were at first too conscious of their Christian duty and restrained their followers. Louis VII refused to accept the advice of some of his nobles and bishops to take arms against the Christian city; and though Frederick Barbarossa toyed with the idea, he controlled his anger and passed by. It was left to the greedy cynics that directed the Fourth Crusade to take advantage of a momentary weakness in the Byzantine state to plot and achieve its destruction.

The Latin Empire of Constantinople, conceived in sin, was a puny child for whose welfare the West eagerly sacrificed the needs of its children in the Holy Land. The Popes themselves were far more anxious to keep the unwilling Greeks under their ecclesiastical rule than to rescue Jerusalem. When the Byzantines recovered their capital Western pontiffs and politicians alike worked hard to restore Western control. The Crusade had become a movement not for the protection of Christendom but for the establishment of the authority of the Roman Church.

The Destruction of Byzantine Culture

The determination of the Westerners to conquer and colonize the lands of Byzantium was disastrous for the interests of Outremer. It was more disastrous still for European civilization. Constantinople was still the centre of the civilized Christian world. In the pages of [contemporary writer] Villehardouin we see reflected the impression that it made on the knights that had come from France and Italy to conquer it. They could not believe that so superb a city could exist on earth; it was of all cities the sovereign. Like most barbarian invaders, the men of the Fourth Crusade did not intend to destroy what they found. They meant to share in it and dominate it. But their greed and their clumsiness led them to indulge in irreparable destruction. Only the Venetians, with their higher level of culture, knew what it would be most profitable to save. Italy, indeed, reaped some benefit from the decline and fall of Byzantium. The Frankish settlers in Byzantine lands, though they brought a superficial and romantic vitality to the hills and valleys of Greece, were unfitted to understand the long Greek tradition of culture. But the Italians, whose connections with Greece had never been broken for long, were better able to appreciate the value of what they took; and when the decline of Byzantium meant the dispersal of its scholars, they found a welcome in Italy. The spread of humanism in Italy was an indirect result of the Fourth Crusade.

The Italian Renaissance is a matter of pride for mankind. But it would have been better could it have been achieved without the ruin of Eastern Christendom. Byzantine culture survived the shock of the Fourth Crusade. In the fourteenth and early fifteenth centuries Byzantine art and thought flowered in splendid profusion. But the political basis of the Empire was insecure. Indeed, since 1204 it was no longer an Empire but one state amongst many others as strong or stronger. Faced with the hostility of the West and the rivalry of its Balkan neighbours, it could no longer guard Christendom against the Turks. It was the Crusaders themselves who wilfully broke down the defence of Christendom and thus allowed the infidel to cross the Straits and penetrate into the heart of Europe. The true martyrs of the Crusade were not the gallant knights who fell fighting at the Horns of Hattin or before the towers of Acre, but the innocent Christians of the Balkans, as well as of Anatolia and Syria, who were handed over to persecution and slavery.

More Stupidity than Sin

To the Crusaders themselves their failures were inexplicable. They were fighting for the cause of the Almighty; and if faith and logic were correct, that cause should have triumphed. In the first flush of success they entitled their chronicles the *Gesta Dei per Francos*, God's work done by the hand of the Franks. But after the First Crusade there followed a long train of disasters; and even the victories of the Third Crusade were incomplete and unsure. There were evil forces about which thwarted God's work. At first the blame could be lain on Byzantium, on the schismatic Emperor and his ungodly people who refused to recognize the divine mission of the Crusaders. But after the Fourth Crusade that excuse could no longer be maintained; yet things went steadily worse. Moralist preachers might claim that God was angry with His warriors because of their sins. There was some truth in this, but as complete explanation it collapsed when Saint Louis led his army into one of the greatest disasters that the Crusaders ever underwent; for Saint Louis was a man whom the medieval world believed to be without sin. In fact it was not so much wickedness as stupidity that ruined the Holy Wars. Yet such is human nature that a man will admit far more readily to being a sinner than a fool. No one amongst the Crusaders would admit that their real crimes were a wilful and narrow ignorance and an irresponsible lack of foresight.

The chief motive that impelled the Christian armies eastward was faith. But the sincerity and simplicity of their faith led them into pitfalls. It carried them through incredible hardships to victory on the First Crusade, whose success seemed miraculous. The Crusaders therefore expected that miracles would continue to save them when difficulties arose. Their confidence made them foolhardy; and even to the end, at Nicopolis as at Antioch, they were certain that they would receive divine support. Again, their faith by its very simplicity made them intolerant. Their God was a jealous God; they could never conceive it possible that the God of Islam might be the same Power. The colonists settled in Outremer might reach a wider view; but the soldiers from the West came to fight for the Christian God; and to them anyone who showed tolerance to the infidel was a traitor. Even those that worshipped the Christian God in a different ritual were suspect and deplored.

Greed, Envy, and Lust for Power

This genuine faith was often combined with unashamed greed. Few Christians have ever thought it incongruous to combine God's work with the acquisition of material advantages. That the soldiers of God should extract territory and wealth from the infidel was right. It was justifiable to rob the heretic and the schismatic also. Worldly ambitions helped to produce the gallant adventurousness on which much of the early success of the movement was based. But greed and the lust for power are dangerous masters. They breed impatience; for man's life is short and he needs quick results. They breed jealousy and disloyalty; for offices and possessions are limited, and it is impossible to satisfy every claimant. There was a constant feud between the Franks already established in the East and those that came out to fight the infidel and to seek their fortune. Each saw the war from a different point of view. In the turmoil of envy, distrust and intrigue, few campaigns had much chance of success. Quarrels and inefficiency were enhanced by ignorance. The colonists slowly adapted themselves to the ways and the climate of the Levant; they began to learn how their enemies fought and how to make friends with them. But the newly-come Crusader found himself in an utterly unfamiliar world, and he was usually too proud to admit his limitations. He disliked his cousins of Outremer and would not listen to them. So expedition after expedition made the same mistakes and reached the same sorry end.

Powerful and intelligent leadership might have saved the movement. But the feudal background from which the Crusaders were drawn made it difficult for a leader to be accepted. The Crusades were the Pope's work; but Papal Legates were seldom good generals. There were many able men amongst the Kings of Jerusalem; but they had little authority over their own subjects and none over their visiting allies. The Military Orders, who provided the finest and most experienced soldiers, were independent and jealous of each other. National armies led by a King seemed at one time to offer a better weapon; but though Richard the Lionheart of England, who was a soldier of genius, was one of the few successful commanders amongst the Crusaders, the other royal expeditions were without exception disastrous. It was difficult for any monarch to go campaigning for long in lands so far from his own. Cœur-de-Lion's and Saint Louis's sojourns in the East were made at the expense of the welfare of England and France. The financial cost, in particular, was appallingly high. The Italian cities could make the Crusades a profitable affair; and independent nobles who hoped to found estates or marry heiresses in Outremer might find their outlay returned. But to send the royal army overseas was a costly undertaking with very little hope of material recompense. Special taxes must be raised throughout the kingdom. It was not surprising that practical-minded kings, such as Philip IV of France, preferred to raise the taxes and then stay at home. The ideal leader, a great soldier and diplomat, with time and money to spend in the East and a wide understanding of Eastern ways, was never to be found. It was indeed less remarkable that the Crusading movement faded away in failure than that it should ever have met with success, and that, with scarcely one victory to its credit after its spectacular foundation, Outremer should have lasted for two hundred years.

A Tragic Episode in History

The triumphs of the Crusade were the triumphs of faith. But faith without wisdom is a dangerous thing. By the inexorable laws of history the whole world pays for the crimes and follies of each of its citizens. In the long sequence of interaction and fusion between Orient and Occident out of which our civilization has grown, the Crusades were a tragic and destructive episode. The historian as he gazes back across the centuries at their gallant story must find his admiration overcast by sorrow at the witness that it bears to the limitations of human nature. There was so much courage and so little honour, so much devotion and so little understanding. High ideals were besmirched by cruelty and greed, enterprise and endurance by a blind and narrow self-righteousness; and the Holy War itself was nothing more than a long act of intolerance in the name of God, which is the sin against the Holy Ghost.

Chapter 5

The Legacy of the Crusades

Turning | Points

IN WORLD HISTORY

The Crusades Led to the Decay of Near Eastern Civilization

J.J. Saunders

At the time of the Crusades, the Byzantine Empire and the Islamic world were the cultural and academic centers of the Mediterranean region, and their influence stretched well beyond their boundaries. In the following selection, taken from his book *Aspects of the Crusades*, J.J. Saunders writes that these ancient civilizations were far superior to Western Europe, which was floundering in the Dark Ages. However, he points out, the Crusades weakened these two civilizations to the point that they ultimately lost their dominance, allowing the culture of Western Europe to ascend to a position of world leadership.

J.J. Saunders taught history at the University of Canterbury in Christchurch, New Zealand, for many years. His books include *A History of Medieval Islam*, *The History of the Mongol Conquests*, and *Muslims and Mongols: Essays on Medieval Asia*. Saunders also edited the anthology *The Muslim World on the Eve of Europe's Expansion*.

In summing up the results of the Crusades, it is usual to say simply that militarily they were a total failure. This is, of course, undeniable: except in Spain—from which Islam was at last ejected in the same year in which Columbus sailed to the discovery of the New World, where the faith of Muhammad was never to gain a footing—the Muslim enemies of the Cross pressed forward relentlessly at the heels of the retreating Franks. Sixty years after the fall of Acre the Ottoman Turks were in Europe, and to this day they retain possession of Constantine's city, while by the mid-sixteenth

Excerpted from J.J. Saunders, *Aspects of the Crusades* (Christchurch, NZ: Canterbury University Press, 1962). Reprinted by permission of the publisher.

century Muslim naval power in the Mediterranean was as great as it had been in the days of the Omayyads. But the military aspect is only one of many. What has not always been fully realised is that the whole religious and cultural balance of the world was upset by the events of the Crusading-Mongol era. The world of 1300 was almost fantastically different from the world of 1100, for it was these two centuries which saw the final ruin of Oriental Christianity and the cultural decay of Western Asia.

Ancient Civilizations in the East

Since the dawn of history the lands . . . stretching from Egypt through Palestine and Syria around the Syrian desert into Iraq had been centres of urban civilized life. Here were located the famous cities of Oriental antiquity: Ur and Lagash, Thebes and Memphis, Nineveh and Babylon, Susa and Persepolis, Tyre and Sidon, Jerusalem and Damascus. From these a more advanced culture had spread eastwards to the Iranian plateau and the Indus Valley, and westwards all round the Mediterranean. Over the greater part of the area a common language (Aramaic) grew up, which became the official tongue of the Assyrian and Persian Empires, supplanted Hebrew among the Jews, resisted the pressure of Greek in the Hellenistic and Roman periods, and in its eastern form (Syriac, the dialect of Edessa) became the principal language of Oriental, non-Hellenic Christianity.

Yet oddly enough, this community of speech never gave birth to an Aramaic or Syrian nation. Syria and Iraq were always the battlegrounds of contending imperial Powers, Egypt and Babylon, the Seleucids and the Romans, the Byzantines and the Sassanids, and were never themselves strong enough to acquire political independence. When in the fifth century their Semitic populations, who had already translated the Bible into their own tongue, rebelled against the decrees of the Greek-dominated Imperial State Church, the way might have seemed clear for the creation of an Eastern Christian nation, which in later times might have opposed a vigorous resistance to the advance of Islam from Arabia.

Islam and the Syriac Churches

Such a nation never emerged, partly because Byzantine authority was too strongly entrenched in Syria and northern Mesopotamia, partly because Semitic Christianity had itself been split between the Nestorians and the Monophysite Jacobites. Thus when Syria and Iraq were at last prised free of the grip of the Byzantine and Sassanid Empires, this liberation was accomplished not by the native peoples themselves but by the Muslim Arabs. Had the conquerors been old-fashioned pagan Bedouins, they would doubtless in time, like the Germans and Vikings in the West, have accepted the Christianity of their subjects, but they had a new religion, a new law and a sacred book which rendered them impervious to Christian influence. Once Islam had come into these lands, the creation of a Syriac Christian nation-State was out of the question.

Fate was against the Syriac Churches. Divided among themselves, having no State as a political base from which to work, they suffered from grave disadvantages which they never overcame. The Nestorians, indeed, set out boldly to convert Asia: even before the coming of Islam their missionaries were preaching in China. But they operated with very slender resources: they were too thinly scattered, they never succeeded in attaching to themselves the ruling class of a powerful organized community, they had no strong State at their back, and they lost their most promising base (Transoxiana) to the Arab invaders around 740. They converted some important and semi-civilized Turkish tribes of Central Asia, but they made only a slight impression on China, as, for that matter, did Islam. The rise of the Mongol power gave them their last chance. Here was a mighty heathen confederacy which, could it be won to the gospel, might deal Islam its death-blow and turn the whole globe Christian.

Yet, notwithstanding that the Nestorians were reinforced by Latin missionaries from the West, the hoped-for evangelization of Asia was never achieved. The chances seemed good, the margin was narrow, but the failure was decisive. None of the great Mongol chiefs ever received Christian baptism. Hulagu died a pagan, Berke turned Muslim and

Kublai adopted Buddhism. Christianity's defeat may be ascribed to the fewness of the missionaries, to the mutual dislike and jealousy of the Nestorians and Latins, to the hidden strength and appeal of Islam, which had long won over the greater part of the Turkish race, and to the solid entrenchment of Buddhism in eastern Asia. The Mamluk victory at Ain Jalut in 1260 may have convinced many of the Mongols that the God of Islam was to be preferred to the God of the Christians. The conversion of the Mongol Il-khans of Persia to the Muslim faith was the final blow to Christian hopes.

The Final Triumph of Islam

It is from this point that we may properly date the final triumph of Islam in Western and Central Asia. When the Crusaders first broke into the Levant they found themselves in a world that was still largely Christian, even after four centuries of Muslim domination. The Jacobites of Syria, the Copts of Egypt, the Armenians of Cilicia, and the Nestorians of Iraq and Persia, formed substantial communities governed by their own patriarchs and bishops. Christians held high office at Muslim courts, and churches and monasteries were almost as numerous as mosques. Bishop James of Vitry, writing about 1220, asserted that the Christians of the Eastern Churches were greater than all the Greeks and Latins put together. Burchard of Mount Sion, a German Dominican who lived for a time in Palestine sixty years or so later, believed that the Christians of all sects outnumbered the Muslims in the East. The Nestorian Church alone, we are told, had twenty-five provinces and seventy dioceses stretching across Asia from China to Mesopotamia.

By 1300 Christianity in Western Asia was in full retreat. There were mass conversions to Islam from two sides: from Christians who despaired of the future, felt themselves deserted by their Western co-religionists, and no longer had the spirit to resist the pressure of the vengeful and triumphant Muslims, and from Mongols who had come to believe after Ain Jalut that Heaven was fighting for Islam and that it would be prudent to submit to Allah. There was some sporadic anti-Christian persecution, and occasionally there was a sharp turn of the financial screw, as when the Mamluk Government forced the Christians of Syria and Egypt to pay for the damage done by the Crusading forces of Peter of Lusignan in the sack of Alexandria in 1365. But on the whole low morale, social stigma and the altered climate of opinion accounted for the widespread abandonment of the old faith in the lands of its birth and early expansion.

As for the dwindling Christian congregations in the oases of Turkestan, they seem to have been finally swept away in the whirlwind of Timur's invasions at the close of the four-teenth century. The catastrophe of Oriental Christianity is vividly illustrated by the disappearance of the Syriac lan-guage. The last noteworthy author to write in Syriac was Bar-Hebraeus, or Abul-Faraj, a Jacobite churchman who died in 1286, and even he found it necessary to translate his principal work, a Universal History, into Arabic, so that it could enjoy a wider circulation. A language whose earliest memorials go back to the eighth century B.C. and which had been carried as far east as China, is now spoken only in three villages in the Anti-Lebanon.

Islam had won a victory. It had prevented the restoration of Christianity in Western Asia and it had converted the pagan Mongols. . . . At Ain Jalut, in René Grousset's words, 'the rough hand of Baybars steered history back to its former course'. The savage heathen who had killed the last Caliph and turned Baghdad into a charnel-house were brought in the end to prostrate themselves in the mosque and to ac-knowledge that there was no God but Allah and that Muhammad was his apostle, while their descendants or suc-cessors, the Turkish Timurids, were destined to erect mighty Muslim empires and to extend the frontiers of Dar al-Islam. Hulagu and Baybars between them exterminated the Assas-sins, and Sunni orthodoxy was re-established almost every-where in the Muslim world. Yet in reality the course of his-tory is irreversible and can never be turned back to what once was. The Islam that emerged from its contest with the Christian Franks and the pagan Mongols . . . was radically different from what it had been in 1100. It was no longer the vehicle of an advanced world-culture.

The End of the Golden Age

The golden age of Islam had been the four centuries from 800 to 1200, during which the science and philosophy of the Greeks, commonly filtered through a Syriac channel, had fertilized the mind of the Muslim world and stimulated it to creative activity of its own. Arabic, already revered as the sacred language of divine revelation, became the *lingua franca* [primary language] of scholarship and letters over a vast segment of the globe from Spain to Transoxiana. In medicine and mathematics, in history and geography, in logic and philology, in music and astronomy, in physics and chemistry, the men of many races who wrote in Arabic enriched mankind by extending the horizons of knowledge and improving the techniques of inquiry, as, for instance, by the use of the so-called Arabic numerals. The brilliant culture of Islam shone the more brightly by contrast with the stagnant Byzantines and the barbarous Latins.

Through Muslim Spain and Sicily the writings of Aristotle and the great Arabic thinkers, scientists and commentators were introduced into the West to inspire the great intellectual awakening which culminated in the Renaissance. From this moment the West steadily advanced towards that mental mastery of the world which is perhaps only now coming to an end. The East, so long the teacher of mankind, fell behind and has never regained its old supremacy. With the death of Ibn Rushd (Averroes), the last great philosopher of Islam, in 1198, the primacy of Arabic-Muslim culture may be said to have come to an end.

Reasons for the Collapse

To what may we attribute this 'transference of civilization'? Firstly, no doubt, to the sheer physical destruction wrought by the Mongol hordes, who not only killed millions of human beings but wrecked whole cities and burnt their colleges and libraries and art treasures. By wantonly smashing the intricate irrigation systems on which the economic well-being of lands like Iraq depended, they inflicted wounds on these ancient centres of culture which have never really been healed. Nothing done by the German invaders of the fifth century, the Arabs of the seventh, or the Vikings of the ninth, equalled the ruin accomplished by the brutal soldiery of the Great Khans. The Mongols left a trail of death and havoc across all the Muslim lands of Western Asia. In Eastern Europe they struck Russia such ferocious blows that the country was plunged back into a barbarism from which it took centuries to emerge. Western Christendom escaped this fearful scourge, and thus acquired an advantage over its competitors. On at least one occasion, however, the Crusaders proved themselves as barbarously destructive as the Mongols: the sack of Constantinople in 1204, if not so bloody an affair as the sack of Baghdad in 1258, was quite as ruinous to culture. Byzantine Hellenism suffered irreparable injury, and Constantinople ceased to be what it had been since its foundation, one of the mother-cities of civilization.

Secondly, the cultural unity of Islam perished in the storms of the Mongol age. Hitherto, the learned had written in Arabic from Spain to Turkestan, an area greater than had ever been dominated by Greek or Latin. The most advanced work in science and philosophy was produced in this universal language; Turks and Persians, Egyptians and Berbers, had composed poems and histories, biographies and medical treatises, in an Arabic which was not their mother-tongue, and the government of the Muslim States was conducted in the same medium. After the Mongol conquests Arabic retreated to those regions west of the Tigris where it was the current vernacular, and in Iran and Turkestan it was supplanted by Persian. . . . Though it was still employed in works of theology and scholastic philosophy, it ceased to be the language of science, poetry, and political administration in the eastern half of the Muslim world. From 1300 onwards the field of secular Arabic literature was restricted to Egypt, Syria and the Maghrib. This linguistic schism destroyed the unitary character of Islamic civilization and checked the diffusion of knowledge and the interchange of ideas. By contrast, the new science and philosophy in the West was propagated in a single language—Latin—which remained the *lingua franca* of European scholarship down to the seventeenth century.

Altering the Spirit of Islam

Finally, the long and bitter struggle against the Crusaders, the Mongols, and the heretics within the fold transformed the spirit of Islam. What had once been expansive, tolerant, intellectually alert and curious, and eager to uncover the processes of nature, now became narrow, rigid, pedantic and suspicious of scientific inquiry. Philosophy was a danger to the Faith. Was not all true knowledge contained in the Koran and the Traditions? The *madrasas* [schools] set up in the Seljuk age to defend orthodoxy . . . were filled with the exponents of an unbending scholasticism. . . .

Apart from the towering and lonely figure of Ibn Khaldun (1332–1406), who left but few disciples and whose brilliant work on the philosophy of history was neglected by his co-religionists and rediscovered by European scholars only in the nineteenth century, Islam produced no more creative thinkers, and in the investigation of the phenomena of Nature it was left far behind by the nations of the Christian West. The latter were the heirs of two traditions: one going back beyond Christianity to the Judaism of the Old Testament and taking God for its centre, the other derived from the secular rationalism of ancient Greece and having Nature as its object of study. Islam had but one, comprehensive, all-embracing religious Law, and secular thought and science could obtain only an uneasy lodgement within it at the risk of being expelled as dangerous and undesirable aliens. Shaken by the threat to the purity of the Faith, as they conceived it, the doctors of the Law clamped down on free scientific inquiry and Islam shut itself up in the past, a past from which it is only now slowly and painfully emerging.

Thus the intellectual leadership of the world passed to the peoples of the West. The age of the Crusades was not only the age of the decay of Byzantium, of Islam and of Oriental Christianity, it also marked the end of the cultural domination of the Mediterranean world which had lasted since the days of the Phoenicians. The future lay with the nations of North-West Europe.

The Crusades Precipitated the Discovery of the New World

Joshua Prawer

Joshua Prawer was a professor of medieval history at Hebrew University of Jerusalem; he served as the dean of the university's Faculty of Humanities from 1962 to 1965. Among his other activities, Prawer was the chairman of the Pedagogical Secretariat for the Israel Ministry of Education for three years, helped to found Haifa University in Israel, and spent many years as editor-in-chief of the *Encyclopaedia Hebraica*.

Prawer wrote numerous articles for scholarly journals and authored several books, including *Crusader Institutions, The Crusaders' Kingdom: European Colonialism in the Middle Ages*, and *The History of the Jews in the Latin Kingdom of Jerusalem*. The following selection is excerpted from his book *The World of the Crusaders*. Even after the Crusades ended, Prawer asserts, Christian Europeans were still influenced by the concept of crusading and the goal of winning back Jerusalem. This influence can be seen in the motivations of the explorers who discovered the New World, he writes. In particular, notes Prawer, Christopher Columbus hoped to discover new routes or gold that would enable the Europeans to fight another Crusade for the reconquest of Jerusalem.

'Before the end of the world, all prophecies have to be fulfilled; the Gospels need be diffused all over the world and the Holy City of Jerusalem has to be given back to the Christian Church.' This was not written by a mystic or would-be prophet of the Middle Ages; it was written by

Excerpted from Joshua Prawer, *The World of the Crusaders* (New York: Quadrangle Books, 1972). Reprinted by permission of the author's estate.

Christopher Columbus, the Italian navigator in the service of Their Majesties, the Most Catholic Kings of Spain, after the discovery of the New World. His caravels carried white sails with red crosses, the traditional sign of the crusaders, and on the deck of one of his ships was a converted Jew, Luis de Torres, as an interpreter of Arabic!

About two hundred years elapsed between the fall of Acre and the discovery of the New World. The crusading idea, though weakened, was not dead. The antagonism between West and East did not disappear, and the notion of a Holy War had not been abandoned. But more and more, circumstances changed the notion of the Holy War from an offensive against Islam into a war to defend the True Faith against the encroaching powers of Islam. For one, Islam was no longer represented only by Arab-ruled states, but by the great Ottoman Empire. Master of Constantinople (renamed Istanbul) from 1453, the Turkish Empire was far more dangerous than its predecessors. . . .

A "Crusade" of Conversion

Not only political and economic factors put an end to the Crusades. No less important, at least in circles which one would today describe as 'intellectual', was the criticism and the growing opposition to the Crusades as an *ideology*. Voices of opposition were heard as far back as the Second Crusade, and each succeeding expedition brought on a new wave of disillusionment and criticism. The many who opposed the Crusades ranged from the light-hearted and impudent troubadours to political thinkers, who deplored the exploitation of the movement for papal interests (for example, the campaign against Frederick II), and even mystics and men of profound faith and piety, who expressed doubts as to the divine inspiration of the movement because bloodshed was opposed to evangelical teachings. It is in these circles that a new idea arose: to preach the Gospels to the Infidels and thereby bring them to conversion. This new ideology of a peaceful mission inflamed the imagination, and it soon rivalled that of the Crusades.

As far back as the middle of the twelfth century, the great

abbot of Cluny, Peter the Venerable, had the Koran translated into Latin and so made it accessible to the West so as
to serve the understanding of Islam and as a solid basis of
anti-Islamic polemics. Some toyed with the idea that since
the Prophets and Jesus were not rejected by Islam, it would
be sufficient to point out the errors of Mohammed in order
to bring Moslems into the fold of Christianity. Missions to
the Mongols in the middle of the thirteenth century were essentially religious missions with the aim of converting the
new power to Christianity. It was the Catalan Raymond Lull
who, at the turn of the thirteenth century, became the most
eloquent apostle of the missionary idea. Under his influence,
the Council of Vienna (1311) decided to establish six schools
of oriental languages to train the future propagandists and
missionaries. Dominicans and Franciscans reached un-
charted areas of the globe, preaching, discussing, baptising
and establishing small local communities. Though some of
their exploits could be classified as thrilling the missions
never became a mass movement. Nonetheless, their existence undermined the idea of the Crusades and furnished a
theoretical basis for opposition or rejection.

The Link Between Crusading and Exploring

Despite handicaps, the ideology of the Crusades continued
to survive, but with time it fixed new aims and consequently
new means of action. The major change took place at the end
of the fourteenth century and became dominant after the
middle of the fifteenth century, when the idea of the Crusades became linked with the great movement of exploration.
It is not always easy to know how much of the new ideal was
window-dressing and how much sincere. It seems that the
movement of exploration drew its inspiration from different
sources influenced and appealed to people on different levels.

The great movement of discoveries began at the beginning of the fifteenth century with Portuguese explorers who
reached the Atlantic islands in the West and contoured the
western coast of Africa in the South. The Infante Enriquez
of Portugal was the moving spirit behind these hazardous
enterprises, which in less than a hundred years had changed

the destiny of man. The Portuguese explorations of the coast of Africa were, in a sense, a continuation of the *reconquista* [reconquest], a transfer of the Holy War—now at its last stages in the Iberian Peninsula—into the neighbouring lands of Islam and paganism. It would be a misreading of history to assign exclusively missionary aims to these explorations or even to presume that conversion to Christianity was a dominant factor. Yet there is no doubt that the daring captains, explorers and even hard-bitten merchants did believe that there was a more sublime purpose to their enterprises than the search for [the legendary kingdom of] Eldorado. The spiritual aspect of the expeditions was linked to the belief in the 'white man's burden' of spreading the Gospel throughout the inhabited world. These latter-day apostles were profoundly Christian, and conversion of the unbelievers and baptism of the pagans were viewed as an integral part of

Christopher Columbus and the Crusades

Dana C. Munro was a professor of history at the University of Wisconsin, the University of Pennsylvania, and at Princeton University in New Jersey. He is considered to be the founder of the American school of historians of the Crusades. The following excerpt is taken from his posthumous book The Kingdom of the Crusaders.

Interest in Crusades continued long after the lands which the early Crusaders had won were all lost. Christopher Columbus—to mention only one instance—was interested not only in discovering the way to the Indies, but also in helping the cause of the Crusades. The two objects were closely bound together in his thoughts. In his journal, under the date of December 26, 1492 (i.e., while he was on his first voyage) he stated that he wished all the profit of his undertaking to be spent in the conquest of Jerusalem, and that he believed that the Spanish sovereigns had promised to do this. When writing his will, he was still intent upon furthering the cause of the Crusades, and he directed the creation of a trust fund which should be used for a Crusade.

Dana C. Munro, *The Kingdom of the Crusaders*, 1935.

their undertakings. Characteristic of this feeling was the fact that after the discovery of the New World, Columbus signed his name as Christoferens, the bearer of the good tidings of Christ to the New World. This missionary aspect is present throughout the period of the Great Discoveries. Christopher Columbus, as well as Vasco da Gama and even the great empire-founder Albuquerque were conscious of it and viewed it as a part of their tasks.

Columbus's expedition and expectations were based partially on the erroneous beliefs about the size of the earth and the notion that sailing westwards, one would reach India directly. Out of these premises grew the notion of an attack on Islam through its back door, that is from the East. The legend of the kingdom of Presbyter John, alternately located in the East and in Africa, and the fantastic descriptions of his riches and military power led to the assumption that an eastern alliance would enable an attack on Islam from two directions.

The New World and the Crusading Vision

When the error became obvious, the Crusader idea was phrased in economic terms, namely that direct contact with the Spice Islands and India would make Europe commercially independent of Egypt, while simultaneously undermining Egypt's main economic resources: the income from duties on international commerce which terminated its Asio-African course in the Nile delta. Europe never succeeded in realising this program, but it was realised by the Ottoman Turks after their conquest of Egypt (1517) and the deviation of commercial routes to their new capital in Istanbul. While this ruined Egypt, it spurred Europe to new exploratory efforts in order to break the Turkish monopoly on commerce with the Far East. Yet the domination of commerce with Asia, as well as the discovery of gold in the New World, still served the vision of the defunct Crusades. While sailing westwards and expanding the distances between the Christian world and the Holy Land, Columbus noted in his shipboard ledger: 'I propose to Your Majesties that all the profit to be derived from my enterprise should be used for the recovery of Jerusalem.'

The Crusades Gave Rise to the Modern Conflict in the Middle East

Karen Armstrong

In the following selection, Karen Armstrong traces the impact of the Crusades on European history and thought from the discovery of the New World to the modern day. The experience of the Crusades, she argues, led directly to the current Middle Eastern conflict between the Israelis and the Palestinians. For example, she maintains, most Europeans and Americans support the Jewish cause and hold deep-seated prejudices against Arabs. These attitudes have their origins in the Europeans' experience of the Crusades, the author contends. Armstrong concludes that the conflict in the Middle East is just another extension of the Holy War that has been fought between Christians, Muslims, and Jews since the Middle Ages.

Karen Armstrong is a writer, editor, translator, and teacher. She has written and presented two British television documentaries: *The First Christian*, on the life of St. Paul, and *Holy War*, on the Crusades and the twentieth-century conflict over Palestine. The following selection is excerpted from Armstrong's book *Holy War*, which was written to accompany her documentary series by the same name. She is also the author of *A History of God: The 4000-Year Quest of Judaism, Christianity, and Islam*, *Muhammad: A Biography of the Prophet*, and *The Gospel According to Women: Christianity's Creation of the Sex War in the West*.

The year 1492 has been called the beginning of the modern period, and, while this is obviously an oversimplification, it is

Excerpted from Karen Armstrong, *Holy War* (London: Macmillan, 1988). Copyright ©1988 by Karen Armstrong. Reproduced by permission of Felicity Bryan Literary Agency.

certainly true that three very important things happened that year in Spain, which had seemed free of the intolerant neurosis that plagued the rest of Europe. In January King Ferdinand and Queen Isabella finally defeated the Muslim Kingdom of Granada, the last stronghold of Islam in Europe. With deep emotion, crowds watched the Christian banner being ceremonially raised on the city walls and throughout Europe church-bells pealed joyfully to celebrate this purging of Muslim filth. Three months later the Jews of Spain were given a terrible choice: they either had to convert to Christianity or leave the country. Many were so attached to Spain that they chose baptism, but about 100,000 Spanish Jews began a new period of exile and homelessness and the Jews of Europe mourned the destruction of Spanish Jewry as the greatest disaster since the loss of Jerusalem in CE 70. But the year 1492 is most famous for another apparently different but in fact deeply connected reason. Present at the ceremony of liberation at Granada was a man whose name was Christopher Columbus and in August he sailed across the Atlantic hoping to arrive in India, but accidentally discovered the New World instead. In India Columbus had hoped to establish a new Christian base from which to attack the Muslims, and his diaries show that years later he was still preoccupied with the reconquest of Jerusalem. As Europe sailed into the modern period that would in so many respects be an entirely new world, she was still obsessed with the old crusading hatreds and enthusiasms that would not die away. . . .

Demonizing the Jews and the Muslims

In the period immediately succeeding the Crusades, 'the Jew' and 'the Muslim' had become surrounded with an aura of absolute dread. Both were seen as capable and desirous of destroying Christendom totally and the external threat was becoming interiorised and institutionalised. This intolerance could not be controlled by reason or common sense; it had become too deeply embedded in the Christian identity and was part of the way people in the West saw the world. During the crusading period, Western Europe had created a new self. This self had pulled Europeans out of the Dark

Ages and would soon impel them to conquer the world. But it was not a very healthy self for it contained a massive repression and paradox. People had sincerely believed that the Crusades were an act of love. Right up to the end of the Middle Ages nobody had seriously questioned the morality of this cruel and aggressive Christianity and if people objected it was usually for more pragmatic reasons. Yet the whole notion of a Crusade was obviously opposed to the loving pacifism of Jesus, who had told Christians to love their enemies. To believe that a war of extermination was an act of love involved a huge suppression and it would seem that this led to the neurotic projection of Christian anxieties on to the Crusaders' victims. In the Christian imagination both 'the Jew' and 'the Muslim' were monstrously violent and bloodthirsty. Surely this must reflect a deep worry about Christian violence? As they groped for a new understanding of who they were and what they stood for, Christians in Europe got used to seeing Jews and Muslims as symbols of all they were *not*. The fantasies they created bore no relation to the objective reality but were unhealthy creations expressive of a flaw in Western integrity. At each stage of Europe's development, Europeans redefined the image of the Jew and the Muslim to make them both the complete opposite and a distorted mirror-image of the Western self. It is a habit they acquired from the Crusaders. . . .

The Rise of Protestantism

Sixteenth-century Germany was the home of the Protestant Reformation and it is important to make clear from the outset that, though the Crusades to the Holy Land were a Catholic project, Protestantism had its own forms of crusading and these would be crucial in forming modern Western attitudes towards Jews, Muslims and the 'Holy Land'. The Reformation may have banned relics, devotion to saints, pilgrimages and the love of holy places, which had all been crucial in crusading religion, but it would continue the crusading tradition of seeing Muslims and Jews in an abnormal way and made its own distinctive and damaging contribution to this Western mythology. . . .

But in the seventeenth century an entirely different Protestant attitude towards the Jews appeared which would have very important consequences. In England some Protestants wanted to abolish the ritual and hierarchy of the Anglican Church and return to a simpler religion of direct intimacy with God, without the intervention of priests and ritual. They were called 'Puritans' by their Anglican and Catholic opponents, because of their concern for moral and religious purity. The Bible is always crucial in any extreme Protestant sect that refuses to conform to the established Church, because it is the Word of God, the chief way in which he has communicated with man, and people usually interpret it quite literally. The Puritans were particularly drawn to the stern ethics of the Old Testament and took St Paul very seriously when he wrote that Christians were the New Israel. Like the Crusaders before them, they insisted that they were God's new elect, the new chosen people. Unlike the Crusaders the Puritans felt not that they had to slaughter Jews, but that it was their duty that God's clearly expressed wishes for them in the Old Testament be carried out. They also applied to their own experience the lessons that God had given to the Jews in the days of the old Covenant. Christians had always done this, but the Puritans took the logical step of identifying with the Jews of the past and gave themselves a rather Jewish identity: they called their children Jewish names like Samuel, Amos, Sarah or Judith, for example. Further they believed that they were living in the Last Days and St Paul had said that before the Second Coming the Jews would be converted. The Jews would, therefore, not be Jews for very much longer. . . .

American Affinity with the Crusades and Zionism

As early as 1620 the first band of Puritans left England in the *Mayflower* and sailed to the New World; from that date more and more settlers joined them in the new settlement that they called the Plymouth Plantation. Every year Americans remember this crucial moment in their history at Thanksgiving and the story and experience of the Pilgrim Fathers has been crucial in shaping the American identity. The very fact that they called themselves 'Pilgrims' like the Crusaders and the early Zionist settlers [who went to Israel in the late nineteenth century] shows how closely allied the Puritan migrations were to the spirit of other religious migrations. It also shows that a crusading enthusiasm is not only embedded deeply in the American identity and crucially formative in American history, but also that there is a natural American affinity with Zionism. Let us examine this more closely.

First, it is important to say that like the Zionists the Pilgrim Fathers were fleeing oppression in Europe. Familiarity with the story of the *Mayflower* can lead us to see this as a rather romantic episode, perhaps not dissimilar to the glamorous way in which some people see the Crusades. But the emigration was painful and dangerous. The voyage was long, perilous and acutely uncomfortable. Some people actually died on the long journey across the Atlantic and when they arrived many more died of disease and hunger. It was in its own way as traumatic as crusading. The country seemed inhospitable. . . . The whole experience was a struggle to achieve a new, independent identity in a new world, not at all dissimilar to the aims of the early Zionists. . . .

The dangers the Puritans had endured in England had given them an apocalyptic sense of an impending catastrophe. . . . This sense of extremity and fear and desperate search for a refuge was as strongly felt by the New England settlers as all their more positive hopes for the country. America has prided itself on being a nation of refugees and for providing a haven for immigrants who have fled oppression and persecution in Europe. The giant Statue of Liberty in New York Harbour must have been a moving sight to all the persecuted, downtrodden Europeans who later made the dangerous and uncomfortable voyage over the Atlantic. America, like Israel later, was a country born out of suffering in Europe.

A Barren Wilderness?

Yet there are closer and more positive similarities. Like the Crusaders, the Pilgrim Fathers and their followers turned spontaneously to the experience of the old chosen people, the Jews, when they were setting up their colony, and as was their wont they interpreted their struggle in the light of the ancient Jewish experience. Indeed they called their colony the 'English Canaan' and gave their settlements in the American wilderness biblical names: Hebron, Salem, Bethlehem, Zion and Judaea. The Zionists too, secular as they were, turned back to the Bible in their colonising effort. In making a Christian presence an 'established fact' in the New World, the Americans also had to grapple with the problem of the native American Indians, whose land they proposed to take away. They came up with the same justification as the Zionists would make use of later when defending their claim against the Palestinians': America was an 'empty' country, a barren wilderness, which the natives were too primitive to develop properly. . . . When they found that gentle persuasion was insufficient to allay Indian hostility, the Puritans turned their migration into a holy war, on the ancient Jewish paradigm in the early books of the Bible. Like the Crusaders and like the Zionists they resorted to extreme and ruthless methods in their holy war against the Pequot Indians during the 1640s. . . .

A Proposal to Return the Jews to Israel

It would have seemed to most Puritans that the first-fruits of the millennium had been manifested not in America but in England, for Oliver Cromwell had led his New Model Army to victory against the royalists in 1649, had beheaded King Charles I and established a Puritan republic in England with himself as 'Lord Protector'. He did not think that New England was important in the least and wrote of America as a 'poor, cold and useless' place. But in Cromwell's Puritan England there were two events that showed the shape of things to come. In the heady days of his victory in 1649 Cromwell had received a petition from the Puritan colony that had been established in Amsterdam, headed by Anne and Ebenezer Cartright, urging him to hasten the Second Coming of Christ. In the Bible it was prophesied that the Jews would be scattered 'to the ends of the earth' (Deuteronomy 28:64; Daniel 12:17) but that prophecy had not been fulfilled for there had been no Jews in England (a country that Jews at that time called Kezer ha-Aretz: the end of the earth) since King Edward I had expelled them from the country. Cromwell, the Cartrights urged, should hasten the coming redemption by bringing the Jews back to England. In the new Puritan republic the Jews would surely be converted to Christianity and this would also hasten the Second Coming of Christ. Secondly, the Cartrights asked:

> That this nation of England, with the inhabitants of the Netherlands, shall be the first and readiest to transport Israel's sons and daughters on their ships to the land promised to their forefathers Abraham, Isaac and Jacob for an everlasting inheritance.

The Cartrights' petition shows how close the Puritans were in spirit to the Crusaders and to extreme religious Zionists today. Instead of waiting passively for the redemption, the Puritans believed that they should hasten it by fulfilling the prophecies themselves. . . .

The Age of Reason

The eighteenth century is often called the Age of Reason. Thinkers like Voltaire and the *philosophes* [philosophers] believed that modern man no longer needed religion and should rise above the old irrational beliefs which had oppressed the people and kept them enthralled to superstition. There was a new search for liberty and freedom, especially in France, which culminated in the revolution of 1789 when the Goddess of Reason was enthroned as the deity of the liberated people. Some rationalists did not abandon religion but tried to make it reasonable. They rejected the idea of revelation, which had produced so many unnatural forms of belief, and created deism, a belief in a God whose existence could be demonstrated by reason alone; and they developed a rational moral code. In many ways the eighteenth century closely resembles our own. We also believe in freedom and strive for a reasonable, secular ideal. Many people thought, until recently, that religion was dead and would never be a force again in major world events. This was a very mistaken view. The eighteenth century shows us that it is not possible to batten religion and irrational emotion down completely. It seems impossible to replace strong emotional habits and opinions with cool reason and logic. These things will out, sometimes more passionately than before because of a period of repression. We seem not to be rational animals but to have strong emotional, religious needs. Even when we try to effect an objective appraisal of a situation or to view our 'enemies' dispassionately, by attempting to see two sides to a question, superstitions, prejudices and fantastic distortions still continue to colour our view. This certainly happened during the eighteenth-century Age of Reason. . . .

Yet one must give the French Enlightenment the credit it deserves. After the French revolution, the Jews were given legal emancipation and enjoyed the same protection and privileges as the Gentiles [non-Jewish people] of France. It marked a great change in the fortunes of European Jews and was the first official sign of acceptance since the Crusades. It was a public acknowledgement, that Jews were normal human beings, equal to Gentiles and entitled to the same human rights. . . . This principle was gradually accepted by the other leaders of Western Europe in the years that followed, and during the first part of the nineteenth century the secular and revolutionary ideals of the Enlightenment spread and the position of the Jews was greatly improved. Even countries like Germany, which had a very long tradition of extreme anti-semitism, emancipated the Jews. European Jews themselves were affected by the new secularism and began to assimilate, seeing themselves as French or German rather than Jewish. It did seem the dawn of a new era and for this we must give full credit to the Age of Reason.

Napoleon's New "Crusade"

But if Napoleon pursued enlightened policies of toleration, he also shows us that the old dreams of the Crusaders were not dead, irrational though they were. . . . In 1798 he made a bid for colonial power that captured the imagination of many Europeans because it revived old buried dreams, but it also showed the new cool sense of superiority that we have seen developed in Europeans during the Enlightenment.

Napoleon wanted to challenge the British empire in India by establishing his own empire in the Middle East, but he was also inspired by older European, crusading fantasies. Until the end of his life he saw the defeat of his Eastern expedition as the moment when his fate had been sealed. Europe seemed too small for his talents, and Napoleon was convinced that his destiny lay in the East. . . .

His plan was to conquer Palestine from the Turks, establish himself in Jerusalem, hand the country over to the Jews and remove his Eastern capital to Damascus. Under France, the Jews would defend the country against all comers. Nothing came of this grand scheme, because Napoleon was defeated in 1799 by the British, who had joined forces with the Turks to prevent this French penetration into the Middle East. To further their own colonial ambitions the British were now prepared to 'help' the Turks, until such time as they managed to eject the Ottomans from the Middle East and establish colonies there. Europeans were now ready to begin a full-scale invasion of the East once more and to do this they would be ready to exploit the Arab or Turkish Muslims and the Jews.

As we move ever closer to our own century, it should be clear in what direction Europe was moving and how this would affect the modern crisis in the Middle East. A rational man like Napoleon still cultivated crusading fantasies and, though there had been a marked shift in the European attitude towards Muslims and Jews, there was no permanent fundamental change. In Europe during the nineteenth century, Jews were certainly acquiring a new dignity and were enjoying a toleration that would hitherto have seemed unimaginable, but as we know only too well, this would not last. During the nineteenth century the old crusading hostility surfaced again and set Europe on the path that led ultimately to the gas chambers of Auschwitz. The Jews were living in the midst of Europe; they were under people's noses, whereas, ever since Europeans had purged their countries of Muslims, Islam had increasingly become a distant threat. That meant that hatred of Arab and Turkish Muslims did not reach the same crescendo of horror. Indeed, during the eighteenth century, Europeans had acquired a confidence which enabled some of them to look down on Muslims as primitives, others to ignore the existence of Islam altogether and still others to use even the weapon of knowledge to exploit and oppress them. The basic aggression that had been originally inspired by the Crusades was still there.

The Romantic Era

The nineteenth century has useful and sometimes chilling lessons to teach us about our own attitudes. In the first place, it marked the end of the Age of Reason and indeed led to the vehement rejection of the cult of pure reason of the Romantic movement. The Romantics, in the early years of the century, began a cult of feeling and imagination. They also encouraged a revival of basic Christian beliefs, to which they gave a new secular form. In particular the ideals of redemption and salvation powerfully affected the imagination of many Europeans and this affected the colonialists, who invaded the Middle East and North Africa during the nineteenth century and set up colonies there. They tended to see themselves as saviours, redeeming the barbarous East from hopeless stagnation. The Crusaders had never exactly seen themselves as saviours of the Muslims; they had, if you like, a more honest attitude and were quite clear that liberation meant elimination or oppression. But the Crusaders *were* like the nineteenth-century colonialists in thinking that their control of the Middle East was of crucial importance to the future of the whole world, which one day the West hoped to conquer. . . .

As people looked towards the Middle East, they all produced inadequate solutions, for one simple reason: they all failed to take into account the interests of all three religions and all three peoples. In France, a Catholic country, people tended to return to the classical crusading attitude of seeing Europeans as a chosen or privileged race, superior to both Arabs and Jews. Frenchmen often ignored or despised both peoples, fusing the two together in the old crusading way. Germany returned to the racial chauvinism and anti-semitism that crusading and crusading myths had fostered for centuries and threw off the new, unfamiliar rational toleration; Britain, a Protestant country, maintained the non-Jewish Zionism that had been the result of Protestant crusading. This took neither peoples seriously enough but was prepared to use the Jews to fulfil a religious dream and oppress the Arabs for their colonial ambitions. Nobody was able to see that an equitable solution meant respecting absolutely the inalienable rights of all three religions and all three peoples. . . .

More and more, the British were turning to the Zionist solution as a means of colonising the primitive East. In 1838 Prime Minister Lord Palmerston had sent William Young to be the first Vice-Consul in the new Consulate in Jerusalem, with special instructions 'to afford protection to the Jews generally'. The British wanted to make use of Jews instead of persecuting them. This latest Zionist initiative came from the great philanthropist Ashley, seventh Earl of Shaftesbury, who was the friend and stepfather-in-law of Palmerston and the mentor of William Young. An ardent evangelical, Lord Shaftesbury was possessed by the old millennial dream of converting the Jews and returning them to Zion to bring the Second Coming of Christ more quickly. He had persuaded Palmerston to send Young to Jerusalem with a special mandate for the Jews, and was convinced that this was an important step towards their final return. As he wrote in his diary: 'What a wonderful event it is. The ancient city of the people of God is about to resume a place among the nations, and England is the first of the Gentile Kingdoms that ceases to tread her down.' Yet this zeal for the Jews was not inspired by true concern for them as a separate people. In fact there was a residual anti-semitism in Shaftesbury, who would vote against Jewish emancipation in 1861. As usual he simply saw the Jews as a tool for the Christian redemption. He also shared the blindness of most Zionists about a possible Palestinian problem because he could not 'see' the Arabs. It was Lord Shaftesbury who coined the slogan, which the Jewish Zionists would later adapt and make their own, that Palestine was 'a country without a nation for a nation without a country'. . . .

In 1917, Foreign Secretary Arthur Balfour issued the famous Balfour Declaration [officially declaring British support for establishing a Jewish homeland in Palestine] and finally brought to fruition a long tradition of non-Jewish Zionism in Britain. Balfour was a typical Zionist. He had a practical and political motive, because he hoped that the declaration would win international Jewish support for Britain during the First World War and he was conscious of the strategic importance of Palestine. But he was also inspired by the Christian Protestant tradition. He had been brought up in the Scottish Church and the biblical image of a Jewish Palestine affected him powerfully: he imagined that there would be a cultural renaissance in the new Israel that would be a light unto the Gentiles. Like all Zionists he was completely indifferent to the claim of the Palestinian Arabs, who had long been regarded by the British as barbarous and unworthy caretakers. As he said with astonishing bluntness in his *Memorandum Respecting Syria, Palestine and Mesopotamia:*

> For in Palestine we do not propose even to go through the form of consulting the wishes of the present inhabitants of the country, though the American Commission has been going through the form of asking what they are. The Four Great Powers [Great Britain, France, Italy, and the United States] are committed to Zionism. And Zionism, be it right or wrong, good or bad, is rooted in age-long traditions, in present needs, in future hopes, of far profounder import than the desires and prejudices of the 700,000 Arabs who now inhabit that ancient land.

Like a true Crusader, Balfour was convinced that 'our' view of the Holy Land put him above ordinary moral considerations. Zionism was by now so firmly established as self-evidently right that it was impossible for Balfour to see that the Arabs had any claim at all to the land they had inhabited for 1200 years. . . .

Anti-Arab Prejudice

Gentile support for the State of Israel in the West was from the beginning complex and neurotic, moulded not simply by political and humanitarian reasons, but by millennial Protestant and biblical ideas, crusading colonialism and crusading anti-semitism. Non-Jewish Zionists were in a very real sense neo-Crusaders, even if they were no longer inspired by the old passion for the Tomb of Christ.

This becomes very clear when we consider the Gentile Zionists' attitude to the 'Arabs'. Yet again the old prejudice came into play and because the Arabs really were, quite understandably, opposed to the Zionist scheme, they were made into the distorted enemy of true civilisation yet again. But this time they were juxtaposed and measured against 'our' new representative, the 'Jew'. . . .

There is little squeamishness about Arab anti-semitism, which seems to be the only socially acceptable form of racism left. Biased and fictional remarks are constantly bandied about in public and in private, and people would, quite properly, be shocked if the same remarks were directed against blacks or Jews. The Middle East conflict has enabled the West to give a new twist to the stereotype of the 'Arab': he is an anti-Jewish-Semite. Now that 'we' are very nervously and stridently against Jewish anti-semitism, the 'Arab' is seen to be essentially and absolutely smouldering with anti-semitic fantasies and obsessed with the annihilation of the State of Israel. This is an oversimplified view and takes no account of the wrong that has been done to many thousands of Arab people during the implementation of the Zionist project, but it is attractive to Western people and gives them a healthy glow of righteousness when they attack the 'Arab'. But it is also indicative of a moral crisis in Europe. . . .

America: A Jewish Refuge

But Europe is no longer the capital of the West nor the capital of Christianity. The leadership has passed to the United States and, though there has been some anti-semitic prejudice there, in general America has not hated the Jews and should have none of these problems. Quite the contrary; we have seen that the Pilgrim Fathers identified with Jews and thought of the New World as another Canaan. America has provided a refuge for thousands of Jews who fled persecution in Europe and has given them a good home. Today many American Jews maintain that America has replaced Muslim Spain, which the Jews lost in the year that Columbus discovered America. They argue either that New York is the new capital of the Jews or that, together with Israel, American Jews 'will create something new for themselves and the world', as Bernard Avishai writes, which will replace the Jewish culture that was lost in Europe. Americans can rightly be proud of this achievement. They have established a strong emotional bond and even an identification with a people whom Europeans have persecuted and massacred ever since the Crusades. . . .

Israel as America's Alter Ego

Like the Jewish Zionists, the American settlers were not just pioneers but refugees who fled oppression in Europe. Both America and Israel are in this sense the creation of Europe. For Americans and Israelis the bond is strong because each recognises the other at a deep level. People who have suffered oppression have a strong bond and empathy that others, who have not suffered in this way, cannot understand. Yet this does not mean that either of these countries of refugees should be able to oppress other people and drive them into permanent exile.

A strong identification, such as America feels for Israel, means that objectivity can be very difficult. A threat to Israel could be seen as a threat to the identity of America itself and as a wound in her integrity. Certainly the United States sees Israel as her *alter ego* in the Middle East. . . .

This glowing image is at variance with the facts. Israel is a country which has conducted an aggressive and illegal occupation for over twenty years and has brutally oppressed the population of the Occupied Territories. In the winter of 1987/8 (the time of writing) the world was shocked to see the cruelty with which Israeli soldiers fired upon and killed unarmed people who were throwing rocks. If this is a model democracy, it is understandable that the people of the Middle East don't think much of it. To call Israel a partner in a war against terrorism is to commit the old crime of not seeing all three sides of the problem. It is to deny that the violence inflicted on the Palestinian people since the earliest days of the Jewish state has also been terrorism. It is to distort the picture by making the Israelis angels and the Palestinians monsters. American identification with Israel and blindness to the Arab position follows the same blinkered pattern as has always infected non-Jewish Zionism. Its causes are less dark and convoluted than the European reluctance to see all sides of the question, but no less deep. When you feel such a strong sense of identification with a country as the Americans feel for Israel, that country's enemies become your own and threaten your own identity, causing a 'dread' that leads to violence. . . .

The Latest Round in the Holy Wars

The wars in the Middle East today are like the Crusades because they are increasingly becoming religious wars. They are also holy wars because they are fought on emotional issues that are felt to be sacred by all three of the participants. A purely rational solution is impossible in this climate of extreme emotion, because people are not just fighting for territory, for rights or for interests that can be tidily sorted out. These wars are the latest round in a conflict that began when the Christian West persecuted and massacred Jews and Muslims in the First Crusade. As far as the West is concerned the issues are not very different from those that dominated the Crusades and they are highly emotive. We must realise that we are not acting sagely and rationally if we denounce anti-semitism and make anti-semitic anti-Arab jokes or claim that Palestinians are terrorists and Israelis only victims of terrorism. To deny a people's identity, as many Western people have long denied the Arab and Islamic reality, is to erase them from our emotional map and thus to annihilate them. We have seen in our own century where such fantasies of annihilation can lead.

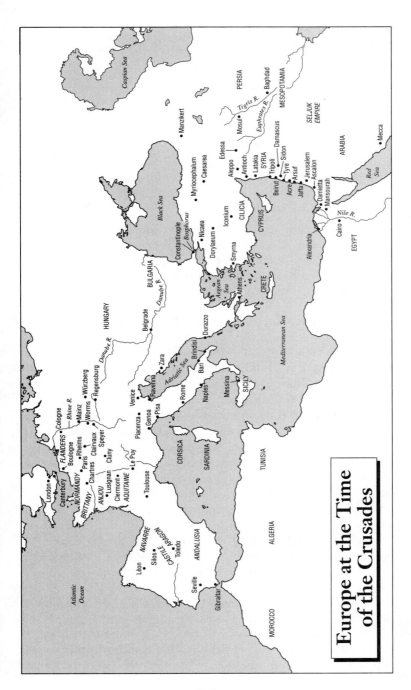

Europe at the Time of the Crusades

Appendix

Excerpts from Original Documents Pertaining to the Crusades

Document 1: A Plea for Aid from Byzantium

In 1093, Emperor Alexius Comnenus of Byzantium sent the following letter to Count Robert of Flanders, in which he describes the atrocities committed by the Turks against the Greeks. Pope Urban II also read this letter, which greatly influenced his decision to instigate the First Crusade.

O illustrious count and great consoler of the faith, I am writing in order to inform Your Prudence that the very saintly empire of Greek Christians is daily being persecuted by . . . the Turks. . . . The blood of Christians flows in unheard-of scenes of carnage, amidst the most shameful insults. . . . I shall merely describe a very few of them. . . .

The enemy has the habit of circumcising young Christians and Christian babies above the baptismal font. In derision of Christ they let the blood flow into the font. Then they are forced to urinate in the font. . . . Those who refuse to do so are tortured and put to death. They carry off noble matrons and their daughters and abuse them like animals. . . .

Then, too, the Turks shamelessly commit the sin of sodomy on our men of all ages and all ranks . . . and, O misery, something that has never been seen or heard before, on bishops. . . .

Furthermore they have destroyed or fouled the holy places in all manner of ways, and they threaten to do worse. Who does not groan? Who is not filled with compassion? Who does not reel back with horror? Who does not offer his prayers to heaven? For almost the entire land has been invaded by the enemy from Jerusalem to Greece . . . right up to Thrace. Already there is almost nothing left for them to conquer except Constantinople, which they threaten to conquer any day now, unless God and the Christians of the Latin rite come quickly to our aid. . . .

Therefore in the name of God and because of the true piety of the generality of Greek Christians, we implore you to bring to this city all the faithful soldiers of Christ . . . to bring me aid and to bring aid to the Greek Christians. . . . Before Constantinople falls into their power, you should do everything you can to be worthy of receiving heaven's benediction, an ineffable and glorious reward for your aid. It would be better that Constantinople falls into your hands than into the hands of the pagans.

Robert Payne, *The Dream and the Tomb: A History of the Crusades*. London: Robert Hale Limited, 1986.

Document 2: Pope Urban II Declares the First Crusade

At the Council of Clermont on November 27, 1095, Pope Urban II called for a Crusade to the Holy Land. Several different versions of his sermon exist. The following excerpts are taken from the account recorded by Fulcher of Chartres. Fulcher was present at the council and probably heard Urban's sermon firsthand.

Since, oh sons of God, you have promised God more strongly than usual to uphold faithfully peace-keeping at home and the preservation of the rights of the Church, it appears worth while for you in addition to turn the vigour of your goodness to a certain other matter, the concern of God and yourselves, now that you have been invigorated by the correction of the Lord. For it is necessary for you to run as quickly as you can to the aid of your brothers living on the eastern shore; you have often been told that they are in need of your help. For, as many of you have already been told, the Turks, a Persian race, have overrun them right up to the Mediterranean Sea, to that strait called the Arm of St George. Occupying more and more of the land of the Christians on the borders of Romania, they have conquered those who have already been overcome seven times by warlike invasion, slaughtering and capturing many, destroying churches and laying waste the kingdom of God. So, if you leave them alone much longer they will further grind under their heels the faithful of God.

On this matter I exhort you, heralds of Christ, with an earnest prayer—not I, but the Lord—so that by preaching frequently you may persuade everyone of no matter what class, be he knight or foot-soldier, rich or poor, to strive to bring aid to the Christian inhabitants in time by driving this infamous race from our territories. I appeal directly to those present; I order those absent; but Christ commands. All men going there who die untimely deaths, whether on the journey by land or by sea or while fighting the pagans, will immediately have their sins remitted. I am entitled to grant this to those about to go by the gift of God. Oh how shameful if a race so spurned and degenerate, the handmaid of devils, should conquer a race endowed with the faith of almighty God and resplendent with the name of Christ! Oh what a great disgrace will be imputed to you by the Lord himself if you do not help those who by the profession of their faith are rated, like you, as Christians! Let those who in the past have been accustomed to spread private war so vilely among the faithful (he said) advance against the infidels in a battle which ought to have been begun already and which ought to end in triumph. Let those who were formerly brigands now become soldiers of Christ; those who once waged war against their brothers and blood-relatives fight lawfully against barbarians; those who until now have been mercenaries for a few coins achieve eternal rewards. Let those who have been wearing themselves out to the detriment of both body and soul labour for a double honour. If they really continue to live in their former state they will be sad and poor, but if in the latter state happy and rich; in the former they will be the enemies of the Lord, in the latter they will be his friends. And those who are about to depart must not delay, but when winter is over and spring has come they must get eagerly under way with the Lord as their leader, after setting their affairs in order and collecting money for their expenses on the journey.

Louise and Jonathan Riley-Smith, *The Crusades: Idea and Reality, 1095–1274.* London: Edward Arnold, 1981.

Document 3: The Rush to Leave

Filled with religious enthusiasm, royalty and peasants alike hurried to embark on the First Crusade. The following description of the economic and social effects of their fervor was written by Guibert of Nogent, a French abbot, in his chronicles of the First Crusade.

So many men were in haste to make their affairs ready for this journey that seven sheep were sold for five *denarii*, to give but one example of the sudden cheapening of all goods. The former scarcity of corn was turned into plenty; for each pilgrim, eager to raise money at all hazards, parted with his goods, not at his own price but at the buyer's, lest he be delayed from treading the *via Dei*, the way of God. So we saw this marvel, that all men bought dear and sold cheap, and a few coins would now purchase the possessions which neither prison nor torture could have wrung from the peasants but a short while before. Nor was it less laughable that the very men who had hitherto derided this foolish selling by their neighbours would then, of a sudden impulse, also sell up for a few pence and march forth side by side with those they had previously mocked.

Thus God Almighty, who is wont to bring many vain beginnings to a pious end, led these simple souls into salvation merely through their good intention. Then you might see a marvellous and most curious sight: a troop of poor folk with two-wheeled carts drawn by oxen which they had shod after the manner of horses. In these little carts were their scant possessions, and often their families also; and their little children, as soon as they came to some walled town, would ask again and again if this was the place to which they were travelling, a place called Jerusalem.

Now, at that time, before this great movement of the nations, the whole of France suffered the cruellest conflicts, with robbery, fire and arson, brigands and bandits on almost every road. Men fought pitched battles for no other excuse but insatiable greed. In a sentence, whatsoever was open to sight was coveted and taken by these rogues. Then, of a sudden, there was a marvellous and incredible change of spirit, by reason of the decree of Pope Urban. Men sought out bishops or priests to invest them with the sign of the cross. And even as the wildest winds are often laid by a little fall of rain, so we beheld this immediate peace, and cessation of customary fights and tumults, by means of a breath that passed invisibly from man to man. And this breath—we cannot doubt it—was of Christ.

Michael Foss, *People of the First Crusade*. New York: Arcade Publishing, 1997.

Document 4: Seeking Redemption Through Crusading

Before starting on the First Crusade, many knights and nobles attempted to make amends for former misdeeds. Around 1096, the nobleman Nivelo signed this agreement with the Abbey of St. Peter of Chartres in France. In exchange for funds from the monks to help with the cost of crusading, Nivelo vows that he and his knights will no longer oppress the poor.

Anyone who is the recipient of pardon through the grace of heavenly atonement and who wants to be more completely freed from the burden of his sins, whose weight oppresses the soul of the sinner and prevents it from flying up to heaven, must look to end his sins before they abandon him. And so I Nivelo, raised in a nobility of birth which produces in many people an ignobility of mind, for the redemption of my soul and in exchange for a great sum of money given me for this, renounce for ever in favour of St Peter the oppressive behaviour resulting from a certain bad custom, handed on to me not by ancient right but from the time of my father, a man of little weight who first harassed the poor with this oppression. Thereafter I constantly maintained it in an atrociously tyrannical manner. I had harshly worn down the land of St Peter, that is to say Emprainville and the places around it, in the way that had become customary, by seizing the goods of the inhabitants there. This was the rough nature of this custom. Whenever the onset of knightly ferocity stirred me up, I used to descend on the aforesaid village, taking with me a troop of my knights and a crowd of my attendants, and against nature I would make over the goods of the men of St Peter for food for my knights.

And so since, in order to obtain the pardon for my crimes which God can give me, I am going on pilgrimage to Jerusalem which until now has been enslaved with her sons, the monks have given me 10 pounds in *denarii* towards the expenses of the appointed journey, in return for giving up this oppression; and they have given 3 pounds to my sister, called Comitissa, the wife of Hugh, viscount of Châteaudun, in return for her consent; 40 *solidi* to Hamelin my brother; with the agreement of my son Urso and my other relatives. . . . If in the course of time one of my descendants is tempted to break the strength of this concession and is convicted of such an act by the witnesses named below, may he, transfixed by the thunderbolt of anathema, be placed in the fires of hell . . . to be tormented endlessly. And so, to reinforce my confirmation of this, I make the sign of the cross with my own hand and I pass the document over to my son called Urso and my other relatives and witnesses for them to confirm by making their signs. And everyone ought to note that I make satisfaction to St Peter for such abominable past injuries and that I will forever desist from causing this restless trouble, which is now stilled.

Louise and Jonathan Riley-Smith, *The Crusades: Idea and Reality, 1095–1274*. London: Edward Arnold, 1981.

Document 5: Persecution of the Jews

Albert of Aix was a clergyman who compiled a history of the First Crusade. Here he writes about a band of crusaders who massacred European Jews on their route to the Holy Land.

At the beginning of summer in the same year in which Peter and Gottschalk, after collecting an army, had set out, there assembled in like fashion a large and innumerable host of Christians from diverse kingdoms and lands; namely, from the realms of France, England, Flanders, and Lorraine. . . . I know not whether by a judgment of the Lord, or by some error of mind, they rose in a spirit of cruelty against the Jewish people scattered throughout these

cities and slaughtered them without mercy, especially in the Kingdom of Lorraine, asserting it to be the beginning of their expedition and their duty against the enemies of the Christian faith. This
slaughter of Jews was done first by citizens of Cologne. These suddenly fell upon a small band of Jews and severely wounded and
killed many; they destroyed the houses and synagogues of the Jews
and divided among themselves a very large amount of money. . . .

Not long after this, they started upon their journey, as they had
vowed, and arrived in a great multitude at the city of Mainz. There
Count Emico, a nobleman, a very mighty man in this region, was
awaiting, with a large band of Teutons, the arrival of the pilgrims
who were coming thither from diverse lands by the King's highway.

The Jews of this city, knowing of the slaughter of their
brethren, and that they themselves could not escape the hands of
so many, fled in hope of safety to Bishop Rothard. They put an infinite treasure in his guard and trust, having much faith in his protection, because he was Bishop of the city. Then that excellent
Bishop of the city cautiously set aside the incredible amount of
money received from them. He placed the Jews in the very spa-
cious hall of his own house, away from the sight of Count Emico
and his followers, that they might remain safe and sound in a very
secure and strong place.

But Emico and the rest of his band held a council and, after sun-
rise, attacked the Jews in the hall with arrows and lances. Breaking
the bolts and doors, they killed the Jews, about seven hundred in
number, who in vain resisted the force and attack of so many thousands. They killed the women, also, and with their swords pierced
tender children of whatever age and sex. The Jews, seeing that
their Christian enemies were attacking them and their children,
and that they were sparing no age, likewise fell upon one another,
brother, children, wives, and sisters, and thus they perished at each
other's hands. Horrible to say, mothers cut the throats of nursing
children with knives and stabbed others, preferring them to perish
thus by their own hands rather than to be killed by the weapons of
the uncircumcised.

From this cruel slaughter of the Jews a few escaped; and a few
because of fear, rather than because of love of the Christian faith,
were baptized. With very great spoils taken from these people,
Count Emico, Clarebold, Thomas, and all that intolerable company of men and women then continued on their way to Jerusalem.

August C. Krey, *The First Crusade: The Accounts of Eye-Witnesses and Participants*. Princeton, NJ:
Princeton University Press, 1921.

Document 6: Sanctifying the Holy Name

The massacre of the European Jews was also recorded by Jewish chroniclers. The following excerpt was originally written in Hebrew shortly after 1096 by a chronicler known as Anonymous of Mainz. In this passage, he describes how many Jews in Mainz decided to kill themselves and their families rather than to be slaughtered by the crusaders.

When the children of the sacred covenant saw that . . . the enemy had overcome them, they all cried out—young men and old men, young women and children, menservants and maidservants—and wept for themselves and their lives. They said: "We shall suffer the yoke of awe of the sacred. For the moment the enemy will kill us with the easiest of . . . deaths—by the sword. But we shall remain alive; our souls [will repose] in paradise, in the radiance of the great light, forever." They all said acceptingly and willingly: "Ultimately one must not question the ways of the Holy One blessed be he and blessed be his Name, who gave us his Torah and commanded us to put to death and to kill ourselves for the unity of his holy Name. Blessed are we if we do his will and blessed are all those who are killed and slaughtered and who die for the unity of his Name. Not only are they privileged to enter the world to come and sit in the circle of the saintly. . . . What is more, they exchange a world of darkness for a world of light, a world of pain for a world of happiness, a transitory world for a world that is eternal and everlasting." They all cried out loudly and in unison: "Ultimately we must not tarry. For the enemy has come upon us suddenly. Let us offer ourselves up before our Father in heaven. Anyone who has a knife should come and slaughter us for the sanctification of the unique Name [of God] who lives forever. Subsequently let him pierce himself with his sword either in his throat or in his belly or let him slaughter himself." They all stood—men and women—and slaughtered one another. The young women and the brides and bridegrooms looked through the windows and cried out loudly and said: "Look and see, God, what we do for the sanctification of your great Name, rather than to abandon your divinity for a crucified one, a trampled and wretched and abominable offshoot. . . , a bastard and a child of menstruation and lust." They were all slaughtered. The blood of this slaughter flowed through the chambers in which the children of the sacred covenant were. They lay in slaughtered rows—the infant with the elderly . . . [making sounds] like those made by slaughtered sheep. . . .

There was a notable lady, Rachel the daughter of R. Isaac ben

R. Asher. She said to her companions: "I have four children. On them as well have no mercy, lest these uncircumcised come and seize them and they remain in their pseudo-faith. With them as well you must sanctify the holy Name." One of her companions came and took the knife. When she saw the knife, she cried loudly and bitterly. She beat her face, crying and saying: "'Where is your steadfast love, O Lord?'" She took Isaac her small son—indeed he was very lovely—and slaughtered him. She . . . said to her companions: "Wait! Do not slaughter Isaac before Aaron." But the lad Aaron, when he saw that his brother had been slaughtered, cried out: "Mother, Mother, do not slaughter me!" He then went and hid himself under a bureau. She took her two daughters, Bella and Matrona, and sacrificed them to the Lord God of Hosts, who commanded us not to abandon pure awe of him and to remain loyal to him. When the saintly one finished sacrificing her three children before our Creator, she then lifted her voice and called out to her son: "Aaron, Aaron, where are you? I shall not have pity or mercy on you either." She pulled him by the leg from under the bureau, where he had hidden, and sacrificed him before the sublime and exalted God. She then put them under her two sleeves, two on one side and two on the other, near her heart. They convulsed near her, until the crusaders seized the chamber. They found her sitting and mourning them. They said to her: "Show us the money which you have under your sleeves." When they saw the slaughtered children, they smote her and killed her. . . . The crusaders killed all those in the chamber and stripped them naked. They were still writhing and convulsing in their blood, as they stripped them. . . .

Subsequently they threw them from the chambers through the windows naked, heap upon heap and mound upon mound, until they formed a high heap.

Robert Chazan, *European Jewry and the First Crusade*. Berkeley: University of California Press, 1987.

Document 7: The End of the People's Crusade

Anna Comnena was the daughter of the Byzantine emperor Alexius Comnenus; in the mid-1100s, Anna wrote the Alexiad, *which recounts the events of her father's reign. Anna herself was a teenager during the First Crusade and provides her own impressions of the crusaders. In this excerpt, she describes the arrival of Peter the Hermit (whom she also refers to as Peter the Cuckoo) and his People's Crusade in Constantinople, as well as their ultimate demise at the hands of the Turks.*

As if he had sounded a divine voice in the hearts of all, Peter the Hermit inspired the Franks from everywhere to gather together with their weapons, horses and other military equipment. There was such universal eagerness and enthusiasm that every highway had some of them; along with the soldiers went an unarmed crowd, more numerous than the sand or the stars, carrying palms and crosses on their shoulders, including even women and children who had left their own countries. To look upon them was like seeing rivers flowing together from all sides, and coming against us in full force, for the most part through Hungary.

The emperor of Constantinople, Alexius I Comnenus, advised Peter to await the other Christian forces. However, he did not; trusting in the large numbers of his [French, German and Italian] followers, he crossed the Bosporus and pitched camp at a small village called Helenopolis. But as many as ten thousand French crusaders separated from the rest of the army and, with the utmost cruelty, plundered the Turkish territory around Nicaea. They dismembered some of the babies, others they put on spits and roasted over a fire; those of advanced years they subjected to every form of torture. When the people inside the city of Nicaea learned what was happening they opened the gates and went out against the crusaders. A violent encounter ensued, but Peter's followers attacked hard, forcing them to retreat.

The raiders then took all their booty and returned to Helenopolis. An argument broke out between them and those who had stayed behind, as usually happens in such cases, when envy inflames the mind. Then some audacious Germans separated from the others, went to the castle of Xerigordos and took it by assault. When the Turkish sultan Qilij Arslan learned what had happened, he sent an adequate force against them. He recaptured Xerigordos, put some of the Germans to the sword and took others captive.

At the same time, he devised a plan against those who had remained behind with Peter the Cuckoo. He placed men in ambush at suitable places, so that anyone heading for Nicaea would fall into the trap and be caught. Further, knowing the Franks' love of money, he instructed two energetic men to go to Peter's camp and announce that the forces had captured Nicaea and were dividing up the spoil from the city. When this report reached the men with Peter, it threw them into total confusion. At the news of plunder and money, they immediately set off along the road to Nicaea, with no semblance of order, all forgetting their military skill and the discipline required of those going out to battle.

The race of Latins is generally noted for its love of money; but when it embarks on the invasion of a country, then it becomes totally unbridled, devoid of all reason. Since these men were advancing in no sort of order or discipline, they fell into the Turkish ambushes near Drakon and were miserably wiped out. Such a large number of Franks became the victims of Turkish swords, that when the scattered remains of the slaughtered men were collected, they made not merely a hill or mound or peak, but a huge mountain, deep and wide, most remarkable, so great was the pile of bones.

Elizabeth Hallam, ed., *Chronicles of the Crusades: Nine Crusades and Two Hundred Years of Bitter Conflict for the Holy Land Brought to Life Through the Words of Those Who Were Actually There.* New York: Weidenfeld and Nicolson, 1989.

Document 8: The First Crusaders Capture Jerusalem

In July 1099, Jerusalem fell to the crusaders, who sacked the city. Raymond of Aguilers, the author of the following account, was a priest who took part in the First Crusade and witnessed the fall of Jerusalem.

Now that our men had possession of the walls and towers, wonderful sights were to be seen. Some of our men (and this was more merciful) cut off the heads of their enemies; others shot them with arrows, so that they fell from the towers; others tortured them longer by casting them into the flames. Piles of heads, hands, and feet were to be seen in the streets of the city. It was necessary to pick one's way over the bodies of men and horses. But these were small matters compared to what happened at the Temple of Solomon, a place where religious services are ordinarily chanted. What happened there? If I tell the truth, it will exceed your powers of belief. So let it suffice to say this much, at least, that in the Temple and porch of Solomon, men rode in blood up to their knees and bridle reins. Indeed, it was a just and splendid judgment of God that this place should be filled with the blood of the unbelievers, since it had suffered so long from their blasphemies. The city was filled with corpses and blood. . . .

Now that the city was taken, it was well worth all our previous labors and hardships to see the devotion of the pilgrims at the Holy Sepulchre. How they rejoiced and exulted and sang a new song to the Lord! For their hearts offered prayers of praise to God, victorious and triumphant, which cannot be told in words. A new day, new joy, new and perpetual gladness, the consummation of our labor and devotion, drew forth from all new words and new songs. This day, I say, will be famous in all future ages, for it turned our labors and sorrows into joy and exultation; this day, I say, marks the justification of all Christianity, the humiliation of paganism, and the renewal of our faith.

August C. Krey, *The First Crusade: The Accounts of Eye-Witnesses and Participants*. Princeton, NJ: Princeton University Press, 1921.

Document 9: The Islamic Response to the Capture of Jerusalem

While the Europeans celebrated the victory of the First Crusade and the deliverance of Jerusalem into Christian hands, the Muslims of the Middle East were shocked and horrified at the turn of events. Abu l-Muzaffar al-Abiwardi, a poet from the region that is now Iraq, called for all Muslims to unite in defense of their brethren.

We have mingled blood with flowing tears, and there is no room left in us for pity.

To shed tears is a man's worst weapon when the swords stir up the embers of war.

Sons of Islam, behind you are battles in which heads rolled at your feet.

Dare you slumber in the blessed shade of safety, where life is as soft as an orchard flower?

How can the eye sleep between the lids at a time of disasters that would waken any sleeper?

While your Syrian brothers can only sleep on the backs of their chargers, or in vultures' bellies!

Must the foreigners feed on our ignominy, while you trail behind you the train of a pleasant life, like men whose world is at peace?

When blood has been spilt, when sweet girls must for shame hide their lovely faces in their hands!

When the white swords' points are red with blood, and the iron of the brown lances is stained with gore!

At the sound of sword hammering on lance young children's hair turns white.

This is war, and the man who shuns the whirlpool to save his life shall grind his teeth in penitence.

This is war, and the infidel's sword is naked in his hand, ready to be sheathed again in men's necks and skulls.

Francesco Gabrieli, *Arab Historians of the Crusades*, trans. E.J. Costello. London: Routledge & Kegan Paul, 1969.

Document 10: Settlers in the Holy Land

Fulcher of Chartres went on the First Crusade and afterwards settled in the Holy Land, living primarily in Jerusalem. Writing in his chronicle of the Crusade in the 1120s, Fulcher comments on the changes experienced by those Western Europeans who remained in the Middle East and established the crusader kingdoms.

Consider, I pray, and reflect how in our time God has transferred the West into the East. For we who were Occidentals now have been made Orientals. He who was a Roman or a Frank is now a Galilaean, or an inhabitant of Palestine. One who was a citizen of Rheims or of Chartres now has been made a citizen of Tyre or of Antioch. We have already forgotten the places of our birth; already they have become unknown to many of us, or, at least, are unmentioned. Some already possess here homes and servants which they have received through inheritance. Some have taken wives not merely of their own people, but Syrians, or Armenians, or even Saracens who have received the grace of baptism. Some have with them father-in-law, or daughter-in-law, or son-in-law, or step-son, or step-father. There are here, too, grandchildren and great-grandchildren. One cultivates vines, another the fields. The one and the other use mutually the speech and the idioms of the different languages. Different languages, now made common, become known to both races, and faith unites those whose forefathers were strangers. . . . Those who were strangers are now natives; and he who was a sojourner now has become a resident. Our parents and relatives from day to day come to join us, abandoning, even though reluctantly, all that they possess. For those who were poor there, here God makes rich. Those who had few coins, here possess countless besants; and those who had not had a villa, here, by the gift of God, already possess a city. Therefore, why should one who has found the East so favorable return to the West? God does not wish those to suffer want who, carrying their crosses, have vowed to follow Him, nay even unto the end. You see, therefore, that this is a great miracle, and one which must greatly astonish the whole world. Who has ever heard anything like it? Therefore, God wishes to enrich us all and to draw us to Himself as His most dear friends.

August C. Krey, *The First Crusade: The Accounts of Eye-Witnesses and Participants.* Princeton, NJ: Princeton University Press, 1921.

Document 11: The Muslims Retaliate

In December 1144, the Muslim army under the leadership of Zangi conquered the Frankish settlement of Edessa. The following account of

Zangi's strategy and victory was written by 'Izz ad-Din Ibn al-Athir, a Muslim scholar and historian.

'Imād ad-Din Zangi ibn Aq Sunqūr seized from the Franks the city of Edessa and other forts. . . . The Franks had penetrated far into this area. . . . Their influence extended from near Mardīn to the Euphrates. . . . These . . . regions west of the Euphrates belonged to Joscelin, the most famous of the Franks and the leader of their army by virtue of his valour and command of strategy. Zangi knew that if he made a direct attack on Edessa the Franks would concentrate there to defend it, and it was too well fortified to be an easy conquest. He moved to Diyār Bakr, to give the Franks the impression that his interests lay elsewhere and that he was in no position to attack their kingdom. When the Franks felt sure that he could not extract himself from the war he was fighting with the Artuqids and other princes at Diyār Bakr, and so felt safe from him, Joscelin left Edessa and crossed the Euphrates to move westwards. As soon as Zangi's spies informed him of this, he issued orders to his army to set out the next day for Edessa. . . .

They besieged the city and attacked it for three weeks. Zangi made several assaults on it, and used sappers to mine the walls. He was straining every nerve in the struggle, for fear that the Franks should marshal their forces and march on him to relieve the fortress. Then the sappers undermined the wall and it collapsed, and Zangi took the city and besieged the citadel. The citizens and their goods were seized, the young taken captive, the men killed. . . .

It is said that a great authority on genealogies and biographies tells the following story: the King of Sicily sent a naval expedition that ravaged Tripoli in North Africa. Now there was in Sicily a learned, God-fearing Muslim whom the King held in great respect, relying on his advice rather than that of his own priests and monks; so much so that the people used to say that the King was really a Muslim. One day, as the King was standing at a window overlooking the sea, he saw a small boat come into the harbour. The crew told him that his army had invaded Muslim territory, laid it waste and returned victorious. The Muslim sage was dozing at the King's side. The King said to him: 'Did you hear what they said?' 'No.' 'They told me that we have defeated the Muslims in Tripoli. What use is Muhammad now to his land and his people?' 'He was not there,' replied the old man, 'he was at Edessa, which the Muslims have just taken.' The Franks who were present laughed, but the King said: 'Do not laugh, for by God this man is incapable of speaking anything but the truth.' And a few days later news came from the Franks in Syria that Edessa had been taken. Certain honest and godly men have told me that a holy man saw the dead Zangi in a dream and asked him: 'How has God treated you?' and Zangi replied, 'God has pardoned me, because I conquered Edessa.'

Francesco Gabrieli, *Arab Historians of the Crusades*, trans. E.J. Costello. London: Routledge & Kegan Paul, 1969.

Document 12: Europe Reacts to the Loss of Edessa

The news of the sack of Edessa took several months to reach Western Europe. Upon hearing it, most Christians were horrified; many blamed the defeat on their own sinfulness. Pope Eugene II expressed similar sentiments in his December 1, 1145, papal bull that called for a new Crusade to help defend the crusader kingdoms.

How much the Roman pontiffs, our predecessors, have labored for the liberation of the Eastern Church, we have learned from the accounts of the ancients and have found written in their acts. For our predecessor, Pope Urban of blessed memory, sounded, as it were, the heavenly clarion and took care to rouse up from the various parts of the world the sons of the Roman Church for the liberation of the East. . . .

Now, however, because of our sins and those of the people—we cannot speak of it without much grief and lamentation—the city of Edessa, called Rohais in our language . . . has been captured by the enemies of Christ. They have occupied many Christian castles and they have killed the Archbishop of the city, his clergy, and many other Christians there. The relics of the saints, too, have been given over to be trampled upon by the infidel and have been dispersed. We are well aware (and we assume that it is not hidden from your wisdom) how much danger thereby threatens the church of God and all of Christendom. . . .

We therefore beseech, admonish, and command all of you, and we enjoin it for the remission of sins, that those who are on God's side—and especially the more powerful and noble men—that they gird themselves manfully and attack the pagan multitudes . . . liberate the Eastern church, and strive to wrest many thousands of our captive brethren from their hands. . . .

We also . . . decree and confirm by the authority given to us by God, the remission of sins (which our aforesaid predecessor, Pope Urban, established) for those who, prompted by devotion, shall undertake and accomplish such a holy and necessary task. We decree, also, that the wives and sons, goods and possessions of these men shall remain under the protection of Holy Church, of ourselves, and of the archbishops, bishops, and other prelates of the Church of God. We forbid, also by the apostolic authority, that any suit be brought concerning those things which they possessed peacefully at the time they took the cross until such time as there shall be certain tidings of their return or of their death. Since, moreover, those who fight for the Lord ought in no way to concern themselves with costly garments, bodily appearance, dogs, hawks, or other things which are signs of licentiousness, we admonish your prudence in the Lord that those who undertake such holy work shall not be taken up with these things, but shall, with all their strength, devote their attention and diligence to arms, horses, and other things with which they may war on the infidel. Those who are laden with debt to another and who shall, with pure heart, begin the holy journey, shall not pay interest for time past. If they, or others for them, are bound by oath or pledge for the payment of interest, we absolve them by the apostolic authority. It shall be allowed to them also that when, after their relations or the lords to whom their fiefs belong, have been warned, if these people either can not or do not wish to lend them money, then they may freely and without contradiction pledge their lands or other possessions to churches, to churchmen, or to any of the other faithful.

James A. Brundage, *Crusades: A Documentary Survey*. Milwaukee: Marquette University Press, 1962.

Document 13: Frederick Barbarossa Threatens Saladin

In March 1188, at nearly seventy years of age, the Holy Roman Emperor, Frederick Barbarossa, vowed to take part in the Third Crusade. During his preparations for his departure for the Holy Land, Frederick wrote to the Muslim leader Saladin, advising him to peacefully surrender Jerusalem lest he face the wrath of the crusaders.

Frederick, by the grace of God ever-august ruler of the Holy Roman Empire, and mighty conqueror of its enemies, to Saladin, protector of the Saracens. I bid you quit Jerusalem as the pharaohs of old fled before the Jews. As befits our majesty, we acknowledge the receipt of many letters sent to us in the past by your highness concerning this difficult business, letters which would have served your purpose better if there had been any sincere intention behind the words. We have now decided to address your majesty by letter in return.

You have profaned that holy land over which we rule by command of the Eternal King, as guardian of Judaea, Samaria and Palestine. Concern for our imperial office demands that we look with serious attention upon a crime of such bold and heinous presumptuousness. Wherefore we require you to give back the land, and everything that you have taken, and, in addition, to pay a fine commensurate with such dreadful crimes, as laid down by divine law.

Otherwise, lest we appear to be initiating an unjust war, we now fix a date a year from 1 November 1188, for a trial by battle, by the merit of the life-giving Cross and in the name of the true Joseph.

With God's help you will find out by experience what our conquering eagles can do, our battalions of many races, the wild German flying to arms even in time of peace, the untamed folk from the source of the Rhine, the young men of the Danube who do not know the meaning of flight, tall Bavarians and crafty Swabians. Then there are the wary Franconians, the sword-players of Saxony, the restless Burgundians and lecherous Alpine tribes; Bohemians eager for death, Bolognians wilder than their own wild beasts, pilots from Venice, sea-captains from Pisa.

In the end, on the day I have named, a day of joy, gladness and reverence for Christ, you will also find out that my own right hand, which you accuse of being feeble with age, has not forgotten how to wield a sword.

Elizabeth Hallam, ed., *Chronicles of the Crusades: Nine Crusades and Two Hundred Years of Bitter Conflict for the Holy Land Brought to Life Through the Words of Those Who Were Actually There.* New York: Weidenfeld and Nicolson, 1989.

Document 14: Saladin's Defiant Reply

Saladin's answer to Frederick Barbarossa's letter expresses his willingness to meet the crusaders on the battlefield and his confidence of the Muslims' superior strength. However, the anticipated battle between Frederick and Saladin never took place, as Frederick accidentally drowned while en route to the Holy Land.

To that true king and our friend, the great and noble Frederick, ruler of Germany, in the name of God the compassionate, by the grace of the one God, the powerful and all-surpassing victor, the everlasting, of whose reign there is no end.

We would beg to inform that true, great and mighty king, our good friend the ruler of Germany, that a certain man called Henry of Dietz has arrived here saying he is your messenger, bringing us a certain document which he says is from you. We have caused this document to be read and, after hearing what he had to say, given him a spoken answer. This is our written reply to the document.

If you are going to reckon up those who share your intention of coming against us, naming them and saying 'the king of this or that country, such-and-such a count, archbishop, marquis, or warrior', and if we wanted to specify those who are in our service, those who obey our command, ready at our word, those who would fight in our forces—all this could not be contained in writing.

If you are counting up numbers of Christians, there are more, many more, Saracens than they. Moreover, there is an ocean between you and your counted Christians, while there is none between the countless Saracens and ourselves, nothing to hinder their coming to our aid. The Bedouins are with us—who would be enough by themselves to deal with our enemies—and the Turks; if we set them loose on our foes they would annihilate them. At our bidding the peasants would fight vigorously against anyone invading their land, plundering them and wiping them out. . . .

And when, as your letter says, you are all gathered together, with the enormous multitude your messenger talks of, it is in God's might that we shall come out against you. The coastal lands will not be enough for us. God willing, we will sail across, and, with his strength, take possession of all your territories. For, if you come, you will bring every resource with you, you will be over here with all your people. We are well aware that no one will be left in your country able to defend himself, let alone safeguard the land. When God, in his strength, has granted us victory over you, all that remains will be the unopposed capture, by that same strength and will, of all your possessions. . . .

Our people are well endowed with lands. God has richly added unto us territories far and wide, held in our power, Egypt with its dependencies, the land of Damascus, coastal Jerusalem, Mesopotamia with its castles, Edessa and India with their adjuncts. By God's grace all these are in our hands and all the rest of the Saracen realm bows to our rule. . . . By God's power and might we have captured Jerusalem with its land; only three cities remain in Christian hands, Tyre, Tripoli and Antioch, and these will inevitably be taken.

Elizabeth Hallam, ed., *Chronicles of the Crusades: Nine Crusades and Two Hundred Years of Bitter Conflict for the Holy Land Brought to Life Through the Words of Those Who Were Actually There.* New York: Weidenfeld and Nicolson, 1989.

Document 15: Showing Kindness to the Enemy

Although the Crusades mainly consisted of brutal warfare, acts of mercy and chivalry occurred on both sides. Saladin's periodic acts of benevolence were attested to by both the Muslims and the crusaders. The following is excerpted from a biography of Saladin written by Baha' ad-Din Ibn Shaddad, who served Saladin as a household retainer and official.

The Sultan [Saladin] was distinguished by the nobility of his conduct, the benevolence of his regard, his great modesty and extraordinary affability to his guests. He would not permit anyone who visited him to leave without eating with him, or to ask for something without receiving it. Everyone who appeared before him was treated with honour, even an infidel. . . .

Once a Frankish prisoner was brought before him in whom the Sultan aroused such fear that the marks of terror and agitation were visible in his face. The interpreter asked him: 'What are you afraid of?' God inspired him to reply: 'At first I was afraid of seeing that face, but after seeing it and standing in his presence, I am sure that I shall see only good in it.' The Sultan was moved, pardoned him and let him go free.

One day when I was on duty I was riding with him ahead of the Franks when a sentry brought up a woman who was in a distracted state, weeping and beating her breast. 'This woman,' said the sentry, 'has come from the Frankish camp and asked to be brought before the Sultan, so we brought her here.' The Sultan told the interpreter to ask her what was the matter, and she said that Muslim raiders had come into her tent the day before and had carried off her little daughter. 'All night long I have been seeking help, until this morning our leaders told me: "The Muslim King is merciful; we will let you leave the camp to go to him, and you can ask him for your daughter." So they let me come, and you are my only hope of getting my baby back again.' Saladin was moved to pity by her plight, and tears came into his eyes. His generous spirit prompted him to order someone to take her to the market-place in the camp to ask who had bought the child, repay him and bring her back. All this occurred in the morning; not an hour passed before the knight returned with the child on his shoulders. As soon as her mother caught sight of her she fell to the ground, rubbing her face in the dust, while everyone there wept with her. She raised her face to heaven, but we could not understand what she said. Her daughter was handed over to her and she was conducted back to her own camp.

Francesco Gabrieli, *Arab Historians of the Crusades*, trans. E.J. Costello. London: Routledge & Kegan Paul, 1969.

Document 16: Women Warriors Among the Franks

'Imad ad-Din al-Isfahani was Saladin's secretary during the Third Cru-sade. In the following passage, he describes the crusader women who fought alongside the men.

Another person to arrive by sea was a noblewoman who was very wealthy. She was a queen in her own land, and arrived accompa-nied by five hundred knights with their horses and money, pages and valets, she paying all their expenses and treating them gener-ously out of her wealth. They rode out when she rode out, charged when she charged, flung themselves into the fray at her side, their ranks unwavering as long as she stood firm.

Among the Franks there were indeed women who rode into bat-tle with cuirasses and helmets, dressed in men's clothes; who rode out into the thick of the fray and acted like brave men although they were but tender women, maintaining that all this was an act of piety, thinking to gain heavenly rewards by it, and making it their way of life. Praise be to him who led them into such error and out of the paths of wisdom! On the day of battle more than one woman rode out with them like a knight and showed (masculine) endurance in spite of the weakness (of her sex); clothed only in a coat of mail they were not recognized as women until they had been stripped of their arms. Some of them were discovered and sold as slaves; and everywhere was full of old women. These were sometimes a sup-port and sometimes a source of weakness. They exhorted and in-cited men to summon their pride, saying that the Cross imposed on them the obligation to resist to the bitter end, and that the com-batants would win eternal life only by sacrificing their lives, and that their God's sepulchre was in enemy hands.

Francesco Gabrieli, *Arab Historians of the Crusades*, trans. E.J. Costello. London: Routledge & Kegan Paul, 1969.

Document 17: A Clash of Cultures

The crusaders and the Muslims varied greatly in cultural practices and social mores. Usamah Ibn-Munqidh, a Syrian writer and courtier who lived during the first three Crusades and interacted frequently with the Franks, examines some of their stranger customs in his memoirs.

Mysterious are the works of the Creator, the author of all things! When one comes to recount cases regarding the Franks, he cannot but glorify Allah (exalted is he!) and sanctify him, for he sees them as animals possessing the virtues of courage and fighting, but noth-ing else; just as animals have only the virtues of strength and carrying loads. I shall now give some instances of their doings and their curious mentality. . . .

The lord of al-Munaytirah wrote to my uncle asking him to dispatch a physician to treat certain sick persons among his people. My uncle sent him a Christian physician named Thābit. Thābit was absent but ten days when he returned. So we said to him, "How quickly hast thou healed thy patients!" He said:

> They brought before me a knight in whose leg an abscess had grown; and a woman afflicted with imbecility. To the knight I applied a small poultice until the abscess opened and became well; and the woman I put on diet and made her humor wet. Then a Frankish physician came to them and said, "This man knows nothing about treating them." He then said to the knight, "Which wouldst thou prefer, living with one leg or dying with two?" The latter replied, "Living with one leg." The physician said, "Bring me a strong knight and a sharp ax." A knight came with the ax. And I was standing by. Then the physician laid the leg of the patient on a block of wood and bade the knight strike his leg with the ax and chop it off at one blow. Accordingly he struck it—while I was looking on—one blow, but the leg was not severed. He dealt another blow, upon which the marrow of the leg flowed out and the patient died on the spot. He then examined the woman and said, "This is a woman in whose head there is a devil which has possessed her. Shave off her hair." Accordingly they shaved it off and the woman began once more to eat their ordinary diet—garlic and mustard. Her imbecility took a turn for the worse. The physician then said, "The devil has penetrated through her head." He therefore took a razor, made a deep cruciform incision on it, peeled off the skin at the middle of the incision until the bone of the skull was exposed and rubbed it with salt. The woman also expired instantly. Thereupon I asked them whether my services were needed any longer, and when they replied in the negative I returned home, having learned of their medicine what I knew not before. . . .

I attended one day a duel in Nāblus between two Franks. The reason for this was that certain Moslem thieves took by surprise one of the villages of Nāblus. One of the peasants of that village was charged with having acted as guide for the thieves when they fell upon the village. So he fled away. The king sent and arrested his children. The peasant thereupon came back to the king and said, "Let justice be done in my case. I challenge to a duel the man who claimed that I guided the thieves to the village." The king then said to the tenant who held the village in fief, "Bring forth someone to fight the duel with him." The tenant went to his village, where a blacksmith lived, took hold of him and ordered him to fight the duel. The tenant became thus sure of the safety of his own peasants, none of whom would be killed and his estate ruined.

I saw this blacksmith. He was a physically strong young man, but his heart failed him. He would walk a few steps and then sit down and ask for a drink. The one who had made the challenge was an old man, but he was strong in spirit and he would rub the nail of his thumb against that of the forefinger in defiance, as if he was not worrying over the duel. Then came the viscount, i.e., the seignior of the town, and gave each one of the two contestants a cudgel and a shield and arranged the people in a circle around them.

The two met. The old man would press the blacksmith backward until he would get him as far the circle, then he would come back to the middle of the arena. They went on exchanging blows until they looked like pillars smeared with blood. The contest was prolonged and the viscount began to urge them to hurry, saying, "Hurry on." The fact that the smith was given to the use of the hammer proved now of great advantage to him. The old man was worn out and the smith gave him a blow which made him fall. His cudgel fell under his back. The smith knelt down over him and tried to stick his fingers into the eyes of his adversary, but could not do it because of the great quantity of blood flowing out. Then he rose up and hit his head with the cudgel until he killed him. They then fastened a rope around the neck of the dead person, dragged him away and hanged him. The lord who brought the smith now came, gave the smith his own mantle, made him mount the horse behind him and rode off with him. This case illustrates the kind of jurisprudence and legal decisions the Franks have—may Allah's curse be upon them!

An Arab-Syrian Gentleman and Warrior in the Period of the Crusades: Memoirs of Usamah Ibn-Munqidh, trans. Philip K. Hitti. Princeton, NJ: Princeton University Press, 1987.

Document 18: A Fiery Fleet

Geoffroy de Villehardouin was a French noble who fought in the Fourth Crusade and took part in the siege of Constantinople. In his chronicle The Conquest of Constantinople, *Villehardouin describes the Greeks' ingenious attempt to destroy the crusaders' fleet.*

Thus the war began; and each side did its utmost to harm the other, both by sea and on land. The two armies fought against each other in many different places, but—God be praised—they never met in battle without heavier losses on the Greek side than on the French. The war went on for a very long time, right into the middle of the winter.

Finally, the Greeks thought of putting a very terrifying plan into operation. They took seventeen great ships, and filled them full of logs and shavings, pitch and tow, and wooden barrels. Then they waited until the wind was blowing from their side of the water. One night, at twelve o'clock, they set fire to the ships, and let them drift with all their sails unfurled to the wind. The flames from them rose so high that it seemed as if the whole world was on fire.

The ships came sailing on towards the Crusaders' fleet; the bugles sounded the alert, and from everywhere in the camp men sprang to arms. The Venetians and others who had ships hastened to get aboard them, and strove with all their might and main to take them out of range of danger. Geoffroy de Villehardouin, who composed this chronicle and was an eye-witness of the incident, affirms that no men ever defended themselves more gallantly on the sea than the Venetians did that night. They leapt into galleys and into longboats, and, in the face of the enemy, laid hold of the fire-ships, all ablaze as they were, with grappling irons, and forcibly pulling them out of the harbour into the main current of the straits, left them to drift burning out to sea.

So many Greeks had come down to the water's edge that there seemed to be no end to them; the noise they made was so great you would have thought both earth and sea were being swallowed up. They clambered into any boats they could find, and shot at our men as they were fighting the flames, so that many of them were wounded.

As soon as they had heard the call to arms the knights in camp had all got ready. Now our battalions poured out on to the plain in somewhat random order, according to the distance from their quarters. They were afraid the Greeks would advance from that direction to attack them.

Our men endured all this toil and anguish till it was light; but by God's help we lost nothing, except for a merchant ship laden with goods from Pisa, which caught fire and sank. We had all been in deadly peril that night, for if our fleet had been burned we should have lost everything, and could not have got away either by sea or by land.

Joinville and Villehardouin: Chronicles of the Crusades, trans. M.R.B. Shaw. New York: Dorset Press, 1985.

Document 19: The Sack of Constantinople

The sack of Constantinople was perhaps the darkest moment of the Crusades, as crusaders looted churches and abbeys of their treasures. The

Greek chronicler Nicetas Choniates bemoans the great sufferings visited on his people by their fellow Christians.

How shall I begin to tell of the deeds wrought by these nefarious men! Alas, the images, which ought to have been adored, were trodden under foot! Alas, the relics of the holy martyrs were thrown into unclean places! Then was seen what one shudders to hear, namely, the divine body and blood of Christ was spilled upon the ground or thrown about. They snatched the precious reliquaries, thrust into their bosoms the ornaments which these contained, and used the broken remnants for pans and drinking cups. . . .

Nor can the violation of the Great Church [St. Sophia] be listened to with equanimity. For the sacred altar, formed of all kinds of precious materials and admired by the whole world, was broken into bits and distributed among the soldiers, as was all the other sacred wealth of so great and infinite splendor. . . .

Nay more, a certain harlot, a sharer in their guilt, a minister of the furies, a servant of the demons, a worker of incantations and poisonings, insulting Christ, sat in the patriarch's seat, singing an obscene song and dancing frequently. Nor, indeed, were these crimes committed and others left undone, on the ground that these were of lesser guilt, the others of greater. But with one consent all the most heinous sins and crimes were committed by all with equal zeal. Could those, who showed so great madness against God Himself, have spared the honorable matrons and maidens or the virgins consecrated to God? . . .

No one was without a share in the grief. In the alleys, in the streets, in the temples, complaints, weeping, lamentations, grief, the groaning of men, the shrieks of women, wounds, rape, captivity, the separation of those most closely united. Nobles wandered about ignominiously, those of venerable age in tears, the rich in poverty. Thus it was in the streets, on the corners, in the temple, in the dens, for no place remained unassailed or defended the suppliants. All places everywhere were filled full of all kinds of crime. Oh, immortal God, how great the afflictions of the men, how great the distress!

Dana C. Munro, *The Fourth Crusade.* Philadelphia: University of Pennsylvania Press, 1901.

Document 20: Sacred Booty

Gunther of Paris also chronicled the sack of Constantinople, but he told the story from the crusaders' point of view. In the following excerpt, Gunther narrates a Catholic abbot's search for holy relics to steal from the Greeks.

While the victors were rapidly plundering the conquered city, which was theirs by right of conquest, the abbot Martin began to cogitate about his own share of the booty, and lest he alone should remain empty-handed, while all the others became rich, he resolved to seize upon plunder with his own sacred hands. But, since he thought it not meet [fitting] to handle any booty of worldly things with those sacred hands, he began to plan how he might secure some portion of the relics of the saints, of which he knew there was a great quantity in the city.

Accordingly, having a presentiment of some great result, he took with him one of his two chaplains and went to a church. . . .

There he found an aged man of agreeable countenance, having a long and hoary beard, a priest, but very unlike our priests in his dress. Thinking him a layman, the abbot, though inwardly calm, threatened him with a very ferocious voice, saying: "Come, perfidious old man, show me the most powerful relics you have, or you shall die immediately." The latter, terrified by the sound rather than the words, since he heard but did not understand what was said, and knowing that Martin could not speak Greek, began in the *Romana lingua* [Latin], of which he knew a little, to entreat Martin and by soft words to turn away the latter's wrath, which in truth did not exist. In reply, the abbot succeeded in getting out a few words of the same language, sufficient to make the old man understand what he wanted. The latter, observing Martin's face and dress, and thinking it more tolerable that a religious man should handle the sacred relics with fear and reverence, than that worldly men should, perchance, pollute them with their worldly hands, opened a chest bound with iron and showed the desired treasure, which was more grateful and pleasing to Martin than all the royal wealth of Greece. The abbot hastily and eagerly thrust in both hands and working quickly, filled with the fruits of the sacrilege both his own and his chaplain's bosom. He wisely concealed what seemed the most valuable and departed without opposition. . . .

When he was hastening to his vessel, so stuffed full, if I may use the expression, those who knew and loved him, saw him from their ships as they were themselves hastening to the booty, and inquired joyfully whether he had stolen anything, or with what he was so loaded down as he walked. With a joyful countenance, as always, and with pleasant words he said: "We have done well." To which they replied: "Thanks be to God."

Dana C. Munro, *The Fourth Crusade*. Philadelphia: University of Pennsylvania Press, 1901.

Document 21: Pope Innocent III's Reprimand

Pope Innocent III was furious when he heard that the Fourth Crusade, instead of going to the aid of the crusader kingdoms, had captured Constantinople. In this letter from July 12, 1204, the pope sharply takes to task one of the papal legates who was with the crusaders at Constantinople.

To Peter, Cardinal Priest of the Title of St. Marcellus, Legate of the Apostolic See.

We were not a little astonished and disturbed to hear that you and our beloved son the Cardinal Priest of the Title of St. Praxida and Legate of the Apostolic See, in fear of the looming perils of the Holy Land, have left the province of Jerusalem (which, at this point is in such great need) and that you have gone by ship to Constantinople. And now we see that what we dreaded has occurred and what we feared has come to pass. . . . For you, who ought to have looked for help for the Holy Land, you who should have stirred up others, both by word and by example, to assist the Holy Land—on your own initiative you sailed to Greece, bringing in your footsteps not only the pilgrims, but even the natives of the Holy Land who came to Constantinople, following our venerable brother, the Archbishop of Tyre. When you had deserted it, the Holy Land remained destitute of men, void of strength. Because of you, its last state was worse than the first, for all its friends deserted with you; nor was there any admirer to console it. . . . We ourselves were not a little agitated and, with reason, we acted against you, since you had fallen in with this counsel and because you had deserted the Land which the Lord consecrated by his presence, the land in which our King marvelously performed the mystery of our redemption. . . .

It was your duty to attend to the business of your legation and to give careful consideration, not to the capture of the Empire of Constantinople, but rather to the defense of what is left of the Holy Land and, with the Lord's leave, the restoration of what has been lost. . . .

How, indeed, is the Greek church to be brought back into ecclesiastical union and to a devotion for the Apostolic See when she has been beset with so many afflictions and persecutions that she sees in the Latins only an example of perdition and the works of darkness, so that she now, and with reason, detests the Latins more than dogs? As for those who were supposed to be seeking the ends of Jesus Christ, not their own ends, whose swords, which they were supposed to use against the pagans, are now dripping with Christian blood—they have spared neither age nor sex. They have committed incest, adultery, and fornication before the eyes of men. They have exposed both matrons and virgins, even those dedicated to God, to the sordid lusts of boys. Not satisfied with breaking open the imperial treasury and plundering the goods of princes and lesser men, they also laid their hands on the treasures of the churches and, what is more serious, on their very possessions. They have even ripped silver plates from the altars and have hacked them to pieces among themselves. They violated the holy places and have carried off crosses and relics.

James A. Brundage, *Crusades: A Documentary Survey.* Milwaukee: Marquette University Press, 1962.

Document 22: Frederick II's Visit to Jerusalem

Frederick II, the Holy Roman Emperor, led the relatively peaceful Sixth Crusade and regained Jerusalem for the Christians. During his brief stay in Jerusalem in 1229, Frederick showed interest in Islam and Middle Eastern culture. This illustrative anecdote was recorded by Syrian author Sibt Ibn al-Jauzi.

The Emperor . . . had a red skin, and was bald and shortsighted. Had he been a slave he would not have been worth two hundred *dirham*. It was clear from what he said that he was a materialist and that his Christianity was simply a game to him. Al-Kamil had ordered the Qadi of Nablus, Shams ad-Din, to tell the muezzins that during the Emperor's stay in Jerusalem they were not to go up into their minarets and give the call to prayer in the sacred precinct. The qadi forgot to tell the muezzins, and so the muezzin 'Abd al-Karim mounted his minaret at dawn and began to recite the Qur'anic [Koranic] verses about the Christians, such as 'God has no son', referring to Jesus son of Mary, and other such texts. In the morning the qadi called 'Abd al-Karim to him and said: 'What have you done? The Sultan's command was thus and thus.' He replied: 'You did not tell me; I am sorry.' The second night he did not give the call. The next morning the Emperor summoned the qadi, who had come to Jerusalem as his personal adviser and had been responsible for handing the city over to him, and said: 'O qadi, where is the man who yesterday climbed the minaret and spoke these words?' The qadi told him of the Sultan's orders. 'You did wrong, qadi; would you alter your rites and law and faith for my sake? If you were staying in my country, would I order the bells to be silenced for your sake? By God, do not do this; this is the first time that we have found fault in you!'

Francesco Gabrieli, *Arab Historians of the Crusades*, trans. E.J. Costello. London: Routledge & Kegan Paul, 1969.

Document 23: Taken Captive

The French nobleman Jean de Joinville accompanied King Louis IX on the Seventh Crusade and later recorded his experiences in The Life of St. Louis. *Here Joinville relates how he and his crew were captured by the Muslims—and how quick thinking and good fortune saved his life.*

We saw four of the sultan's galleys coming towards us, with a good thousand men aboard. So I called my knights and the rest of my men together and asked them which they would prefer—to surrender to the sultan's galleys or to the Saracens on shore. We all agreed that we would rather surrender to the sultan's galleys, because in that way we should remain together, than yield ourselves to the enemy on land, who would separate us, and sell us to the Bedouins. . . .

Then one of my crew said to me: 'My lord, unless you give us leave to say you're the king's cousin, they'll kill everyone of you, and us along with you.' So I told him I was quite willing for him to say what he liked.

As soon as the men on the foremost galley, which was coming towards us to ram us amidships, heard this man's announcement, they cast anchor alongside our boat. At this juncture God sent me a Saracen from the Emperor of Germany's land. He came swimming across the stream, clad in breeches of unbleached linen, and got aboard our ship. He clasped me round the waist and said to me: 'My lord, unless you act quickly and resolutely you are lost. What you must do is to leap from your ship on to the prow that overhangs the keel of this galley. If you do this, no one will notice you, for they're thinking only of the booty to be gained from your ship.' A rope was flung to me from the galley, and by God's will I leapt on to the projecting deck. I was, however, so unsteady on my feet, that if the Saracen had not leapt after me to hold me up I should have fallen back into the water.

I was drawn forward into the galley, where there were a good two hundred and eighty of the enemy, while the Saracen still kept his arms around me. Then they threw me to the ground and flung themselves on my body to cut my throat, for any man who killed me would have thought to win honour by it. But the Saracen still held me in his arms, and cried: 'He's the king's cousin!' All the same they twice bore me to the ground, and once forced me to my knees. It was then I felt the knife at my throat. But in this ordeal God saved me with the help of the Saracen, who led me to one of the castles on the ship where the Saracen knights were assembled. . . .

The admiral in command of the galleys sent for me and asked

me whether I really were the king's cousin. I answered 'No,' and told him how and why the sailor had said I was. The admiral told me I had acted wisely, for otherwise we should all have been put to death. He asked if by any chance I happened to be related to the Emperor Frederick of Germany. I replied that I had reason to believe that my lady mother was his first cousin; whereupon the admiral remarked that he loved me all the more for it. . . .

He subsequently had all my crew brought before me, and told me that every one of them had renounced their faith. I warned him not to put any trust in them, for just as lightly as they had left our side so they would leave his, if they saw either time or opportunity to do so. The admiral replied that he agreed with me, for as Saladin used to say, one never saw a bad Christian become a good Saracen, nor a bad Saracen become a good Christian.

Joinville and Villehardouin: Chronicles of the Crusades, trans. M.R.B. Shaw. New York: Dorset Press, 1985.

Document 24: Baybars's Victory

Sultan Baybars of Egypt captured the Christian city of Antioch in May 1268, slaughtering or enslaving the inhabitants. Prince Bohemond of Antioch (who was also the count of Tripoli) was absent from the city when Baybars's forces overran it. Therefore, Baybars sent Bohemond the following letter to break the bad news.

The Glorious Count Bohemond, magnificent and magnanimous, having the courage of a lion, being the glory of the nation of Jesus, the head of the Christian church and the leader of the people of the Messiah, who no longer bears the title of Prince of Antioch, since Antioch has been lost to him, but is reduced to a mere count, may God show him the way and give him a good death and help him to remember my words. . . .

We took Antioch by the sword on the fourth hour of Saturday on the fourth day of Ramadan, and we destroyed all those you had chosen to guard the city. All these men had possessions, and all their possessions have passed into our hands.

Oh, if only you had seen your knights trampled by our horses, your houses looted and at the mercy of everyone who passed by, your treasure weighed by the quintal, your women sold in the market-place four for a gold *dinar.* If only you had seen your churches utterly destroyed, the crucifixes torn apart, the pages of the Gospels scattered, the tombs of the patriarchs trodden underfoot. If only you had seen your Muslim enemy trampling down your altars and holy of holies, cutting the throats of deacons, priests and bishops, the patriarchate irremediably abolished, the powerful reduced to powerlessness! If only you had seen your palaces given over to the flames, the dead devoured by the flames of this world before being devoured by the flames of the next world, your castles and all their attendant buildings wiped off the face of the earth, the Church of St. Paul totally destroyed so that nothing is left of it, and seeing all this you would have said: "Would to God that I were dust! Would to God! Would to God that I had never received the letter with these melancholy tidings!". . .

This letter is sent to congratulate you that God has seen fit to preserve you and to prolong your days. All this you owe to the fact that you were not in Antioch when we captured it. If you had taken part in the battle, then you would either be dead, or a prisoner, or riddled with wounds. You must take great joy in being alive, for there is nothing so joyful as escaping from a great calamity. Perhaps God gave you this respite so that you could make amends for your former disobedience toward Him. And since no one from your city survived to tell you the news, it has fallen upon us to give you these tidings; and since also no one from your city is in any position to congratulate you on your own survival, this too has been left to us. Nor can you accuse us of saying anything false, nor do you need to go elsewhere to learn the truth.

Robert Payne, *The Dream and the Tomb: A History of the Crusades*. London: Robert Hale Limited, 1986.

Document 25: The Fall of Acre

The Muslim conquest of Acre in May 1291 marked the beginning of the end for the crusader kingdoms and the Western European presence in the Holy Land. This account of the fall of Acre was written by a chronicler known only as the Templar of Tyre.

Henry II of Lusignan, king of Jerusalem and Cyprus, had summoned his forces in Cyprus; he collected them, left Famagusta, and arrived in Acre on 4 May 1291.

A few days after King Henry arrived, envoys were sent to the sultan. The sultan left his tent and went to the gate in the town called the Legate's Gate; all shooting was forbidden.

The envoys came unarmed into the sultan's presence. He asked, 'Have you brought me the keys of the town?' But the envoys replied that this was not a city to be surrendered so easily and they had come to ask him to show some sort of mercy to the poor people. To this Sultan al-Ashraf Khalil answered, 'I will do you this much grace: give me nothing but the stones; take everything else and go out and go away. I do this for the sake of your king who is young, as I am myself.'

The envoys told him that this was not possible and he said, 'Then go away, for I will not do anything else for you.'. . .

The envoys went back into Acre and both sides resumed shooting at each other with mangonels [missile-throwing engines], and behaving like enemies. When the new tower, known as the King's Tower, was taken, most men sent their wives and children out to sea in ships. In the morning of Thursday 17 May, the weather was so bad and the sea so rough that the women and children could not bear it and went back to their homes.

Then on Friday 18 May 1291, before daybreak, there came the loud and terrible sound of a kettledrum, and as the drum sounded, the Saracens assaulted the city of Acre on every side. The place where they first got in was through this damned tower which they had taken.

They came in countless numbers, all on foot; in front came men with great tall shields, after them men throwing Greek fire, and then men who shot bolts and feathered arrows so thickly that they seemed like rain falling from the sky.

When Henry of Lusignan, king of Jerusalem and Cyprus, witnessed this disaster, he went to the master of the Hospitallers; they saw clearly that no advice or help could do any good, so they fled and went aboard the galleys.

That day was appalling, for nobles and citizens, women and girls were frantic with terror; they went running through the streets, their children in their arms, weeping and desperate; they fled to the sea-shore to escape death, and when the Saracens caught them one would take the mother and the other the child, they would drag them from place to place and pull them apart; and sometimes two Saracens would quarrel over a woman and she would be killed; or a woman was taken and her sucking child flung to the ground where it died under the horses' hooves.

Elizabeth Hallam, ed., *Chronicles of the Crusades: Nine Crusades and Two Hundred Years of Bitter Conflict for the Holy Land Brought to Life Through the Words of Those Who Were Actually There.* New York: Weidenfeld and Nicolson, 1989.

Document 26: A Crusader Bids his Love Farewell

During the crusading period, many songs were composed about the heartache felt by crusaders who were leaving their homes and their loved ones for a dangerous journey from which they might not return. The date of this anonymous French song is not known, but it surely expresses the feelings of many crusaders throughout the two hundred years of the crusading movement.

To have perfect joy in paradise
I must leave the land I love so much,
Where she lives whom I thank every day.
Her body is noble and spirited, her face fresh and lovely;
And my true heart surrenders all to her.
But my body must take its leave of her:
I am departing for the place where God suffered death
To ransom us on a Friday.

Sweet love, I have great sorrow in my heart
Now that at last I must leave you,
With whom I have found so much good, such tenderness,
Joy and gaiety to charm me.
But Fortune by her power has made me
Exchange my joy for the sadness and sorrow
I will feel for you many nights and many days.
Thus will I go to serve my creator.

No more than a child can endure hunger—
And no one can chastise him for crying because of it—
Do I believe that I can stay away
From you, whom I am used to kiss and to embrace,
Nor have I in me such power of abstinence.
A hundred times a night I shall recall your beauty:
It gave me such pleasure to hold your body!
When I no longer have it I shall die of desire.

Good Lord God, if I for you
Leave the country where she is that I love so,
Grant us in heaven everlasting joy,
My love and me, through your mercy,
And grant her the strength to love me,
So that she will not forget me in my long absence,
For I love her more than anything in the world
And I feel so sad about her that my heart is breaking.

Louise and Jonathan Riley-Smith, *The Crusades: Idea and Reality, 1095–1274.* London: Edward Arnold, 1981.

Discussion Questions

Chapter 1: The Origins of the Holy Wars

1. Alfred Duggan outlines the historical events that preceded the First Crusade. According to Duggan, what crucial turning points led to the attempt by Western Europeans to regain Jerusalem? What role did the Battle of Manzikert play in the decision to declare the First Crusade?

2. Sidney Painter argues that the solidification of the feudal system and the Clunaic reforms of the Catholic Church in the eleventh century enabled the Crusades to occur. In his opinion, what were the advantages and disadvantages of feudalism? In what ways did the Clunaic reforms change the operations of the church?

3. Robert Payne asserts that Urban II was the ideal pope to spur the crusading movement. What qualities did Urban possess that allowed him to gain popular support for the First Crusade? What were Urban's motives in preaching the Crusade? What authority did he hope to secure for the Catholic Church?

4. Urban's presentation of the First Crusade as an armed pilgrimage was important to his success, in Marcus Bull's opinion. How were pilgrims to Jerusalem treated by "the infidels," according to accounts of Urban's speech at Clermont? In what ways was the German pilgrimage of 1064–65 a precursor of the First Crusade?

5. Hans Eberhard Mayer writes that Western Europe's economic problems caused many young men to decide to find their fortune in the Holy Land. What was the only other "safety valve" allowed to younger sons, according to Mayer, and why did many of them consider crusading a superior choice?

Chapter 2: Why Participants Went on the Crusades

1. Crusaders went to the Holy Land for many reasons, not all of them noble or spiritual in nature, as Ronald C. Finucane describes. How did the typical crusader interpret the promise of the Crusade indulgence, in Finucane's opinion? What practical benefits might have motivated the crusaders? Provide examples from the text.

2. Jonathan Riley-Smith depicts the ceremony of "taking the

cross" and the symbolism surrounding it. According to the author, of what elements did the ceremony typically consist? What special legal rights were conferred on those who took the cross? What spiritual benefits did they hope to obtain?

3. Henry Treece examines two important military orders that arose in the Holy Land. What was the original function of the Knights Hospitallers, according to Treece, and how had its primary purpose changed by 1118? What were the three classes of the Knights Templar, and which services did each class perform? What characteristics of the military orders enabled them to significantly affect life in the Middle East?

4. The Children's Crusade was one of the strangest and most tragic events of the crusading movement. In the view of Norman P. Zacour, why did these peasant children believe they could conquer the Holy Land when kings and nobles had failed? Why was the Children's Crusade tolerated more than the Shepherds' Crusade of 1251? In which areas of Europe did movements of intense religious enthusiasm often arise, and why?

Chapter 3: Social Changes and Cultural Influences of the Crusades

1. Crusaders who settled in the East eventually adopted many customs of the region, explains Antony Bridge. According to the author, which two aspects of the crusader kingdoms never changed? What two things prevented the Franks from fully assimilating with their Muslim neighbors?

2. The relations between the European crusaders and the Eastern Christians were uneven, maintains R.C. Smail. How did the Western Christians who settled in the crusader kingdoms regard the Eastern Christians of the area? In what ways did the Christians of the Middle East have more in common with their Muslim neighbors than with the crusaders? Cite the text to support your answer.

3. Ronald C. Finucane explores the impact of the Crusades on women and Jews. What types of women went crusading, according to Finucane, and what perils did they face? What rationale did the crusaders use to justify their atrocities against the European Jews? How did the First Crusade massacre influence European attitudes toward Jews?

4. According to Hilmar C. Krueger, what material gains did the

crusaders achieve in the Holy Land, and how did these gains often create situations that harmed the crusader kingdom? In what ways did the Crusades stimulate capitalistic expansion in Europe? Provide examples from the text to support your answer.

5. Martin Erbstösser describes how the Crusades stimulated the influx of knowledge from the Middle East into Western Europe. In which three categories did Arabic culture most affect Europe? Give examples from the text of the many products and ideas introduced to Europe from the Middle East and their effects on European society.

Chapter 4: Were the Crusades a Success?

1. T.A. Archer and Charles Lethbridge Kingsford contend that the Crusades were a success. What do the authors believe were the two primary objectives of the Crusades? How well were these goals achieved? How would the history of the Byzantine Empire and Western Europe have differed if the Crusades had not occurred?

2. In James A. Brundage's opinion, the Crusades were a mixed success. He argues that the crusaders failed in their stated goals but achieved success in ways they never imagined. Cite the examples he gives in support of this argument. Do you feel that the successes he cites outweigh the failures? Defend your answer.

3. Steven Runciman maintains that the Crusades were an unmitigated disaster for all three cultures involved. Examining his essay, which culture do you think suffered the most from the Crusades? Which suffered least? Use examples from the text to support your answer.

4. The three essays in this chapter present differing opinions on the results of the Crusades. Which of the three arguments do you find most convincing? Why?

Chapter 5: The Legacy of the Crusades

1. The Crusades greatly weakened Near Eastern civilization, in the opinion of J.J. Saunders. In his view, when was the golden age of Islam? How did the Muslims' long struggle against the crusaders affect the spirit of their religion, and thereby the intellectual and cultural leadership of the Islamic world?

2. Joshua Prawer states that many explorers to the New World were influenced by the old crusading idea. Which elements of

crusading ideology remained in this era? What changes had occurred in the ideology over the centuries? How was Columbus's
search for a direct westward path to India related to the hope of
launching a new Crusade against the Islamic countries?

3. How did the medieval Western Europeans commingle their
image of Jews and Muslims, according to Karen Armstrong?
Why did the Pilgrims and other Protestants begin to identify
with the Jews? In what ways do Christian Zionists resemble the
crusaders? How have these changes in Christian opinions toward Jews affected American actions concerning the modern-
day conflict in the Middle East?

Chronology

638

Muslim forces conquer Jerusalem, which had been under Christian control.

1054

The Great Schism splits the Christian Church into the Roman Catholic Church in Western Europe and the Greek Orthodox Church in the Byzantine Empire.

1071

At the Battle of Manzikert, the Byzantines are defeated by the Seljuk Turks and lose nearly all of Asia Minor, including Armenia, Antioch, and Edessa. The Seljuks also wrest control of Jerusalem from its Egyptian rulers.

1095

In March, Byzantine Emperor Alexius Comnenus sends envoys to Pope Urban II at the Council of Piacenza, asking for assistance against the Turks. On November 27, at the Council of Clermont, Urban proclaims the First Crusade.

1096

Persecution of Jews in Europe begins in the winter, lasting until June. In the spring, the People's Crusade departs for the Holy Land, only to be decimated by Sultan Qilij Arslan and his Seljuk forces near Nicaea on October 21. From August to October 1096, French and Italian nobles set out with their armies.

1097

The various contingents of the crusader army arrive in Constantinople throughout the winter and spring. From May to June, the crusaders and the Greeks besiege Nicaea, capturing it on June 19. In July, the crusaders defeat Qilij Arslan and his army at Dorylaeum. In August, they conquer Qilij Arslan's capital city of Iconium. In September, Baldwin of Boulogne and Tancred split their contingents off from the main army and head into Cilicia, taking a number of cities. The main army reaches Antioch on October 21 and begins a prolonged siege.

1098

In February, Baldwin of Boulogne conquers the province of Edessa and assumes the title of count. On June 3, the main army captures Antioch; Bohemond of Taranto claims the city and assumes the title of prince. The Egyptians regain Jerusalem from the Seljuks.

1099

The crusaders take over several towns on their way to Jerusalem, which they reach on June 7. On July 15, Jerusalem falls to the crusaders, who sack the city. On July 22, the Latin Kingdom of Jerusalem is established, with Godfrey of Bouillon elected as its ruler. Godfrey refuses the title of king and is instead designated the Advocate of the Holy Sepulchre. On August 12, the crusaders defeat the Egyptian army at Ascalon.

1100

In April, the Muslim rulers of Ascalon, Caesarea, and Acre submit to Godfrey as tributaries. Godfrey dies on July 18; he is succeeded by his brother, Baldwin of Boulogne, who is crowned king of Jerusalem on December 25 in Bethlehem.

1101

The Italian mercantile republics of Venice and Genoa begin to aid the Kingdom of Jerusalem. Baldwin I conquers Arsuf and Caesarea.

1104

The crusaders capture Haifa and Acre, while Alexius Comnenus wrests control of Cilicia from the Franks.

1105–1110

Baldwin I continues to expand and fortify the crusader states. In 1105, his forces defeat the Egyptian army at Ramleh. The Franks regain Cilicia in 1108. During 1109 and 1110, Baldwin captures Tripoli, Beirut, and Sidon.

1118

Baldwin I dies while leading a campaign against the Egyptians; he is succeeded by a relative, Baldwin II.

1119

On June 28, Turkish forces destroy the Frankish army of Antioch.

1123–1124

On April 18, 1123, the Seljuks capture King Baldwin II and decimate his army; Baldwin is ransomed from captivity in 1124. On May 29, 1123, the crusaders beat back an invasion of Egyptians at Ibelin and destroy their fleet off Ascalon. On July 7, 1124, Baldwin II takes Tyre from the Egyptians.

1128–1130
'Imad ad-Din Zangi, the Turkish governor of Mosul, captures Aleppo in 1128. He invades Antioch in the spring of 1130 but eventually agrees to a truce and retreats.

1131
Baldwin II dies in August; his son-in-law, Fulk of Anjou, becomes king of Jerusalem.

1137
Zangi lays siege to the Franks in the castle of Montferrand; in July, King Fulk agrees to surrender Montferrand in exchange for the safe conduct of the Franks inside.

1139–1140
In 1139, Zangi besieges the Muslim city of Damascus but fails to take it. The next year, the ruler of Damascus signs a treaty of alliance with King Fulk to provide mutual defense against Zangi.

1143
Fulk dies on November 10; his son Baldwin III ascends the throne on December 25.

1144
Led by Zangi, the Seljuk Turks invade the county of Edessa, take several castles, and then lay siege to the city of Edessa. In late December, the city falls to the Seljuks, who massacre the Frankish inhabitants.

1145
News of the bloodshed at Edessa reaches Western Europe by summer. On December 1, Pope Eugenius III proclaims the Second Crusade.

1146
St. Bernard of Clairvaux preaches the need for the Second Crusade in France and Germany. Persecution against the Jews breaks out in the Rhineland. On September 14, Zangi is murdered. His sons di-

vide his realm: Saif ed-Din assumes leadership of Mosul, while Nur ed-Din takes control of Aleppo.

1147

In the spring, Louis VII of France and Conrad III of Germany depart on the Second Crusade. Conrad's army of crusaders is devastated by the Turks near Dorylaeum on October 25. Conrad retreats and meets Louis in Nicaea.

1148

Louis VII, Conrad III, and Baldwin III decide to attack Damascus, which up to this point has been the one Muslim ally of Jerusalem. On July 24, the crusader army surrounds Damascus, but Nur ed-Din quickly sends armies to reinforce the city's defenses. On July 28, the crusaders withdraw from Damascus and retreat to Jerusalem, bringing the Second Crusade to an end.

1149–1154

On June 29, 1149, Nur ed-Din defeats the army of Antioch near Inab. In 1151, he takes the last remaining fortress of the county of Edessa. Damascus falls to Nur ed-Din on April 25, 1154.

1162

Baldwin III dies in February and is succeeded by his brother, Amalric I.

1163–1169

During these years, Amalric I maintains an uneasy truce with Nur ed-Din while leading four military expeditions against the Egyptians. Nur ed-Din also sends expeditions into Egypt. Saladin, a young Kurd who is one of Nur ed-Din's lieutenants, begins to rise in power. On March 23, 1169, Egypt submits to Saladin, who becomes vizier of Egypt. Amalric mounts his fifth Egyptian campaign in October 1169, with Byzantine assistance. His army sieges Damietta until December, then retreats in failure.

1174

On May 15, Nur ed-Din dies. Saladin establishes himself as the independent ruler of Egypt and solidifies his control over Damascus. Amalric I dies on July 11. His young son Baldwin IV, who is afflicted with leprosy, ascends to the throne.

1175–1180

In May 1175, Saladin gains official rule of Syria. At the Battle of

Myriocephalum in 1176, the Seljuk Turks destroy the Byzantine army. The following year, Saladin invades the crusader states but is defeated by Baldwin IV's army at Mont Gisard. However, Saladin continues to harry Baldwin's territories while the Egyptian fleet raids Frankish ports. In May 1180, Saladin and Baldwin IV agree to a truce.

1181–1183
In 1181, Reynald of Châtillon, ruler of Antioch, breaks the truce between the Franks and Saladin by attacking a Muslim caravan on its way to Mecca. Saladin responds by taking a ship of Christian pilgrims hostage. Not only does Reynald refuses to negotiate with Saladin, but in 1182 he also begins to raid Muslim ports on the Red Sea. Saladin conquers Edessa in 1182 and Aleppo in 1183. In October 1183, Saladin mounts a siege on Reynald's castle but withdraws his forces in December and agrees to another truce with Baldwin IV.

1185–1186
In March 1185, Baldwin IV dies and his young nephew, Baldwin V, ascends to the throne. However, Baldwin V dies in August 1186 and is succeeded by his mother, Sibylla, and her husband, Guy of Lusignan.

1187
Reynald again breaks the truce between the Franks and the Muslims by attacking a caravan. In May, the Muslims rout a small army of Knights Templar near Nazareth. On July 4, Saladin scores a decisive victory at the Battle of Hattin, soundly defeating the Frankish army. He executes Reynald and holds Guy of Lusignan captive. Throughout the rest of the year, Saladin's forces conquer almost all the important Frankish fortresses and cities, including Jerusalem on October 2. Pope Gregory VII proclaims the Third Crusade on October 29. In the winter, Conrad of Montferrat successfully foils Saladin's siege of Tyre.

1188
Henry II of England, Philip II of France, and Frederick I (Barbarossa) of Germany take the cross and begin to raise funds and crusader armies. In July, Saladin frees Guy of Lusignan, who joins the Christian resistance at Tyre. King William of Sicily sends a fleet to Tyre to help in the defense of the city.

1189

Frederick I sets out for the Holy Land in May. On July 6, Henry II dies; his son Richard I (Lionheart) becomes king of England. In August, Guy of Lusignan begins to siege Acre, aided by an armada of Danish and Flemish ships. Richard I departs for the Holy Land in December. English mobs start to attack Jewish communities, culminating in a massacre of 150 Jews in York the following year.

1190

On May 18, Frederick's army captures Iconium. However, on June 10, Frederick drowns while fording a river in Cilicia, and his troops disperse. His son, Henry VI, succeeds to the throne. Remnants of Frederick's army arrive at Antioch in late June. On July 4, Philip II and Richard I meet in Vézelay and start out for the Holy Land.

1191

Philip II arrives in Acre on April 20, adding his forces to the siege. Richard I is blown off course and conquers the Byzantine island of Cyprus before resuming his journey. He arrives in Acre in early June, and the city falls to the crusaders on July 12. Philip departs for Europe on July 31, leaving Richard in command. On August 20, Richard orders the execution of the 2700 Muslim survivors of the siege, including women and children. At the Battle of Arsuf on September 7, Richard defeats Saladin's forces. The crusaders take Jaffa shortly thereafter.

1192

In January, Richard retakes Ascalon. During the summer, Saladin and Richard skirmish at Jaffa but realize that they have reached a stalemate. On September 2, they conclude a treaty wherein the Franks keep a narrow coastal strip from Tyre to Jaffa but leave Jerusalem and other cities in the hands of the Muslims. Acre becomes the new capital of the crusaders' kingdom. On October 9, Richard leaves for Europe.

1193

Saladin dies on March 4; the ensuing struggle between his sons and his brother results in the division of his empire.

1197

In September, an army of crusaders sent by Henry IV of Germany arrives in Acre. They quickly seize Sidon and Beirut, but Henry's death in Messina on September 28 causes the German Crusade to collapse.

1198

On July 1, the Franks and the Muslims sign a truce recognizing Christian possession of Beirut. In August, Pope Innocent III proclaims the Fourth Crusade to recover Jerusalem.

1201

In April, the crusaders sign a treaty with the Venetians, agreeing to give one-half of their conquests to Venice in return for transportation and supplies. Alexius Angelus, the heir to the throne of Byzantium, asks the crusaders to oust his uncle, Emperor Alexius III.

1202

The crusaders agree to detour to the city of Zara on the coast of Dalmatia, which is under the control of the king of Hungary, and to conquer it for Venice. Zara falls to the crusaders on November 15 and is pillaged. The crusaders stay in Zara over the winter, during which time they agree to seize Constantinople on behalf of Alexius Angelus.

1203

Alexius Angelus joins the crusaders at Zara on April 25. The crusader army arrives at Constantinople on June 24 and enters the city on July 17. Alexius III flees.

1204

Alexius Angelus, now Emperor Alexius IV, proves to be a weak and imprudent leader. A son-in-law of Alexius III stages a coup, has Alexius IV strangled, and ascends the Byzantine throne as Alexius V. In March, the crusaders decide to take Constantinople for themselves. On April 12, they overrun the Greek defenses and then plunder Constantinople for three days. The sack of Constantinople marks the end of the Fourth Crusade, which never reaches the Holy Land. The crusaders set up Latin rule, electing Baldwin of Flanders as emperor, establishing Catholicism, and renaming the conquered lands Romania. The Byzantine royal family creates a government in exile at Nicaea.

1212

Young German and French peasants travel through Europe toward the Holy Land on a Children's Crusade that ends disastrously.

1213–1221

Pope Innocent III proclaims the Fifth Crusade in April 1213 but finds it difficult to fire up enthusiasm among Europe's nobility. The first contingent of crusaders, under King Andrew II of Hungary, does not set out until the summer of 1217; they accomplish little and leave for home the following January. However, in April 1218, large armies of Frisian, German, and Italian crusaders begin to arrive at Acre. The crusaders decide to attack Egypt, and on May 27, 1218, they besiege Damietta. The city finally falls to the crusader army on November 5, 1219. The crusaders remain in Damietta until July 1221, when—after the arrival of more German troops—they advance into Egypt. In August, they find themselves trapped at Mansourah and capitulate, signing a truce with the Muslims and evacuating Damietta in September.

1227–1229
Frederick II of Germany, who had earlier reneged on his vow to go on the Fifth Crusade, sets off for the Holy Land in the summer of 1227 but becomes ill and stops in Italy while sending his fleet on to Acre. Believing that Frederick is again hesitating to fulfill his pledge, Pope Gregory IX excommunicates him in September and forbids him to continue crusading. Nevertheless, Frederick sets sail in June 1228 and arrives in Acre on September 7. He enters negotiations with the sultan of Egypt and on February 18, 1229, reaches an agreement whereby the Christians regain Jerusalem and other territories. Frederick is crowned king of Jerusalem on March 18, 1229, and leaves for Europe in May, having successfully concluded the Sixth Crusade without ever fighting a battle.

1244
On August 23, Jerusalem falls to the Khorezmian Turks, who sack the city and burn many of its churches. The Franks form a coalition with the Syrians, while the Khorezmians join forces with the army of Egypt. The Egyptians and Khorezmians shatter the Frankish-Syrian forces at the Battle of Harbiyah on October 17. In December, Louis IX of France takes the cross and begins preparations for the Seventh Crusade.

1249–1254
Louis IX arrives near Damietta on June 5, 1249, capturing the city on the following day. On February 8, 1250, Louis and his crusaders battle the Egyptians at Mansourah and almost take the city. Louis remains encamped outside Mansourah until the Egyptians cut off his supply lines. In April he attempts to retreat but is forced to sur-

render to the Muslims and is taken prisoner, along with his entire army. On May 6, Louis is released in return for ransom money and the surrender of Damietta to the Muslims. He stays in the Holy Land until 1254, refortifying Acre, Caesarea, Jaffa, and Sidon.

1261
On July 4, Baybars, a Mamluk Turk, becomes the sultan of Egypt. Emperor Michael VIII Palaeologus of Nicaea recaptures Constantinople for the Greeks on July 25, bringing an end to the Latin empire of Romania.

1265–1268
Baybars begins to attack the crusader kingdoms, taking Caesarea and Arsuf in 1265, Safed in 1266, and Jaffa and Antioch in 1268.

1270
Louis IX sets out on his second Crusade, landing in Tunisia on July 18. However, during the campaign Louis becomes ill; he dies in Tunisia on August 25. In November, Louis's brother, Charles of Anjou, makes a treaty with the ruler of Tunisia and then returns to France. Prince Edward of England (later King Edward I) arrives in Tunisia just as the truce is being finalized.

1271–1272
Refusing to accept the truce, Edward and his small army of crusaders land at Acre in 1271, where they learn that Baybars has captured the last major castles of the military orders. Edward conducts a few raids but achieves little, and in May 1272 the city of Acre agrees to a ten-year truce with Baybars, ending hostilities. Edward leaves for Europe in September 1272.

1274–1276
Pope Gregory X tries to launch a new Crusade but cannot obtain sufficient support from the kings and nobles of Western Europe.

1277–1279
Baybars dies on July 1, 1277; a two-year battle for succession follows. In 1279, Qalawun, the commander of the Syrian troops, takes over the government and proclaims himself sultan. During these years, the crusader kingdoms are embroiled in disputes among themselves.

1285–1287
Qalawun begins to advance against the crusader states, capturing

the Hospitallers' castle of Marqab and the town of Maraqiyah in 1285 and the port town of Latakia in 1287.

1289

Qalawun conquers and sacks the port town of Tripoli on April 26; a few days later, his troops take Botron and Nephin. Concerned that the Christians might try to recapture Tripoli from the sea, Qalawun razes the city to the ground and rebuilds it a few miles inland. Acre, now the only major crusader stronghold remaining in the Holy Land, sends pleas for assistance to Europe.

1290

In August, a small force of Italian crusaders arrives in Acre to serve as reinforcements. Soon after their arrival, they run amok, killing any Muslim they meet. Enraged, Qalawun vows not to leave a single Christian alive in the city. On November 4, he sets out toward Acre with his army, but he suddenly becomes ill and dies on November 10. His son, al-Ashraf Khalil, succeeds him as sultan.

1291

Al-Ashraf Khalil musters an enormous army and heads for Acre in March. He lays siege to the town on April 6 and conquers it on May 18. In the bloody aftermath, he spares only a few Christians and orders the city's buildings destroyed. The remaining crusader towns (Tyre, Sidon, Beirut, Haifa) quickly capitulate and the Franks retreat to Cyprus, thus ending the period of the crusader kingdoms in the Holy Land.

For Further Research

Books

Malcolm Billings, *The Crusades: Five Centuries of Holy Wars.* New York: Sterling, 1996.

T.S.R. Boase, *Kingdoms and Strongholds of the Crusaders.* Indianapolis, IN: Bobbs-Merrill, 1971.

Ernle Bradford, *The Sword and the Scimitar: The Saga of the Crusades.* New York: Putnam, 1974.

Robert Chazan, *European Jewry and the First Crusade.* Berkeley: University of California Press, 1987.

Penny J. Cole, *The Preaching of the Crusades to the Holy Land: 1095–1270.* Cambridge, MA: Medieval Academy of America, 1991.

Michael Foss, *People of the First Crusade.* New York: Arcade Publishing, 1997.

John France, *Victory in the East: A Military History of the First Crusade.* New York: Cambridge University Press, 1994.

John Godfrey, *1204: The Unholy Crusade.* New York: Oxford University Press, 1980.

Michael Goodich, Sophia Menache, and Sylvia Schein, eds., *Cross Cultural Convergences in the Crusader Period.* New York: Peter Lang, 1995.

George Zabriskie Gray, *The Children's Crusade: A History.* New York: W. Morrow, 1972.

E.J. King, *The Knights Hospitallers in the Holy Land.* London: Methuen, 1931.

Harold Lamb, *The Crusades.* New York: Bantam Books, 1962.

Stanley Lane-Poole, *Saladin and the Fall of the Kingdom of Jerusalem.* New York: Putnam, 1898.

Ralph-Johannes Lilie, *Byzantium and the Crusader States: 1096–1204,* trans. J.C. Morris and Jean E. Ridings. New York: Oxford University Press, 1993.

Dana C. Munro, *The Kingdom of the Crusaders.* New York: D. Appleton-Century, 1935.

Thomas Patrick Murphy, ed., *The Holy War.* Columbus: Ohio State University Press, 1976.

Richard A. Newhall, *The Crusades*. New York: Holt, Rinehart & Winston, 1963.

Zoé Oldenbourg, *The Crusades*, trans. Anne Carter. New York: Pantheon, 1966.

James M. Powell, *Anatomy of a Crusade: 1213–1221*. Philadelphia: University of Pennsylvania Press, 1986.

Joshua Prawer, *The Crusaders' Kingdom: European Colonialism in the Middle Ages*. New York: Praeger, 1972.

———, *The History of the Jews in the Latin Kingdom of Jerusalem*. New York: Oxford University Press, 1988.

Donald E. Queller and Thomas F. Madden, *The Fourth Crusade: The Conquest of Constantinople, 1201–1204*. Philadelphia: University of Pennsylvania Press, 1997.

Jonathan Riley-Smith, *The Crusades: A Short History*. New Haven, CT: Yale University Press, 1987.

———, *What Were the Crusades?* Totowa, NJ: Rowman & Littlefield, 1977.

John J. Robinson, *Dungeon, Fire, and Sword: The Knights Templar in the Crusades*. New York: M. Evans, 1991.

Steven Runciman, *A History of the Crusades*, 3 vols. Cambridge: Cambridge University Press, 1951–54.

Kenneth M. Setton, ed., *A History of the Crusades*, 6 vols. Madison: University of Wisconsin Press, 1969–89.

Elizabeth Siberry, *Criticism of Crusading: 1095–1274*. New York: Oxford University Press, 1985.

R.C. Smail, *Crusading Warfare: 1097–1193*. New York: Cambridge University Press, 1995.

Periodicals

C.M. Brand, "Byzantines and Saladin, 1185–1192: Opponents of the Third Crusade," *Speculum*, April 1962. Available from the Medieval Academy of America, 1430 Massachusetts Ave., Cambridge, MA 02138.

Marcus Bull, "The Roots of Lay Enthusiasm for the First Crusade," *History*, October 1993. Available from Blackwell Publishers, 350 Main St., Malden, MA 02148.

Penny J. Cole, "Christians, Muslims, and the 'Liberation' of the Holy Land," *Catholic Historical Review*, January 1998. Available from the Catholic University of America Press, 620 Michigan Ave. NE, Washington, DC 20064.

H.E.J. Cowdrey, "Pope Urban II's Preaching of the First Crusade," *History*, June 1970.

John France, "The Destruction of Jerusalem and the First Crusade," *Journal of Ecclesiastical History*, January 1996. Available from Cambridge University Press, 40 W. 20th St., New York, NY 10011.

Bernard Hamilton, "The Impact of Crusader Jerusalem on Western Christendom," *Catholic Historical Review*, October 1994.

Norman Housley, "Saladin's Triumph over the Crusader States: The Battle of Hattin, 1187," *History Today*, July 1987.

Robert Irwin, "Muslim Responses to the Crusades," *History Today*, April 1997.

Charles Issawi, "Crusades and Current Crises in the Near East: A Historical Parallel," *International Affairs*, July 1957.

Bernard McGinn, "Violence and Spirituality: The Enigma of the First Crusade," *Journal of Religion*, July 1989. Available from The University of Chicago Press, Journals Division, PO Box 37005, Chicago, IL 60637.

Jonathan Phillips, "Who Were the First Crusaders?" *History Today*, March 1997.

Joshua Prawer, "Settlement of the Latins in Jerusalem," *Speculum*, October 1952.

Jonathan Riley-Smith, "Crusading as an Act of Love," *History*, June 1980.

John Rosser, "Crusader Castles of Cyprus," *Archaeology*, July/August 1986.

Steven Runciman, "Decline of the Crusading Ideal," *Sewanee Review*, Autumn 1971. Available from The University of the South, Sewanee, TN 37383.

Tim Severin, "Retracing the First Crusade," *National Geographic*, September 1989.

Franc Shor, "Conquest of the Holy City," *National Geographic*, December 1963.

Delno West, "Christopher Columbus, Lost Biblical Sites, and the Last Crusade," *Catholic Historical Review*, October 1992.

Index

Abdul-Faraj, 179
academics, Arab/Islamic influences
  on, 147–51
Acre, fall of, 37–38
Adelard of Bath, 148
agriculture
  crisis in, 74–75
  Oriental influences on, 144–45
Ain Jalut, 178, 179
Al-Ashraf Khalil, 37
Albert of Aix, 127
Albuquerque, 187
Alexandria, 179
Alexius Angelus, 33
Alexius I Comnenus (Byzantine
  emperor), 20, 22, 24, 28, 47
Alexius III (Byzantine emperor), 33
Al-Haitami, 149
al-Hakim (Fatimid Caliph), 70
Al-Khwarizmi, 148
Al-Kindi, 148
allodial land, 75
allods, 52
al-Rashid, Haroun, 44
Al-Razi, 148
America
  affinity with Crusades and
    Zionism, 191–93
  as refuge for Jews, 200–201
Anjou, counts of, 52
Antioch, 24–25, 47
  as crusader kingdom, 110
  siege of, 23, 117
Arabic language, 121, 180
  influences on Western languages,
    143–44
  after Mongol conquests, 181
Arabic numeral system, introduction
  in West, 150
Arab-Islamic culture
  contributions to West from, 180
    agricultural products, 144–45
    arts and crafts, 145–47
    language, 143–44
    scholarly works, 147–48
    scientific knowledge, 147
    trade goods, 145

see also Islam
Aramaic, 176
Archer, T.A., 153
Archimedes, 148
Aristotle, 148, 180
Armenians, 46–47, 121, 178
  support in creation of Edessa, 123
Armstrong, Karen, 188
artisans, 146
Asia Minor
  ancient civilizations of, 176
  first appearance of Turks, 45
  frontier of Christendom in, 43
  see also Outremer
Aspects of the Crusades (Saunders), 175
Atiya, Aziz S., 137
Avishai, Bernard, 201
Ayubites, 165

Baldwin I of Boulogne, 23, 28, 94,
  96, 126, 138
  creation of Edessa by, 123
Baldwin III, 116
Balfour, Arthur, 198–99
Balfour Declaration, 199
Barabdaeus, Jacob, 120
Barbarossa, Frederick (emperor of
  Germany), 31
Bar-Hebraeus, 179
bar Isaac, Meschulam, 131
Bartholomew, Peter, 24
Baybars, 36, 179
Benedictines, 55, 94
benefices (landed estates), 51–52
Bernard of Clairvaux, 86, 92, 133
Billings, Malcolm, 21
Blanche of Castile, 106
Bohemond of Taranto, 23, 25, 88
"Book of Optics" (Al-Haitami), 149
Bridge, Antony, 20, 109
Brundage, James A., 157
Bull, Marcus, 63
Bulst-Thiele, Marie Luise, 95
Burchard of Mount Sion, 178
Byzantium, 15
  Crusades' effects on, 168–69
  culture, destruction of, 169–70

extent of, 41–42
and First Crusade, 155
Seljuk invasion of, 18–19
treatment of Jews under, 17
Caliphate, 165
Canterbury, Archbishop of, 81
Capetian kings, 52
Cartwright, Anne and Ebenezer, 193
Charlemagne, 44
Charles I (king of England), 193
Chazan, Robert, 21
chemistry, 149
Children's Crusade, 107
  beginning of, 101–102
  fate of, 104–105
  route taken, 103
Christ, interest in humanity of, 67
Christendom
  Eastern, effects of Crusades on,
    167–69
  Western
    Crusades as first united effort of,
      154
    effects of Crusades on, 163–65
    eleventh century expansion of, 43
    frontier of, in Asia Minor, 43
    traditions influencing, 182
Christianity
  Eastern versus Roman, 42
  conflicts between, 123–24
  Eastern/Western division of, 15–16
  Semitic, split in, 177
Cilicia, 138
Clement III, 81
Clermont, Council of, 21
Cleymund, John, 82
Cluny, Abbey of, 55–56
college of cardinals, creation of, 56
Columbus, Christopher, 182, 186
  missionary vision of, 187, 189
commerce, 137
  Crusades were not crucial to, 163
  con, 140–41, 158–59
  establishment of credit system,
    141–42
  products of, 145
  trade routes
    establishment of, 12
    Ottoman monopoly of, 187
Comnena, Anna, 83
Comneni, Empire of. See Byzantium
Conrad III (emperor of Germany),

in Second Crusade, 30
Constantine the Great (Roman
  emperor), 41, 67, 69
Constantinople, 15, 41
  Fourth Crusade's attack on, 33–34,
    181
  as turning point of Crusades, 158
Coptic Christians, 121, 178
Council of Nablus, 111
Council of Vienna, 185
Cromwell, Oliver, 193
crosses, as symbol of Crusades,
  86–87
Crusade, Commerce, and Culture
  (Atiya), 137
crusader kingdoms
  governments of, 119–20
  interactions with indigenous
    peoples of, 121–22
  Jerusalem, 110
    efforts to hold/recapture were
      inept, 162
    establishment of, 27–29
    religious communities in, 120–21
  see also Outremer
crusaders
  criticism of, 89
  incentives for, 60, 84
    economic, 82, 136
    faith, 171
    greed, 83, 171–73
    indulgences, 80
    legal privileges, 88
    as penance, 82
    temporal privileges, 81–82
  similarity with 19th century
    colonists, 197
Crusaders in Syria and the Holy Land,
  The (Smail), 119
Crusades
  contribution to Western European
    society, 12, 158
  as crowning glory of Middle Ages,
    156
  effects on Eastern Christendom,
    167–69
  ended Mediterranean era, 182
  and exploration, 185–87
  failed to reconcile
    Eastern/Western Churches, 159
  Fifth, 34
    women in, 128
  First, 14

battle for Jerusalem, 25–27
leaders of, 83–84
persecution of Jews during, 132
siege of Antioch, 23–24
size of, 22
success of, and idea of Holy War,
    91
Fourth, 32–34
benefits of First were undone by,
    155, 159
target of, 164
and growth of commerce, 140–42,
    145, 163
as ideology
of conversion, 184–85
idealism behind, 153–54, 157
opposition to, 184
and Islam, 165–67
Italian merchants and, 138–39
as part of pan-European
    expansionism, 135–36
as pilgrimage for warriors, 68
Protestant forms of, 190
Second, 29–31
persecution of Jews during, 132
Seventh, 35
Sixth, 34–35
as social safety valve, 76
Third, 31–32, 84, 162
women as members of, 126
risks taken by, 126–28
Crusades, The (Erbstösser), 143
Crusades, The (Mayer), 73

da Gama, Vasco, 186
Damascus, defeat of Second Crusade
    at, 30
Dark Ages, 11
de Lagery, Eudes. See Urban II
de Villehardouin, Geoffroy, 80
Dominicans, 149, 185
Druze, 44
Duby, G., 74
Ducas, Andronicus, 46
Ducas, Michael, 46
Duggan, Alfred, 40
Durand of Le Puy, 100, 101

Edessa, 29, 138
as crusader kingdom, 110
creation of, 123
Edward (English prince), 36
Edward I (king of England), 194

Egypt
attack on, by Fifth Crusade, 34
defeat of, at Jerusalem, 27–28
under Ottomans, 187
and recovery of Jerusalem, 25
Eleanor of Aquitaine, 126
Emicho of Leiningen, 130
England
cost of Crusades to, 173
Jews in, 193–94
non-Jewish Zionist movement in,
    198–99
Erbstösser, Martin, 143
Erdmann, Carl, 68
Etheria of Aquitaine, 126
Euclid, 148
exploring, and crusading, link
between, 185–87

fairs, 142
Ferdinand (king of Spain), 189
feudal system
advantages of, 53
economic incentive to barons,
    136–38
eleventh century expansion of,
    51–53
hierarchy of, 52
warfare purpose of, 53–54
Fibonacci, Leonardo, 150–51
Finucane, Ronald C., 79, 125
foods, 113–14
France
cost of Crusades to, 173
19th century views of Arabs and
    Jews, 197
Franciscans, 149, 185
Franks, 29
destruction of Byzantine culture
    by, 169–70
of Outremer
changes in personal habits,
    112–13
hindrances to assimilation,
    117–18
new foods introduced to, 113–14,
    144
orientalization of, 110–11, 117
relations with Muslims, 117
Frederick II (emperor of Germany),
    34, 163, 169, 184
frérêche, 75, 76
Fulcher of Chartres, 116, 117, 138

Fulk Doon of Châteaurenard, 86

Gerald of Wales, 83
Gerard of Cremona, 148
Germany, 19th century views of
  Arabs and Jews, 197
Gesta Dei per Francos, 170
*Gesta Francorum et Aliorum
  Hierosolimitanorum*, 83
Gibbon, Edward, 166
Glaber, Ralph, 69
glass production, 146
Godfrey of Bouillon, 27
  death of, 28
Godwinsson, Sweyn, 44
Great Schism, 16
Greek Empire
  expansion of, 44
  Turkish raids of, 46
Gregory VII, 20, 58–59
  and concept of Holy War, 90–91,
    153, 154
Gregory X, 36
Grousset, René, 179
Guibert of Nogent, 66, 140
Guiscard, Robert, 45
Gunther of Bamberg, 71

Hadrian (Roman emperor), 41
Hakim (Caliph of Cairo), 18, 44
Hameln, children of, 105–106
Harbiyah, Battle of, 34
Hattin, Battle of, 31
Henry of Champagne, 142
Henry III (Holy Roman emperor),
  55, 56
Henry III (king of England), 81, 82
Heraclius (Byzantine emperor), 42–43
Herlihy, David, 74, 129
Hildebrand. *See* Gregory VII
History of the Crusades (Runciman),
  161
Holy War
  as act of intolerance, 173
  change in philosophy of, 184
  concept of, 89–90
    rejection of, by Eastern Church,
      159
Holy War (Armstrong), 188
Horns of Hattin, 31
Hospitallers, 93–94, 122
  power of, 96–97
Hugh of Payens, 94

Hugh II of Le Puiset, 88
Hugo of Bologna, 150
Hugo of Lucca, 150
Hulagu, 179
Hungary, conversion to Christianity,
  69

Ibn Daud, 147–48
Ibn Jubayr, 112
Ibn Khaldun, 182
Ibn Rushd (Averroes), 180
Ibn Sina, 148, 149
indulgences, 80
inheritances, division of, 74–75
Innocent III, 32, 80, 81, 158
Iraq, 176
Isaac II (Byzantine emperor), 33
Isabella (queen of Spain), 189
Islam
  change in spirit of, 182
  Crusades' effects on, 165–67
  defeat of last European stronghold,
    189
  end of golden age, 180
  fall of, 180–81
  Jerusalem under, 43–44
  under Ottomans, 184
  spread of, 16, 43–44
    Crusades delayed, 156
  see also Arab-Islamic culture;
    Muslims
Israel
  as America's alter ego, 201–202
  Gentile support of, 199–200
Italy, 149, 173
  benefits to
    from Crusades, 138–41
    from decline of Byzantium, 170
Ivo of Chartres, 88

Jacobites, 121, 122–23, 124
Jacques de Vitry, 83
James of Vitry, 123, 178
Jerosolimitanus, 88
Jerusalem
  Arab control of, 17, 18, 43–44
    under Hakim's rule, 18
    as motivation for Crusades, 65–66
  battle for, by First Crusade, 24–26
    massacre following, 26–27, 117
  capture by Persians, 42
  Christian activities in, 67
  control by Seljuk Turks, 19

as crusader kingdom, 110
  efforts to hold/recapture were
    inept, 162
  establishment of, 27–29
  estates of knightly families of,
    76–77
  liberation by Heraclius, 42–43
  under Muslim rule, 17–18, 43–44
  political system in, 97
  under Roman Empire, 41
Jews, 43
  assimilation of, 195
  attempts to protect, 133–34
  Christian attitudes toward,
    129–30
  legacy of First Crusade, 132–33
  demonization of, 189–90
  massacres of, 130–32
  19th century attitudes toward,
    196–98
  persecution of, 21
  Puritans' view of, 189–90
  revolts against Rome by, 40–41
  of Rhineland, persecution of, 130
  treatment under Muslim rule,
    17–18
Jibrin, Beit, 122
John of Seville, 147
John of Spain, 147
Judaism, 182

Kempe, Margery, 126
Khorezmians, 34
Kingdom of the Crusaders, The
  (Munro), 186
Kingsford, Charles Lethbridge, 153
Knights Templar, 94–96
Koran, 182, 185
  translation of, 149
Krueger, Hilmar C., 135

language
  Arab/Islamic influence on, 143–45
  liturgical, 121
Latin, 181
Lietbert of Cambrai (bishop), 70
Lloyd, Simon, 21
Louis IX (St. Louis), 34–35, 106,
  171, 172
Louis VII (king of France), 126, 169
  preparatory rituals of, 86
  in Second Crusade, 29–30
Lull, Raymond, 185

magnetism, 150
Mainz, Jewish massacre at, 131–32
Mamluks, victory at Ain Jalut, 178
Mansourah, 34, 35
Manzikert, Battle of, 18, 46–47
Maronites, 121, 122
marriage
  between Franks and Moslems,
    110–11
  of priests, 56
  restriction of, 75
Martel, Charles, 51
Martin, Everett Dean, 100
mass psychosis, 100–101
mathematics, 148, 180
Mathilda of Tuscany, 91
Mayer, Hans Eberhard, 73
medicine/medical care
  Arab influence on, 149, 180
  in Outremer, 116
Meletos the Syrian, 122
Memorandum Respecting Syria,
  Palestine and Mesopotamia (Balfour),
  199
Michael the Syrian, 122
military orders. *See* Hospitallers;
  Knights Templar
monarchy, effects of Crusades on,
  163
Mongols, 180
  conversion to Islam, 178
Monophysite Jacobites, 177, 178
Moslems, decline of, 164–65
Munro, Dana C., 11, 24, 186
Muslims
  demonization of, 189–90
  Egyptian
    defeat of, 27–28
    and recovery of Jerusalem, 25
  and Franks of Outremer, 117–18
  19th century European attitudes
    toward, 196–98
  Sunni, 179
  and Syrian Christians, 124
  treatment of Christians by, 43–44

Napoleon, 195
Nestorians, 120, 124, 177, 178
Nicaea, 23, 47
Normans
  expansion into Eastern
    Mediterranean, 168
  southern migration of, 45

Nur ed-Din, 30

Omar (Caliph), 43
Origin of the Idea of Crusade, The
   (Erdmann), 68
Ottoman Empire, 158
   assumption of Islamic states by,
      165–66
   British alliance with, 196
   decline of, 162
   Islam under, 184
   monopoly on trade route, 187
Otto of Freising, 83
Outremer
   colonists in, 29, 171–72
   crusader kingdoms in, 109
      everyday life, 110–14
      French influence on, 110
      trades and pastimes, 114–15
   power of Christian military orders
      in, 94–97
   social structure, 94–96
   see also crusader kingdoms

Painter, Sidney, 50
Palestine, Napoleon's plans for, 196
Palestinians, 198
Palmerston, Lord, 198
Papacy
   Crusades enhanced prestige of, 158
   effects of Crusades on, 163–64
   strengthening of, 56–57
paper production, 146
Paris, Matthew, 106
Paschal II, 91
Patzinaks, 48
Payne, Robert, 24, 50
peers, 52
People's Crusade, 22
Peoples of the Book, 17, 43
Peregrinus, Petrus, 150
Persia, capture of Jerusalem by, 42
Peter of Lusignan, 179
Peter the Hermit, 21, 127
Peter the Venerable, 185
Petrus of Maricourt, 150
Philip of Tripoli, 148
Phillip IV (king of France), 173
Phillip II (king of France), 31
philosophes (philosophers), 194
pilgrimages
   debt of Crusades to, 72
   difficulties of, 70, 71–72

and Holy War, contrasts between,
   90
   to Jerusalem, 41
   under Muslim rule, 44
   routes taken, 45
   linkage of Crusades to, 66–67
   penitential, 82
   symbols of, 86
Pilgrims, as religious migrants,
   191–92
Pius II, 161
Portuguese, explorations of Africa,
   186
poulains, 111
Prawer, Joshua, 183
Presbyter John, 186
primogeniture, 75
Protestantism, rise of, 190–91
Puritans, attitude towards Jews, 191

Qalawun, 37
Qilij Arslan (Seljuk sultan), 23

Raymond of Toulouse, 25, 126, 138
Reason, Age of, 194–95
relics, enthusiasm for, 67
Renaissance, contributions of Islam
   to, 158, 180
Reynald of Châtillon, 30
Richard I (king of England), 31, 32,
   126, 172
Richard of Saint-Vanne, 67, 70
Richard II of Normandy, 70
Riley-Smith, Jonathan, 85
Robert the Monk, 64, 65
Roman Catholic Church
   and concept of Holy War, 91, 159
   versus Eastern Church, 42, 123–24
   reforms of, 54–55
   revitalized strength of, 11
Roman Empire
   division of, 15
   Jerusalem under, 14–15
   Jewish revolts against, 40–41
Romanus IV Diogenes (Byzantine
   emperor), 19
   defeat at Manzikert, 46–47
Rotrou of Mortagne, 88
Roussel de Balliol, 47
Runciman, Steven, 18, 36, 37, 161

Saladin, 30–31
   treaty with Richard I, 32

Saracens, origin of term, 28–29
Sargent-Baur, Barbara N., 60
Saunders, J.J., 175
scientific knowledge, Arab/Islamic
   influences on, 147–51, 180
Seljuk Turks, 18
   advance of, after last Crusade,
      161–62
   first appearance in Asia Minor, 45
   Islam under, 182
   surrender of Romanus to, 46–47
Shaftesbury, Earl of, 198
Shepherds' Crusade, 106–107
Sicilian war, 164
Sicily, 163
silk production, 146
Smail, R.C., 119
Spain, 149, 180
   destruction of Jewry in, 189
   Muslim invasion of, 16–17
St. Benedict, 55, 94
Stephen of Antioch, 148
Stephen of Blois, 24, 83
St. Helena, 41, 69
St. John the Almsgiver, 93
Story of the Crusades, The (Duggan), 40
Strayer, Joseph R., 11, 24
St. Willibald, 69
Syria, 44, 119, 168, 176
   factions in, 48
   Western Europe's control of,
      119–20

taking the cross, 85
Tancred, 23, 138
textiles, 114
Tiberias, capture by Saladin, 30–31
Timur, 179
trade. See commerce
trade routes, 145
   establishment of, 12
Treece, Henry, 17, 93
Tripoli, 138
Truce of God, 61, 62
True Cross, 42
Turcopoles, 123
Turks. See Ottoman Empire; Seljuk
   Turks

Urban II, 12, 48–49, 136
   address at Clermont, 19, 61–62, 63
   audience for, 64
   exaggerations in, 65–66
   linkage of Crusades to
      pilgrimages, 66–67
   response to, 21
   appeal by Alexius to, 20
   and concept of Holy War, 90, 91,
      153, 154
   introduction of cross as symbol of
      commitment, 86–87
   motives of, for calling Crusades, 59
   diversion from feudal wars, 61
   objectives of, 154–55
Usamah (Arab prince), 112

Varangian Guard, 48
Venerabilis, Petrus, 149
Villehardouin, 169
Visigoths, 15
Voltaire, 194

war, as act of penance, 90–91
   see also Holy War
William of Aquitaine, 55
William of Normandy, 54
William of Tyre, 116, 123, 133
windmills, 146
women
   on the home front, 129
   as members of Crusades, 126
   risks taken by, 126–28
   sexual abuse of, 127
   as warriors, 128
Worms, Jewish massacre at, 130

Young, William, 198

Zacour, Norman P., 99
Zangi, Imad ad-Din, 29
Zara, 33
Zionism
   American affinity with, 192–93
   and British colonial expansion, 198
   non-Jewish, 199
Zoroastrians, 43

DATE DUE

3/4			

909.07   BC#33909010101619
CRU   The Crusades

Waterloo Middle School